Lost farms of Brinscall Moors

Lost farms of Brinscall Moors

The lives of Lancashire hill farmers

David Clayton

Copyright © David Clayton, 2011

First published in 2011 by
Palatine Books, an imprint of
Carnegie Publishing Ltd,
Carnegie House,
Chatsworth Road,
Lancaster LA1 4SL
www.carnegiepublishing.com

British Library Cataloguing-in-Publication data
A catalogue record for this book is available from the British Library

ISBN 978-1-874181-76-7

Designed and typeset by Carnegie Book Production, Lancaster
Printed and bound in the UK by Halstan Press, Amersham

Contents

Brinscall, The Moors and The Farms

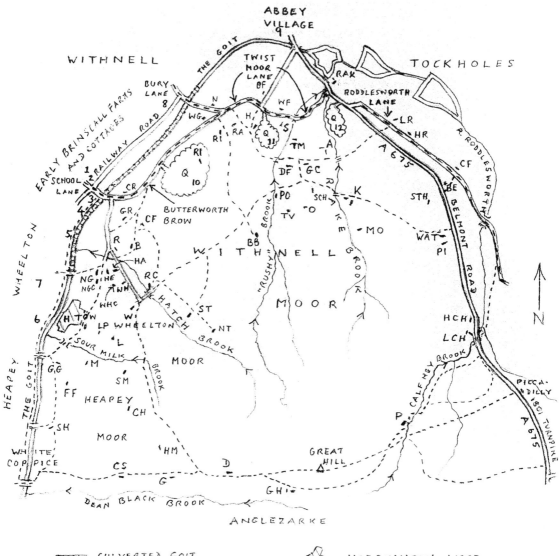

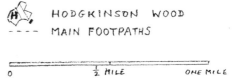

ⅢⅢ	CULVERTED GOIT	Ⓗ	HODGKINSON WOOD
≡≡≡	PRE-TURNPIKE (PRE-1801) ROAD	----	MAIN FOOTPATHS
Ⓠ	QUARRY		

0   ½ MILE   ONE MILE

1	Brinscall Station (site of)
2	Brinscall Row
3	Brinscall Baths
4	The Lodge
5	Brinscall Bleach Works (site of)
6	Brinscall Print Works (site of)
7	Brinscall Hall
8	Withnell Mill (site of)
9	Abbey Mill
10	Brinscall (ex-Withnell) Quarry
11	Central Quarry
12	Birch Clough Quarry

The Lost Farms

Heapey

CH	Calico Hall
CS	Coppice Stile
FF	Fir Farm
G	Grime's
GG	Goose Green
HM	Heapey Moor Farm
M	Marsden's
SH	Sharrock's
SM	Sour Milk Hall

Wheelton

D	Drinkwater's
GH	Great Hill Farm
HA	Hatch Place
HE	Heaton's
L	Liptrot's
LP	Leigh Place
NG	New Ground
NGC	New Ground Cottages
TOW	Top O' Th' Wood
W	Whittle's
WH	White Hall
WHC	White Hall Cottages

Withnell

A	Aushaw's
B	Beardsworth's
BB	Botany Bay (Summer House)
BE	Besom Hall
CF	Cocker's Folly
DF	Dale Fold
GC	Grouse Cottage
GR	Greenlands
H	Hillock
HCH	Higher Calf Hey
K	Keck
LCH	Lower Calf Hey
MO	Mosscrop's
NT	New Temple
O	The Oaks
P	Pimm's
PO	Pope's
R	Ripping
RAK	Rake
RC	Ratten Clough
RI	Richmond's
S	Snape's
SCH	Scott Hall
ST	Solomon's Temple
STH	Stake Hill
TM	Twist Moor House
TV	Tower View
WG	Whave Gate

The Surviving Farms

BF	Baron's Fold
CF	Cliff Fold
CR	Crosby's (Butterworth Barn)
HR	Higher Roddlesworth
LR	Lower Roddlesworth
N	Norcross
PI	Pickering's
RA	Ramsden's
WAT	Watson's
WF	Wood's Fold

Acknowledgements

THROUGHOUT THE WHOLE PROCESS of researching, preparing and writing this book I have been greatly indebted to my good friends John and Jean Fisk for their constant encouragement and support. To John in particular I am especially grateful for his typing and editing skills and for his wise judgement on matters of selection and style. For her enthusiasm for the subject and her expertise when reading drafts and offering positive and critically useful advice I owe much to fellow Brinscall resident Julie Colvin.

My understanding and my knowledge of farming life in this part of Lancashire have been enlarged and refined through many a warm and lively conversation with farmer and historian Stuart Whalley, and with farmers Alan Tattersall and John Smith.

Similarly, many of the realities of life as it was in these hill farms have been described to me with a specialist awareness 'from the inside' during my conversations with Mrs Vera Briggs (Mayor), Mrs Barbara Butler (Moss) and Mrs Dorothy Boyle (Bennett). To these ladies and also to Mrs Maureen Cottam (Fisher) I am grateful for loans of both family photographs and also rare and precious photographs of buildings now departed – essential illustrations for a book which otherwise might have had none. I thank David Fairclough for photographs he has kindly provided and I especially thank Mrs Fazakerley for the 1929 photograph of the 90-year-old Mrs. Sarah Shorrock. I have, in addition, learned to admire the astute judgements and map-making skills of Barbara Butler's grandfather, Richard Robinson – 'A Moorland Lad'. Mr Robinson had grown up at Botany Bay in the 1880s and 90s.

Other most helpful Brinscall friends who have offered information and advice include Brian and Gillian Banks, Carol Myerscough, Jack Rossall, Jack Murray, Harold Gomersall, Dawn O'Dea and Brian Fairbrother.

Finally I thank my colleagues at Carnegie Publishing for their special expertise and enthusiasm and my friend Paul Jennings for his early assistance in pursuit of census returns. I thank Colin Entwistle of Studio Twelve in Chorley for the significant enhancement of several of the older photographs. I also thank the helpful staffs of the Lancashire Record Office, the Cumbria Record Office (particularly Kate Holliday) and the Chorley Reference Library. I acknowledge permission to use two photographs – of Heather Lea and **Drinkwater's** Farm – belonging to the George Birtill collection now in the care of Chorley Community History Library.

Introduction

W HY HAVE I written this book?
Two special reasons predominate, in addition to my familiarity with the area and my admiration for those who knew these moors centuries ago.

Firstly I want to create a historical archive for this particular stretch of the West Pennine Moors, celebrating those who lived and worked in the ruined farms before they were demolished, and I want to do this while at least faint memories of the farms still remain among the local population. I intend thereby to preserve and publicise a record of names of people and places, and to revive details of a way of life that was still familiar 100 years ago but which, now, is almost totally forgotten, along with the silent tumbled heaps of stone themselves.

Secondly I wish to give moorland walkers an extra pleasure in their walking, a cheerful eye-opener, an awareness in depth of what they are looking at when they come across one and then another of these scattered heaps of stone, so thoroughly collapsed but still so numerous, mysterious and challenging. I know of no other area of such modest size where farmstead ruins occur so frequently. In the space of little more than five square miles there are no fewer than 48 farms waiting to be found, identified and quietly lingered over.

Even in the 10 square miles of the nearby Anglezarke and Rivington combined, famous locally as they are for their own farm ruins and for their recorded history, there are only 33 abandoned farmsteads – a sad number in itself, but a small catastrophe compared with Brinscall's losses in an area only half the size. As it is, just one of Brinscall's ruined farms can now never be found and can only be imagined, a suspended ghost-house hanging precariously in the mind, 150ft above a quarry floor.

While becoming expert in the rise and decline of hill farming in Lancashire you will find yourselves sharing in a tale of national, not just local significance. Join me now in a journey of exploration and discovery. The sites of 48 farms await you.

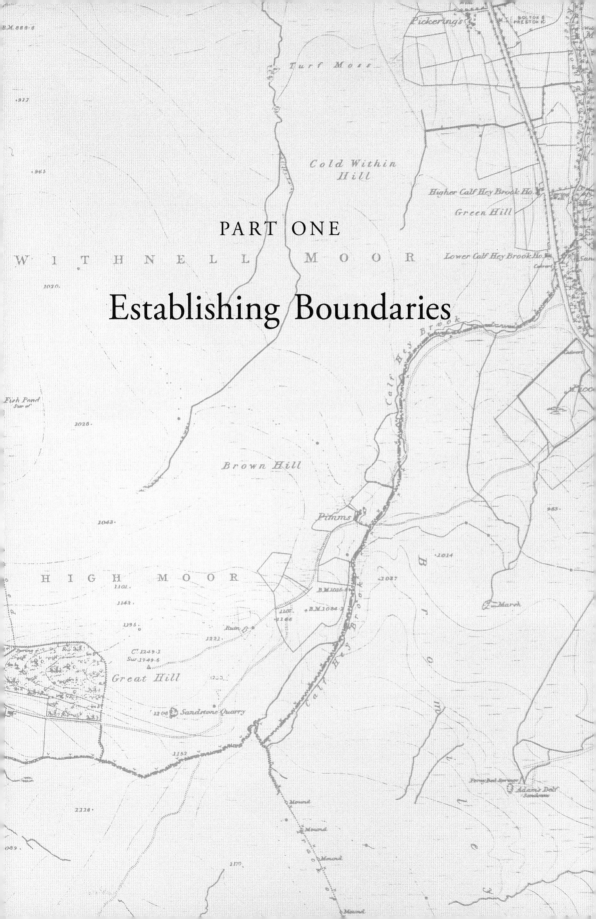

PART ONE

Establishing Boundaries

Mrs Sarah Shorrock, aged 90, photographed at Ratten Clough in 1929.

CHAPTER ONE

The Scene

WELCOME to the village of Brinscall in Lancashire, and to Brinscall Moors, a special part of the West Pennine Moorland scene. Come to Brinscall initially to observe for yourself, at a little distance, the wide expanse of your future expeditions. There are extensive and exhilarating views to be had of the hillsides and the moor-tops, the whole area indeed of your impending walks, searches and discoveries.

Start, I suggest, half-way up Brinscall's School Lane, next to the Oak Tree Inn, the oldest and the original inn hereabouts. From the Oak Tree, looking eastwards across the valley, you will see the pattern of field boundary walls on the slopes, and already, here and there, the isolated clumps of sycamores and hawthorns that mark the site of ruined farms. (Even now you perhaps begin to feel the warm stirrings of sympathetic admiration for those who hewed, shaped and placed the stones to make those dry-stone walls on the hillside? No quick post and wire boundary fences for them. By no means enough suitable metal for wire fences – even if they had been thought of – in eighteenth-century England.)

Notice, quite high up, a particular feature, a short section of close, parallel field walls (convenient for gathering sheep for lambing or for shearing) that still lead up to the sycamores of **Cocker's Folly**, the ruined farm on the hillside's edge. They are a feature, these close parallel walls, that you will find not infrequently elsewhere on the moors too – just east of **Coppice Stile House**, for instance.

While looking at the distant field walls, notice also the zigzag lines of walling that reveal tracks by which farmers and their carts climbed most easily up from the valley floor to their loftier fields and farmsteads. There are at least eight of these zigzag tracks up the sharp hillsides between Abbey Village and White Coppice.

Next, move up School Lane to the area near the cricket field, just beyond and above Windsor Drive. By now the view of the whole of Brinscall Moors is opening up, well beyond **Cocker's Folly**, over to **Ratten Clough** and **Whittle's** at the top of Edge Gate Lane. Then – if you walk as far as Sandy Lane – there is a glimpse, overall, of the high, curved dome – or upturned saucer, as it appears from this angle – of Great Hill. There are more field boundary walls. There are more isolated clumps of sycamores.

For the final part of your preliminary survey it is well worth visiting a pleasant footpath that cuts across fields – green pastures, indeed – to meet Harbour (formerly Windy Harbour) Lane, at National Grid Reference 619216. There are two ways to reach this from the School Lane–Sandy Lane junction you have just met.

The first of these involves your crossing School Lane to walk, in a south-westerly direction, past the primary school and along Harbour Lane itself for about 200m. If you do this, please take care in the presence of motor traffic. Harbour Lane is occasionally a quite busy local route. Single file walking is very wise. Having, after 200m, reached and climbed over the stile on your left, the view facing you is a fine reward. You may proceed easily over two level fields, crossing a second stile on the way, until you reach a third stile, at which it would be a good idea to pause.

An alternative route from the School Lane-Sandy Lane junction means re-tracing your steps past the cricket field (properly the Brinscall and Withnell Athletic and Recreational Association Sports and Social Club) until you almost reach Windsor Drive again. There, cross School Lane to its southern side and take a sign-posted footpath just past the house number 145. After a short distance you will find yourself crossing a stile and then walking along the eastern edge of a football field to a second stile – after which you are in a level pasture with the remains of an ancient ditch and hawthorn hedge on your left. Soon you will reach the stile at which a pause has already been recommended to the Harbour Lane walkers. The two routes now coincide, though it should be said that, among those who have just walked past the football field, any keen watchers for another brief vision of Great Hill will have to stroll in the Harbour Lane direction for 150m or so before turning to gaze upon

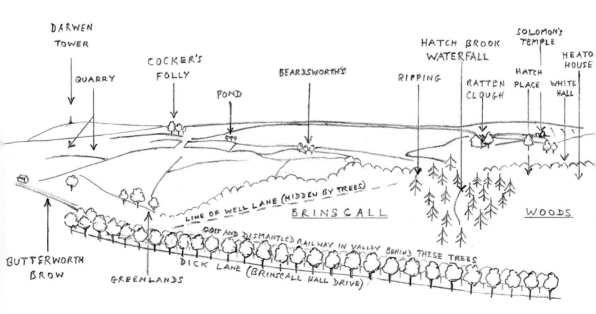

Looking east-south-east from the Windy Harbour Ridge.

the now-revealed summit. Having achieved this they should return to the stile and assume a pause.

It is a firm and substantial stile — worth standing upon, briefly, to increase one's elevation. The view from it, eastwards and south-eastwards, is striking. Eastwards it includes the moor-tops, the lush vegetation of Brinscall Woods on the hillside opposite and the tree-lined avenue of Brinscall Hall Drive (Dick Lane) below. South-eastwards you can see the full extent of the Brinscall Valley down to White Coppice and beyond, with an obvious zigzag route, a grassy track, up the slopes from **Goose Green** to **Fir Farm** and eventually to **Calico Hall** and **Heapey Moor** on the tops. There is also an excellent view of Healey Nab and Grey Heights, with a tantalising glimpse of the Anglezarke reservoir (more easily seen in winter than in summer, unless you walk briefly southwards alongside the wire fence for about 30m).

Then, looking eastwards from the stile, towards Abbey Village, Tockholes and Darwen Tower, you can make out the discreetly camouflaged but quite extensive quarry that has developed during the twentieth century off Butterworth Brow, partly obscured by Withnell Plantation. The quarry was known originally as Withnell, but is now more generally (and typically) known as Brinscall Quarry. It has devoured only one of our farms so far! Beyond the quarry lie your future tracks to **Botany Bay (the Summer House)** and to all the 19 ruined farms of the Twist Moor-Roddlesworth-Calf Hey area.

Before you leave the stile and begin the descent from level pastures down to Brinscall Hall, you might try a small effort of visual imagination. Try to imagine the hillside opposite without its dense mass of trees, without its delightful Brinscall Woods of closely packed birch, sycamore, oak, ash, beech, elder, alder, hawthorn, rowan, holly and conifers. This is how it looked — almost completely tree-less — 100, 200 years ago, a bare hillside with exposed field-boundary walls and with numerous greystone farmhouses and barns dotted across the slopes as well as on the high moors above. Peat-fire smoke would be drifting from house chimneys for much of the year. Cooking, quite apart from the need for hot water and for warmth in the house, required that.

An attractive landscape it is now in very many respects, with the varying early-summer shades of green from new-grown grass on the sheep pastures and newly opening leaves in the rich woodlands. And in the autumn the glowing colours — the reds, golds and browns — are magnificent. But in the eighteenth and nineteenth centuries it was a different place entirely, a busily inhabited farming community, with more people determinedly living and working on the tops and higher slopes than lived in the valleys, in the few short stone terraces (still to be seen) of School Lane, for example, in 1800 or 1850. What we now call Brinscall Woods is largely an early twentieth-century artificial plantation, hiding the boundary walls and farm ruins, concealing 200 years of human striving and a whole way of life indeed. The mossy ruins of farms and boundary walls are still there in the woods for you to find, however, as also are the bare stones more plainly and poignantly exposed in the highest fields

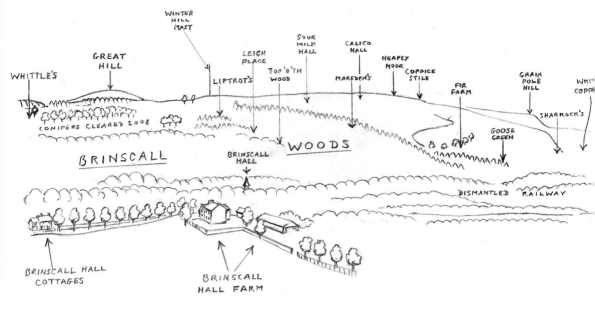

Looking south-east from the Windy Harbour Ridge

where winds and rains batter the rough foundations and sun brings out the subtle colour-blends of fallen stone.

Having with leisurely concentration enjoyed your view of the hillside and the moors, both as they are now and also, in your mind's eye, as they must have been a century ago, it is now time to return, still with the view to inspire you, to your starting point at the Oak Tree Inn. (There is no need, I suppose it should be said, to try to imagine the white wisps and rhythmic poundings from a steam locomotive forcing its way up the steep gradient from Chorley and Heapey to Brinscall and Blackburn along the now-disused line, as it might have been doing in the valley below you at any time between 1869 and 1967.) If you follow the footpath, on the far side of the stile, south-eastwards down the slope, it will take you gradually to the Brinscall Hall Farm, a proudly surviving set of buildings, though no longer a working farm, apart from its occasionally visiting and grazing sheep and cattle. From there you can make your way along the tree-lined route provided by Dick Lane (the Hall Drive) back to School Lane and the Oak Tree Inn.

CHAPTER TWO

Why Brinscall?

N ow that we have observed, preliminarily and approximately, the upland area where our ruined farms are to be found, it is high time to explain and justify the use of the name 'Brinscall' to identify these moors including Great Hill, and the woods, the extended village and indeed much of the region from Anglezarke and White Coppice northwards towards Abbey Village and the A675 Bolton-Belmont-Preston road. It may be increasingly common practice to refer to Brinscall in this way, both among the local population and among outside visitors, but it is a relatively recent custom and not yet an entirely accurate one. Certainly, if you were a punctilious geographer or a high-minded local authority official, you might be troubled if not confused by the confident but loose attaching of the term 'Brinscall' to so wide an area.

The fact is that until 1840 or so, Brinscall (Brendscoles in medieval times or Bronscale on Greenwood's Lancashire map of 1818) was simply a tiny and inconspicuous settlement, most of it within the far larger rural area or township of Withnell. It was similar in size and significance to the small hamlets of Ollerton, Brimmicroft and Stanworth which were also minor settlements within Withnell. Oddly, but typically, some Brinscall dwellings, including its Tudor hall (and the 1876 Victorian replacement) and its water-powered corn mill (later Logwood Mill) were actually contained within the administratively quite extensive township of Wheelton, not in Withnell at all. Indeed, until 1899, one side (the north side) of Brinscall's only main street (School Lane) was in Withnell while the other (its southern side) was in Wheelton. Adjustments to the Withnell–Wheelton boundary have eventually brought Brinscall Hall painlessly into Withnell, though Brinscall – or Logwood – Mill and Brinscall Brook are still resolutely in Wheelton.

On School Lane, about the year 1800 and through the early years of the nineteenth century, there was just the one inn (the Oak Tree) plus a mere eight short and scattered groups of small stone cottages. One of these groups, a terrace of seven cottages on the north side, still firmly surviving in the twenty-first century and still happily inhabited (as numbers 12–24 School Lane) was prominently named on early Ordnance Survey maps as 'Brinscall Row' – a significant feature evidently, in addition to the inn, the hall and the water mill, in the little world of 1830s Brinscall. (See Part Two, Chapter

Five on the early cottages of School Lane, many of them contemporaries of the farm buildings on the higher slopes and the moors.)

Given the established size and administrative jurisdictions of both Withnell and Wheelton, and the similar authority of Heapey township to the south, it is not surprising that our 'Brinscall Moors' had already, by the fourteenth century, been divided (with clearly prescribed boundary lines) into three quite separate sections. Seven hundred years later we still have, on present-day Ordnance Survey maps, the plainly differentiated Withnell Moor, Wheelton Moor and Heapey Moor. There is, literally, no sign of 'Brinscall Moors' on an OS map. If you are striving to find your way by map and compass in a thick and clinging mist across these very moors, it is as well to know this. Similarly, if you are looking for details of 1840s tithe maps and lists of payments, field by moorland field, that were due to be made by tenant farmers to the Vicar of Leyland (whose long-standing right it was to receive these), you must search under the separate listings for Withnell, Wheelton and Heapey. Even more significantly, if you are searching the fascinating nineteenth-century census returns for details of all our moorland farming families, you must again look under the separate statistics for Withnell, Wheelton and Heapey. None of our lost 48 farms is, or was, technically in a parish or township called Brinscall.

It will not greatly surprise readers to learn that even in the early twenty-first century, Brinscall householders, in paying their annual local rates, not only pay to Lancashire County Council and to Chorley Borough Council but also to Withnell Parish Council. There is no Brinscall Parish Council.

Why, then, do I use the term 'Brinscall Moors' to describe the Anglezarke to Abbey Village upland scene, our special and distinctive chunk of rough pastures, rough tracks, fallen enclosure walls and crumbled farmhouses? For four reasons. Firstly because it has a unity of character and experience in which division into three townships is ultimately meaningless and irrelevant; secondly because all names and boundaries are artificial anyway and are often temporary and partly accidental; thirdly because we are simply and realistically adopting what has become common parlance among those who know and care about the area; and fourthly because the area did once have a single name. This was before the Withnell, Wheelton and Heapey jurisdictions were imposed, before the de Hoghtons, or Whalley Abbey, or the Parke or Wood families exercised their authority in Withnell, Wheelton and the moorlands and before the Standishes of Duxbury held sway in parts of Heapey as well as Anglezarke. Before the creation of the tripartite ownership system, our moors north of the Dean Black and Calf Hey Brooks, north of a line, that is, from White Coppice to the Belmont Road, were known by the single, expressive and evocative name of Gunolfsmores.

I do not propose, however, to resurrect the name or reputation of an early medieval chieftain, if there ever was a Gunolf, exciting and imaginative though that might be. But I do propose to employ the concept of a single area with, in the eighteenth and nineteenth centuries at any rate, a similar range of human activities, similar problems and similar opportunities. I propose to use the current normal, familiar, everyday expression 'Brinscall Moors' to cover the whole area, without pedantically separating Withnell from Wheelton, for example. Where I do, in a list of farm names to go with a sketch map, group the farms according to the parishes or townships they formerly (or formally!) belonged to, I do so simply to make it easier for readers to use an Ordnance Survey map in their strollings or to retrieve census information. Where I group the farms by my own sub-regional definitions (e.g. The Twist Moor Group, the Central Group) I do so simply to ensure that walkers do not try to visit too many ruined farms in one day, or on one expedition.

So, given that 'Brinscall Moors' is the practical and familiar, though not the official, description of our slopes and uplands, it has also to be admitted that 'Brinscall Woods' is not the proper or official name for the tree-clad slopes here either. Rather it is as 'Wheelton Plantation' that they appear on Ordnance Survey and United Utilities maps – ludicrous though this may be, since their northern section (beyond the **New Ground** track) is technically in Withnell, and their southern section (beyond the Sour Milk Brook) is technically in Heapey. This is no important matter to the inhabitants of these parts, however. It is as 'Brinscall Woods' that the plantation is almost universally known, and the bluebells of Brinscall Woods do smell every bit as sweet as those of Wheelton Plantation. In any case there was no Wheelton Plantation until the early twentieth century. What there was at that time was a relatively small area of fine beech trees (many of which remain) known as 'Hodgkinson Wood' – at the top of which (for it was on a steep slope) was a farm known as **'Top o'th' Wood'**.

Why then has the name 'Brinscall' rather taken over, locally, as the normal title for both the Woods and the Moors? I can offer four further explanations, all of them convincing, of course, and all of them involving significant social change in the nineteenth and twentieth centuries.

In the first place, with the development in the valley of the Brinscall Bleach Works and Brinscall Print Works during the 1840s (both of these built and owned by the Wood family of Brinscall Hall) there was a significant increase in the population of Brinscall village. Additional School Lane cottages were slotted in among older ones, and complete new and stylish terraces (some of stone, some of brick) were built on School Lane and along Lodge Bank, Butterworth Brow and Quarry Road, as well as along the then recently completed Railway Road and its side streets. There was a daily influx of factory workers, too, walking from as far away as Chorley and Leyland, and returning there at night. If asked in a morning where they were walking to, the walking workers would naturally reply "Brinscall", even though both Bleach Works and Print Works were technically in Wheelton. They would not say "Wheelton" because they were already walking through the widespread Wheelton township (past the Leeds and Liverpool Canal, say) on their way from Chorley or Leyland. Thus the name Brinscall was inevitably becoming known among a wider public.

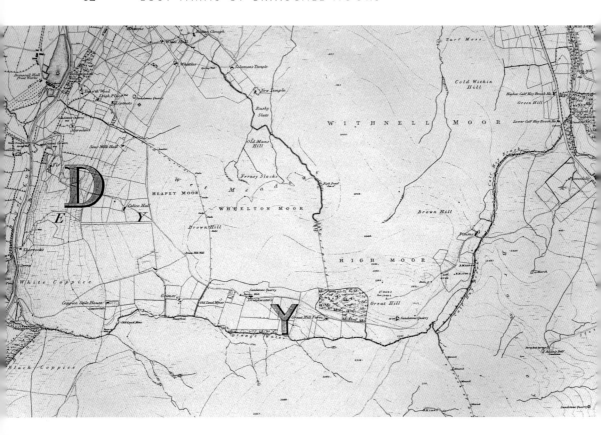

Secondly, and perhaps most importantly, the coming of the railway in 1869 gave Brinscall what could be described as nationwide prominence. The building of a new line between Wigan and Blackburn meant the construction of four new stations between Chorley and Cherry Tree. One of these was to be at School Lane near the line's summit. The station's official name might logically have been 'Wheelton' if it had been built on School Lane's south side, or 'Withnell' if built, as indeed it was, on the north side. But the station at Abbey Village was to be called 'Withnell' so, perhaps because the School Lane station was built next to the cottages of Brinscall Row, 'Brinscall' became its formal name.

Brinscall therefore appeared significantly on the nation's railway timetables. In 1922, on Mondays to Fridays, 14 passenger trains each way stopped at Brinscall, and 16 each way on Saturdays. There was easy access from Brinscall to London Euston via one change at Wigan.

The Wigan–Blackburn line had been built (jointly by the Lancashire Union and the Lancashire and Yorkshire railway companies) primarily for the quicker transporting of coal and cotton cloth between the two towns. However, Brinscall rapidly became a centre for traffic in other goods as well, especially in livestock, milk and other agricultural produce, and lime (for land improvement). There were also at least five additional spur lines and sidings in the Brinscall area serving local quarries and textile factories, making the station a focal point of economic activity for a wide region. The region included much of Withnell and most of the farms of Wheelton. "Within two miles of Brinscall Station" was a typical claim on advertisements for farm sales. From 1869, the life of a farmer on Wheelton Moor, for example, might well revolve, to a greater or lesser extent, around Brinscall's railway station.

Thirdly, two patriotic and public-spirited gestures by the Parke family, in 1902 and 1911, added further, even if unintentionally, to Brinscall's comparative fame. The Parkes had owned the Withnell and Wheelton moors through much of the nineteenth century until the 1898 compulsory purchase by the city of Liverpool. The Parkes had also owned the Withnell Fold paper works, the Withnell Mill (cotton spinning and weaving) at Bury Lane (before Marriage and Pinnock) and the Abbey Mill (before the Birtwistles). They decided to celebrate Edward VII's coronation in 1902 by setting up a Coronation Hospital on healthily high land near the junction of School Lane and Harbour Lane. It rapidly became known as Brinscall Hospital, firmly in Withnell Parish though it is. In 1911, to mark George V's coronation, the Parkes funded a public, heated, indoor swimming pool near the junction of School Lane and Lodge Bank (Croft Bottoms) in what was by then Withnell but until 1899 had been Wheelton. It was a famous rarity. People walked all the way from Horwich to swim in it. Chorley had no pool of equal quality. It rapidly became known as Brinscall Baths, as it still is.

Our fourth factor is an offshoot of a typical piece of twentieth-century technology – the telephone. In the days until comparatively recently when it was usual to have an area code name but not a code number, and then a code name AND a code number, there was only one official GPO code name for the whole of Withnell (including Withnell Fold, Abbey Village and Brinscall) and Wheelton (including Lower and Higher Wheelton). It was, of course, 'Brinscall'. Anyone who lived anywhere in Withnell or Wheelton used to answer their telephone by, in effect, announcing that they lived in Brinscall.

I expect it is now quite clear why I have used the term 'Brinscall Moors' and the term 'Brinscall Woods' to indicate the areas where you will be looking for, and finding, the lost, the collapsed, the demolished, the sad, the late-lamented farms of Withnell, Wheelton and Heapey Moors. And now we need to define this area even more exactly so that you may find your way easily, safely and cheerfully.

CHAPTER THREE

The Moorland
Triangle Defined

I N A N Y E N Q U I R Y, historical, scientific or aesthetic, it is necessary in practice to define, to set limits and boundaries to, the area to be researched, the topics to be considered, the conclusions to be attempted. Otherwise, enquiries have a habit of being never-ending, once the process of discovering and interpreting has begun. In this case, my area of moorland to be covered can be clearly defined. It has precise and physically obvious boundaries, and a certain 'cultural' unity – an almost complete unity of life-style and outcome, at any rate – and, in plan on the map, the satisfying shape of a round-headed triangle. It is bounded in the south by the Dean Black Brook and the Calf Hey Brook (Great Hill providing the watershed between the two); in the east by the A675 (the former Sharples-Hoghton Turnpike of 1801) and the valley of the Roddlesworth River; in the north and west by the Goit (built in 1852–57). The area is entirely the property of United Utilities, formerly North West Water, and before that, after the compulsory purchases of 1898–1902, of Liverpool Corporation Water Works. It is almost entirely Open Access Countryside.

Brinscall Moors are north of Anglezarke, north of Rivington, and north, therefore, of that well-known peak of television and radio masts, the 1,498ft (456m) Winter Hill. Brinscall's highest point is not quite so tall, and it carries not a single mast. But its Great Hill at 1,249ft (381m) is nevertheless a shapely and dominating height, impressive when looked up to from the streets of Chorley or the fields of Croston, and exhilarating to look down from after you have ascended its slopes. Great Hill also possesses to its west, north and east the supporting heights of a fine upland wilderness of fascinating character, a great undulating and open moor of heather and coarse grass tussocks, narrowing and falling gradually as it nears Abbey Village.

Green Hill, Brown Hill, Old Man's Hill, Cold Within Hill, Twist Moor, Roddlesworth Moor and Millstone Edge are the distinctive names that have attached themselves over centuries to some of the minor eminences. It is an extensive and high enough place to give an impression of splendid remoteness. Yet it also provides on

The Goit Bridge at Goose Green.

clear days a remarkable vista towards Pendle, Pen-y-Ghent, Ingleborough, the Lake District mountains (from Black Combe across the Coniston range to the Langdale Pikes) and, from its western edge, the mountains of Snowdonia.

The moor is drained by six streams. Five of these have formal names: Dean Black Brook, Calf Hey Brook, Rake Brook, Hatch Brook and Sour Milk Brook (the latter being occasionally bone-dry and occasionally spectacularly in spate). The sixth stream, just about the longest, is curiously nameless both on maps and among local residents. However, George Birtill of Chorley (the well-known local journalist and historian) gave it the name "Rushy" Brook, and I most happily adopt his suggestion. Sour Milk Brook, incidentally, though sometimes dry, does run frequently enough for it officially to mark the boundary between Wheelton and Heapey for much of its length down to the Goit.

Such are the natural features of the moor, together with many of their names. In the centre of the area north of Great Hill there remains an extensive space which is, and apparently always has been, unenclosed 'waste'. There are some basic field-drain ditches on Old Man's Hill near **New Temple Farm** (possibly dug by Liverpool Corporation personnel to direct surface water more quickly into the "Rushy" Brook) but otherwise no obvious signs of human activity beyond **New Temple**, no intake walls and no farm ruins. If you search carefully, however, it is possible that you might find signs of the alleged former fishpond perhaps established by the monks of Whalley Abbey though this is in a decidedly trackless area. It is round the edges of the moors, comparatively speaking, that intake walls and farm ruins are found, and that cart tracks, or the faint signs of these, survive. Here nature has to an extent, but impermanently, been tamed. The Goit, however, is far from a natural feature. This waterway runs, smooth and free, as persistently and purposefully as it has ever since its construction was completed in 1857.

The Goit is a canalised, artificial watercourse 21ft wide and three and a half miles long. It runs roughly north to south through a conveniently open-ended valley, itself the relic of an Ice-Age glacier's edge and of the pre-Ice Age 'slipped strata' – the so-called Brinscall Fault. It takes water from the Roddlesworth and Rake reservoirs via Brinscall and White Coppice to join the Anglezarke reservoir near 'Waterman's Cottage', and thus ultimately contributes very considerably to the filling of the two Rivington reservoirs. It was a triumph of a Victorian surveyor's observation-powers and engineering acumen – this using of the gentle fall in altitude through the valley from Abbey Village to White Coppice, and this capturing of water that would otherwise flow into the rivers Darwen or Lostock. The Goit took it instead all the way round the north and west of the Brinscall Moors, sending it on its way to Prescot and Liverpool. On its course through the open-ended Brinscall Valley it also receives the waters of the Hatch, the Sour Milk and the Dean Black brooks, plus the oozings of many minor or occasional streamlets. The Goit is very largely the reason why there are 48 abandoned and dismantled farms on Brinscall Moors. (We shall discover the connection in due course.) The engineer Thomas Hawksley (1807–93) certainly had a long-term impact.

For 40 years from 1857 to 1897, however, the Goit seemed to present no threat to the lives of the people who inhabited the farms and cottages of the moors, at least once the navvies who built it had left, and the farms had ceased to double as alehouses. On the contrary, stone bridges over the Goit had helpfully been built by Liverpool Corporation at all those points where there was an existing roadway or track crossing the valley floor and leading up to the higher farms. Five of these bridges survive in more or less original condition, double-arched, substantial stone structures, having round-headed parapets and firm end-pillars with low-pyramid toppings. Minimum width of the roadways over them is at least 3m – broad enough for a decent size cart. These solid statements of Liverpool's goodwill can be found and admired at Bakehouse Lane (below Brinscall Hall, giving access to **New Ground** and Edge Gate Lane in the east above) and at **Goose Green**, at **Sharrock's**, at White Coppice and at a point near Margery Place below Stronstrey Bank not far from Waterman's Cottage.

At Bury Lane-Norcross Brow, and at School Lane-Butterworth Brow-Well Lane, the bridges have been widened to cope with more frequent and heavier traffic. In any case the widened bridges were crossing the Goit at points where, from 1906, it had been culverted for the protection of the water's purity. North of Bury Lane, where the culverting starts, a grand new tunnel entrance, with smooth brick and decorative stonework finish, was installed. You will no doubt find four of the original bridges (but not including the Margery Place bridge, probably) very useful in your comings and goings when approaching the moors from the west on foot. The two widened ones will be useful, too, when travelling by car.

The 1850s stonework of the bridges, and of the walls that run, here and there still, on each side of the Goit, makes an interesting contrast now to the stonework of the earlier (eighteenth century) farm enclosure and intake walls at the lower edge of the valley sides. Goit stonework can also be compared to the stonework of the slightly later (1867–69) walls running in many places on each side of the former railway trackbed. Indeed, near the Bakehouse Lane–**New Ground** bridge, all three types of walling are to be seen in close proximity, their similarities and differences plainly revealed. There is no doubt that Victorian architects and builders intended their stone structures to be grandly permanent. The (mainly eighteenth-century) farm enclosure walls were of traditional dry-stone construction, needing regular maintenance. They have in many places ignominiously collapsed. The Goit walls and the railway walls mainly stand firm, except where they have been deliberately damaged or where material from them has been removed for use elsewhere. Yet, such is the ephemeral nature of human endeavour and achievement that none of the three types of wall now performs any necessary function. None of them keeps anybody out of what they once contained and protected. All are basically ignored. Their permanence was an illusion. Their function is nil.

What is in a sense more impressive than the walls is the steepness of the eastern slopes of the valley, and the plethora of massive, round-edged erratic boulders and large pieces of former quarry debris that in some parts litter the slopes. In creating this sharp and stony edge to the moors, the ice-sheet of 10,000 years or so ago, in its grinding and pushing, produced a more permanent obstacle than any wall-building stone mason.

The fact is that from the hills overlooking the Roddlesworth farms, through the Twist Moor Lane area and especially from Norcross Brow onwards, the northern and western boundaries (the A675 and then the Goit, that is) of our great triangle of moorland follow increasingly closely the natural barrier of this formidably steep and stony edge. The steepness becomes really obvious by the **Whave Gate** site and the Withnell Plantation, with the view from Butterworth Brow down to Railway Road. It is even more obvious from the **Cocker's Folly** site and then by the middle of Brinscall Woods and the view downhill from Heather Lea and the **Top o'th' Wood** site. The magnificent view from **Fir Farm**, which itself is only half way up the slope above **Goose Green**, is breath-taking – especially if you have just climbed up to it.

The steep (Ice Age) slope in Brinscall Woods, with scattered erratics.

We are talking of a slope of a one-in-two, or even in places a one-in-one steepness. This continues to White Coppice and the steep path from the cricket field there up towards **Coppice Stile**. Beyond White Coppice, Stronstrey Bank openly emphasises the height and abruptness of this unusual eight-mile-long geological feature. The slope continues through Anglezarke and into Rivington, to the area of Lord Leverhulme's terraced gardens below the Pike. It does not begin to run out until George's Lane meets Chorley Old Road at Bottom o'th'Moor, south-east of Horwich. On the OS map its contour lines are often tightly packed, as on a Lake District slope such as the Grisedale face of St Sunday Crag, though we are dealing in Brinscall, Anglezarke and Rivington with a 400, not a 1,400ft or more rise (120m rather than 450m, say).

Vigorous quarrying has been a source of additional employment among the families of Brinscall farmers for many centuries at several points along the length of this sharp moorland edge. Quarrying still continues now at one point at least. The availability of good quality millstone grit so near the surface has been irresistibly tempting. 'Old sandstone quarry' appears frequently on nineteenth-century maps.

Above the A675 when we are overlooking the Roddlesworth valley, there are on the surface of the hillside fields some splendid examples of huge crudely shaped chunks of raw stone, tumbled together as if in a triumphant family gathering. Nearby are the remains, close to the Rake Brook, of the very considerable Birch Clough quarry. Moving west, beyond **Snape's Farm** and Wood's Fold, we find the still larger Central quarry. Above that are ancient delvings in the pock-marked surface of Millstone Edge where, in one hollow, if you search the hollows persistently, you will find a surviving complete and awe-inspiring millstone, almost ready for use, grass protruding at present through its central axle-hole.

Off Butterworth Brow and overlooking the former Withnell Mill and Bury Lane is the still-working and intimidatingly massive Brinscall (formerly Withnell) quarry. At the top of Well Lane, where the Hatch Brook tumbles over into a high sylvan waterfall, there are the remains of Hatch quarry. Above **Liptrot's Farm** are the remains of a delightful domestic-sized delph with the stone walls of a small storage workshop beside it. At White Coppice and beyond the Dean Brook at Black Coppice are the clear signs of a good deal of quarrying which continued well into the twentieth century. In Anglezarke are the impressively high cliffs of Leicester Mill quarries. And above Bottom o'th'Moor we come finally to the large workings of Montcliffe quarries.

So much for the quarries, for the time being. But thinking, still, of the Ice Age relic itself, the long steep slope I have been describing, it is the case that only two of our 48 farms, **Goose Green** and **Sharrock's**, could be said to have taken advantage of the shelter it provides. Both of these nestle comfortably at its foot, and find themselves very close to the waters of the Goit. On fine summer days and even on calm winter days, the air is often charmingly tranquil and notably warm by **Goose Green** and **Sharrock's**. Do they even qualify as moorland farms indeed? Conditions for those living there must have been very different on a stormy winter's night from the noise and commotion endured by fellow tenant farmers on the open tops above, in **Calico Hall**, for example.

And yet, when we examine the siting of all the farms, it is remarkable how frequently clever use has been made of the immediate lie of the land to provide some protection from the fiercest and coldest winds. Only perhaps four of the 48 could be said to be totally exposed to strong winds from every direction. The identifying of the indefatigable four could be a topic of lively debate among readers and walkers, but, as a starter, I will offer, contentiously: **Solomon's Temple, Sour Milk Hall, Calico Hall and Heapey Moor Farm.** If I had to I could defend my exclusion (from the most exposed category) of the highest three of the 48 – **Great Hill, Drinkwater's and Pimm's.** I also so far exclude several others fairly remote from the western slopes and fairly obviously exposed to severe weather: **New Temple, Higher Calf Hey, Mosscrop's, Stake Hill, Scott Hall, The Oaks, Tower View and Botany Bay (the Summer House).** To take an effective part in this debate you really will have to walk the moors and visit the farms in a variety of conditions.

PART TWO

The Archive

Paterfamilias George Daniel Mayor,
farmer of Higher Healey, circa 1880.

CHAPTER ONE

The Origins

THE CLEAR AND OVERRIDING purpose of farming on the moors was the rearing and shearing of sheep, the raising and the caring and ultimately via much use of woollen clothing, the wearing. And, of course, to an extent it still is, though wool now faces competition from many other fabrics, and meat production has become a major aspect of hill-farming under the European Union system. But the sight and sound of young lambs in the Spring, newly born or perhaps just a few weeks old and already gaining their confident adventurousness, is one of the delights of a walk on Brinscall Moors. This you can enjoy and take part in on the gentle green slopes by **Ratten Clough** and **Solomon's Temple** or over on Twist Moor by **Grouse Cottage** and **Aushaw's**. (Be sure you entirely respect the ewes and their innocent offspring, meanwhile. Keep your dog absolutely under control.)

Sheep farming for the monks of medieval abbeys was a serious if not quite a sacred pursuit, and Whalley Abbey certainly engaged in this worthy (and lucrative) business on Withnell and probably on Wheelton Moors. The de Hoghtons had interests in the area in the fourteenth century but significantly increased their control only after the 1539 Dissolution of the abbey and the 1540 purchase of its lands. But, so far as we can know, for the de Hoghtons and for the Standish family, their moors of Withnell, Wheelton and Heapey were, before 1600 or so, primarily of interest for their sporting potential. West of our triangle of moorland, towards Chorley and Leyland and beyond, sparsely populated though Lancashire was (compared with Norfolk and Suffolk, say) there were already by 1600, or by soon after, small numbers of substantial manorial-type farm houses, with even double-height mullion and transom windows. The further towards the west they were the more likely it was that they would be of brick rather than stone construction, however. Local stone examples (quite close, indeed, to the moorland) include Higher Healey and Morris farms near Healey Nab, High Bullough (the later 'Manor House') in Anglezarke, Hollinshead Hall in Tockholes, Brinscall Hall (the Tudor version), Stanworth Farm and Roddlesworth (demolished circa 1914 but with a large barn of 1674 and another of 1755, both still standing in good condition and in use near the remaining cottage). But on the higher moors which are the main subject of this book, there was in 1600 almost certainly not a single farmhouse, and there were almost certainly no enclosure or intake walls.

The infamous Tudor Enclosures of the sixteenth century, transforming much English arable land into sheep pasture for the more profitable producing of wool, seriously affected employment and food production in the Midlands, the South and the East but not yet in the North where there was comparatively little arable land anyway. Just as 'classical' architecture, with Graeco-Roman detail, with symmetry and sash windows, was slow to appear in Lancashire, so it was not until the late seventeenth century that enclosures for sheep farming and the actual erecting of groups of moorland farmhouses began in earnest. It seems that the majority of our 'Lost Farms' were built in the fairly short and busy period between circa 1680 and circa 1740. The carved dates and family initials that appear on such main outer doorway lintels as survive (chiefly in Rivington, on the working farms of Wilcock's and Moses Cocker's, for instance, and on those hefty lintels that survive in the Rivington Church and Chapel graveyards – a grimly appropriate place for the remnants of demolished houses) suggest that 1680 to 1740 was the hectic time. Why was it so? Two possibilities suggest themselves.

Firstly, the political and religious compromises of the Restoration (1660) and the 'Glorious' Revolution (1688) had the effect of signalling a probable end in England to major civil wars and social insecurities. The defeat of Louis XIV by 1713 and of the Jacobite Rebellion in 1715 gave the same message. In the new circumstances of late Stuart and early Georgian England, major landowners were now beginning, in an unashamedly commercial way, to regard the making of maximum profit from their estates as right and proper. How else could Hoghton Tower and Duxbury Hall, for instance, be improved and sustained? It might now seem a little less risky, at any rate, to push ahead with a sort of colonising of what had previously been regarded as hostile and unproductive wasteland. Tenant farmers who could make money out of sales of wool might now be worth investing in for the sake of the future rents that they could pay.

Secondly, this was the period when the population of England began its inexorable rise, a rise that continued right through to the twentieth century. As families in west Lancashire and more locally began to expand, how else was living space to be found? The moors were empty and waiting. The soil might be thin and rather acidic. The weather might be on occasion a little harsher. But where grass might be deftly enriched and where sheep might safely graze, a living could be made. Indoor occupations – spinning and handloom weaving, for instance – could augment an income made from sales of wool. Then there was always quarrying. And in a tightly built stone house, with firm and heavy stone-flagged roof on rough but stout timbers, and well-made (double-thickness) inner and outer stone walls, thoroughly packed and infilled with rubble, one could be snug, and warmed by a peat fire, on even the stormiest nights. (You can see the stone wall construction when standing on the plainly obvious foundation remains of **Calico Hall** or **Sour Milk Hall** or **Mosscrop's**, for instance.)

Fresh water was plenteously available. One could provide one's own modest food supplies, with a wholesome if repetitive fresh and cooked diet.

Subsistence farming was the normal experience for the vast majority of English people in 1700, say, if they did not live in a trading town, a London or a Bristol. Life was a continuous working hard to a pattern, a just getting by, a keeping going day by day, a keeping oneself and the youngsters fed and clothed, a preparing for inevitable winter shortages, a sometimes having a little left over if fortune smiled and the weather was kind. There was no retirement age. One did not miss having time to read, for one could not read. One did not have complex philosophical doubts. One could take a pride in one's practical skills and one's physical strength. One did not need or 'deserve' a holiday by the sea or anywhere else. Sundays and occasional 'Holy Days' sufficed for days of rest. One did have family discussions, but on severely practical matters. One did not have privacy in a one-up, one-down cottage with attached barn. One did expect to marry, for the sake (among other things) of the efficient and conventional separation and specialisation of tasks. One hoped to have both sons and daughters.

We can now wonder whether the Thomas Drinkwater and the Elizabeth Beardsworth, respectively bachelor and spinster from 'Winnell' (Withnell) who were married at Leyland Parish Church (their nearest church) on April 13 1669, were among those who chose to bring up their family in a new cottage with attached barn on the moors. And what of George Hatch of Brindle and Ellen Marsden of Withnell, married at Leyland on August 10 1669? Or Robert Whittle of Withnell who married Elizabeth Witton of Blackburn on August 24? The **Drinkwater's, Beardsworth's, Hatch, Marsden's** and **Whittle's** farms are there still on the moors, silently waiting for you to find them. What of Thomas Hodgkinson of Wheelton (had he a connection with Hodgkinson Wood, now part of Wheelton Plantation?) who married Jane Peers of 'Brinscow' on August 10 1669? This is not to mention (though of course it is) the union of William Clayton and Alice Hornby (both of Withnell) who married at Leyland on August 28 1671. Land near to Ramsden's farm was also known, as late as 1831, as Clayton Closes.

And what of James Marsden of Withnell and Mary Hooker of Whalley, married on May 6 1704, Richard Marsden of Withnell and Mary Walker of Tockholes, married on November 12 1705, John Whittle and Jennet Gorton, both of Withnell, married on August 26 1706, and Richard Richmond of Withnell and Sarah Bleasdale of Tockholes, married on August 10 1710? It is not surprising that there was a **Richmond's** Farm too, as well as the **Marsden's** and the **Whittle's**. And although the surname 'Dale' appears only once in the Leyland Parish Registers from c.1650 to c.1710, there was certainly a marriage between Alice Dale of Withnell and Richard Bateson, also of Withnell, on December 21 1704. **Dale** (sometimes 'Deal' on differing maps) **Fold** near Twist Moor Lane in Withnell appears prominently on a 1793 map of Lancashire.

While the majority of the surnames (including the Leighs) in these registers are obviously place names in origin, there are also plenty of Sharrocks or Shorrocks,

Harrocks or Horrocks, Cockers, Popes, Scots or Scotts, Snapes and Liptrots too. There is, however, not one Grime, Heaton, Pimm, Ripping, Keck, Mosscrop or Aushaw in the Leyland Parish lists of marriages in this 1650–1710 period.

It is also apparent that while marriages did happen in April, May, November and December, August does seem to be the favourite month for marriages in an agricultural community – after haytime and before harvest!

CHAPTER TWO

The Buildings

a)   Plans

Photographs of the farms in their pre-demolition state suggest that they were not at all intended to be objects of special beauty or refinement. They were plainly practical and utilitarian solutions to the need for shelter and accommodation. Given that several of their inhabitants were not only 'farmers' but also 'quarrymen' and very used to handling and shaping the local stone, the strong likelihood is that many of the houses and barns were built, and certainly repaired and extended, by those who lived and worked in them.

When you consider the structure, the actual plan, of those many farms whose surviving foundations and even low walls you can actually examine and measure, one thing is obvious right away. The majority of them were traditional stone longhouses. All those apparently built in the 1680–1740 period at any rate followed the customary plan of a one-room-deep rectangle, with four or occasionally three or occasionally five sections or bays making up the length. The width was usually a little less or a little more than 20ft (circa 6m). **Marsden's** was unusually narrow in being only about 16ft (circa 5m) wide. Once you had built the first section it was comparatively easy to add as many further sections or bays as the family numbers or the farm's acreage seemed likely to require. Thus a small farm like **Coppice Stile**, with a total of three fields amounting to five acres (plus one rod and three perches, according to the Tithe lists for Leyland Parish) had a building of three bays only, one of which was the domestic or family end, and two of which formed the barn and shippon. The whole building was something like 54ft (say 17m) long, by the usual 20ft wide. That meant that the family of two parents and (as on the photograph) three children had just one ground-floor living room of 20 by 20ft and one bedroom above it also of 20 by 20ft. There was no porch or lean-to extension.

The larger (84ft long) **Calico Hall**, on the other hand, with attached land of 18 acres, had five bays, with a domestic end of almost certainly two bays (two downstairs rooms and two bedrooms above them) for the two parents (both aged 47 in 1851)

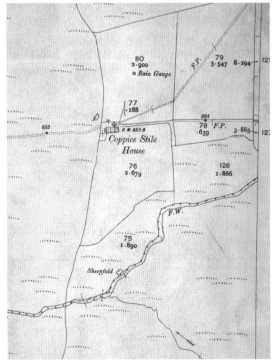

Coppice Stile House, circa 1890: three young daughters watch while poultry are fed and a barrowload of peat arrives.

and their nine children (aged 25, 22, 21, 19, 17, 15, 12, 9 and 5). Clearly, however, for a smaller family, accommodation of one up, one down, with each room being about 20ft square, was considered to be quite adequate. Seventeenth- and eighteenth-century farmworkers in Suffolk, for example, in their timber (not stone) houses, would share a semi-detached timber-framed and thatch-roofed pair of cottages. Each cottage would have one circa 18ft square living room and one circa 18ft square bedroom above it,

Ratten Clough while still complete and habitable, 1960.

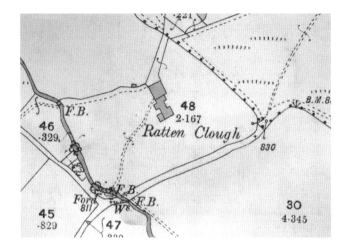

with just one joint brick chimney stack holding the structure together in the centre and providing a large ingle-nook fireplace for the living room on each side. Their barns were normally separate structures.

Our Brinscall Moors longhouses often had a porch (to cut out some draught intrusion) over the main exterior doorway and sometimes a lean-to extension at the shippon end. Occasionally, as at **Ratten Clough, Dale Fold** or **Drinkwater's**, there was a further full-height bay added at the house end to provide an additional cottage (with porch too, at **Ratten Clough**). This might be for a permanent extra labourer or family member or for occupation by temporary extra labourers at lambing or shearing time. Sometimes, as at **White Hall** and **New Ground**, the cottage or cottages would be in a separate building well away from the main longhouse structure.

At both **Keck** and **Aushaw's**, neighbouring farms, one on each side of the Rake Brook valley, there appear to be two separate structures, close together but at right angles to each other as if they housed two separate families at each site, rather than being, as one might initially assume, one large house and one large barn. The reality is revealed by the 1881 census returns.

There were indeed two separate families at **Aushaw's**: firstly the Southworths, James and Ellen, aged 45 and 44, and their three sons aged 19, 15 and 11 months and their four daughters aged 21, 8, 7, and 2; and secondly the Millers, James and Mary, aged 63 and 60, and their son and son-in-law, both aged 30, their daughter aged 24, their three granddaughters aged 7, 5 and 3 and their grandson aged one, plus a charwoman boarder, Margaret Aspin, aged 60. **Keck**, by comparison, had fewer persons in the two households: William and Mary Moulden, aged 53 and 58, plus one 74-year-old former 'indoor servant' from a farm in Kendal, in the main farm house; and one unmarried female 'cotton winder', Mary Bolton, aged 38, in the **Keck Cottage**.

If these human statistics whet your appetite – these fascinating revelations about the numbers, ages and types of persons living in Brinscall Moors longhouses – then please look forward to further social disclosures when we come to consider 'the way of life' in more detail in chapter three. Almost all the longhouse dwellers were tenants, of course, not owners. For the time being, however, let us continue our analysis of the buildings themselves, now that we know a little more about the sorts of families they were intended, or were able, to contain.

b) Walls

The basic longhouse design included a full-height gable wall at each end (i.e. no 'hipped ends'), usually with roughly shaped but large and very effective corner-stones (quoins) to hold the whole building together. (Later – nineteenth-century – structures had more finely dressed quoins.) The sides (both sides, that is) and end walls of the eighteenth-century buildings were normally 'random stone' built – i.e. like the dry-stone field walls but with a tough mix of mortar binding together the outer and

Dale Fold, the house, with cottage and barn, circa 1890.

the inner stones of these double-thickness walls. Unlike the field walls, both the actual outer and inner faces of the farm walls contained stones that were carefully flattened and smoothed, the inner face to take a layer of plaster for interior 'decorating' (painting or even wall-papering!) – as can still be seen at **Pimm's**, for example.

It is evident from the 1890s (or so) photograph that the outer walls of **Coppice Stile** have been lime-washed to reduce rainwater penetration. (There is no guttering on that house.) The south-west-facing gable wall of **Dale Fold** has also been rendered and then lime-washed for the same reason. (The side walls there do have guttering.) At one ruined farm, but only one, there are some remaining heavy ridging stones lying scattered about amid the debris. At just two of the ruined farms there are still some carefully stacked roofing flags, leaning together on the ground with the securing nail holes clearly exposed. You are permitted – even recommended – to think of the farming families, including the young children, whose lives and labours and whose sleep during the wildest storms were protected and safeguarded by those very stones. Who took away the roofing flags and ridge stones of all the other farms?

There are some signs at some farms (**Marsden's** for example) as among Brinscall's

School Lane cottages that fairly carefully dressed stone (but not quite top ashlar condition) was beginning to be used in layered courses in the nineteenth century to make up the 'front' walls of a farmhouse. Random stonework remained normal, however, for the gable ends and the 'rear' – in so far as the terms 'front' and 'rear' mean anything in these detached farm buildings. There was little sense on the moors of a street or entrance-façade frontage even of a School Lane kind, let alone a Bath Crescent or Chatsworth kind. But carefully layered courses of dressed stone are apparent in those two non-farms of Brinscall Woods, Heather Lea and Blackhurst, which clearly are, in character, Victorian gentlemen's suburban villas rather than working farms. They are more like slightly reduced versions of the 1876 Brinscall Hall, indeed. Compare the remaining low walls of Blackhurst with those of the nearby **Top o'th'Wood**. There is a most significant difference. The intriguing underground stables opposite the two houses are also more Blackhurst than **Top o'th'Wood** when you examine the stonework closely. A gentleman's residence would need stables, surely, as well as a garden (an elegant, fashionable, rock-and-grotto garden in the Blackhurst case).

c) Windows

The size and shape of such surviving ground floor stone window ledges as can still be seen in the moorland ruins suggest that the early eighteenth-century house windows were of the mullion and casement kind (they certainly were at **Coppice Stile**) while later eighteenth- or nineteenth-century windows, as at **Dale Fold** and **Whittle's,** were of the sash kind. The surviving, and obviously nineteenth-century, Watson's and Pickering's

Whittle's, abandoned and beginning to be demolished, circa 1920.

(near the A675 Belmont Road) have sash windows. **Ratten Clough**, on the other hand, has (largely now infilled) mullion and casement windows in the rear wall of one early bay of the house ('rear' wall as in 'opposite-side-to-porch-and-main-door'). The surviving, and busily sheep-farming Baron's Fold has good renewed mullion and casement windows meanwhile. It has a cottage that has been added to the north end of the house. It also used to have a large, detached barn, now partly pulled down and replaced by a considerable number of modern storing and sheltering structures.

d) Surviving Originals

Habitable longhouses remain aplenty in the region to the west of Brinscall allowing one to see what might have been made of some of our moorland farmhouses if people had still been able – and willing – to adapt them for twentieth-century living and even working. A slow car journey or a cautious (because of traffic) stroll along the full length of Harbour Lane is instructive. There are no fewer than seven inhabited longhouses quite close to and quite visible from the road. Six of the seven have received, and perhaps benefited from, various levels and qualities of refurbishment or even improvement. One of the six is clearly better than the rest in its maintenance of authentic character. Two of the six, while surviving, and now exhibiting the appearance of converted barns, had obviously been replaced as houses in the late nineteenth century by big, square, high-roomed Victorian mini-mansions erected in front of them.

There is, however, just one of the original seven which retains its full longhouse style with a glorious indifference to 'improvement'. Its walls, its long flag roof, its windows, its porch, its proportions (one third house, two thirds barn) are just as they should be for a genuine example of a Lancashire uplands longhouse. Perhaps **Heapey Moor Farm** or **Pimm's** looked very like this. There are, I happily admit, delightful flowers in the garden, and the interior is very smart and comfortable, with all modern conveniences tastefully provided. It is a perfect reminder of what might have been.

e) Different Plans

'What might have been' is an apt phrase to describe my initial puzzlement when first examining the ground plan of two other individual moorland farms. They manifestly are not simple longhouses, but what were they, what was their appearance, particularly their roof structure, and how old were they? Had they been added to, or oddly modified? Certainly the ground plans of **Botany Bay** (built, probably, about 1805) and **Solomon's Temple** were at first sight a conundrum in each case. It is not that there are few stones left. There are many. The complete foundations and considerable sections of low wall are plainly there to be seen. There seem to be two living rooms

Causeway House, Heapey, a typical seventeenth-/eighteenth-century longhouse still flourishing in 2010.

side by side at both farms, those at **Solomon's Temple** having an undoubted domestic fireplace in one and undoubted domestic outer window ledges in the other. What, therefore, could have been their roof structure? A very wide and very tall one? Two separate ones with a central valley between them? The answer is supplied by a recently seen representation (based on a photograph) of **Botany Bay**.

At that farm the original house was doubled in ground-floor size (at some time between a map of 1848 and a map of 1894) by the addition of a large lean-to building all the way along the north side of the original. The lean-to roof would mean limited first-floor accommodation, of course. But what sort of farm was **Botany Bay**? The quality and surviving height of its boundary and field-enclosure walls speaks of nineteenth-century firmness. Beyond the walls is decidedly rough waste. And in the outer walls of the house itself and of the barn too are carefully dressed stones – for quoins and for door jambs – with sophisticated bevelled edges. Even the gateposts are of rather superior style. So **Botany Bay** (its name suggesting remoteness and surviving under challenge, as in early nineteenth-century Australia) was perhaps not always a year-round working farm but was also used, as it certainly was in the early twentieth century, as a base for grouse-shooters and beaters. Therefore, perhaps, the use of the alternative name – **Summer House**? There were nevertheless 10 persons (with ages varying from 64 years to one year) living there in 1891. It was a farm of 12 acres in 1881 with residents numbering five.

Solomon's Temple, on the other hand, was quite a large (36 acres) establishment with a variety of subsidiary buildings (one of which must have been a sizeable lean-to structure added between 1848 and 1894) within a well-walled farmyard. Once you look now in detail at the stonework quality of the surviving house walls of **Solomon's Temple** it becomes obvious which is the original structure and which is the additional lean-to. Besides the wide and long main buildings there was also a separate block with excellent quoins. What there also was on the east (or slightly uphill) side of the farm was a fine well. On the west (or slightly downhill) side was, until very recently, a complete outside lavatory, a stone-built, sloping-roofed small shed, inside which was a level stone seat with circular central hole. One loo, of course, for two parents and six children in 1851.

Botany Bay (the Summer House), having lost its barn and its upper storey, circa 1950.

Grouse Cottage, with smartly repainted walls, circa 1950. The wind-powered electricity generator is visible above the store room.

f) Water

Wells and lavatories were regular and normal outside provisions (appropriately and judiciously sited) in eighteenth- and nineteenth-century farms. There was no internal provision, of course. Not one of our 48 farms ever had mains water or mains sewage pipes. None ever had mains electricity, though **Grouse Cottage** did have its own wind-driven generator to provide electric lighting into the 1950s. Equally remarkably it also eventually had its own independent water supply, installed by its resident Liverpool Corporation employee in the late 1940s. Traces of the piped supply route can still be found in the fields above, and also by the brook just above **Pope's Farm**. Otherwise and elsewhere, water could be carried into the house in pails from the well (or from the stream when there was one nearby) and stored in barrels. A small pond, as at **Heapey Moor** or **Cocker's Folly** where streams were distant, provided water for poultry, sheep and cattle. Water for washing – of persons, utensils, clothing – in the do-for-all living room – was carried in, every drop, and of course carried out when used, unless it could drain out from a simple shallow stone sink positioned by an outside wall.

There are really good wells, stone-lined and practically designed, square-shaped, rather than circular, at **Heaton House** (where there is also a good horse-trough), **Hatch Place, Leigh Place, Scott Hall, Aushaw's, Marsden's** and **Fir Farm**, in addition to the often-noticed **Drinkwater's**. There is also an arched, stone-lined well and an underground supply route down to the house, in the walled garden area above and behind Blackhurst. Heather Lea had a large, concrete-lined water tank sunk into the private ground behind the house.

At **Ratten Clough**, at the edge of the farmyard to the west of the house, is one of the best remaining outside lavatories. Within the little building can still be seen the upright supporting stone on which rested the stone seat. If, without being too imaginative, you care to glance behind the lavatory building, at the field side away from the house, you might notice that there is a deliberate break in the foundation stonework, allowing, as it were, seepage from within the lavatory into the field below. But of course the removal and emptying of the tub beneath the stone seat was one of the regular physical household duties to be undertaken by family members. That would certainly have been necessary at **Grouse Cottage** where the lean-to small lavatory building survives intact outside the north-eastern gable-end of the former house.

Whatever type of waste-disposal system had been thought adequate in the eighteenth century there is no doubt that later Manchester and London cholera outbreaks, and

Goose Green farm, circa 1935. Lavatory block on the left. Print Works chimney on the right. Two sisters are standing by the house door: Bessie Mayor (wife of Ben Mayor) and Florrie Chadwick.

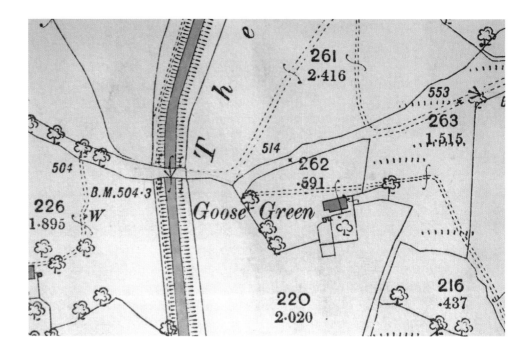

Victorian Public Health Acts, made the provision of at least one small outside lavatory block absolutely a normal feature of every farm whose detailed plan appears on Ordnance Survey maps by 1894. Close to, but discreetly separate from, the main longhouse in plan after plan, is the little square building that contains the "necessary", the "convenience", the "privy", the "lavvy". The photograph of **Goose Green** shows a quite generously sized block (whose purpose was freely acknowledged by the supplier of the photograph) away from the house at the bottom of the garden.

g) "Hutched Up"

When I think carefully now of the sites of all 48 of the ruined farms, I can think of only one farm which was not built on a more or less levelled site, specially levelled, that is, even where the surrounding land was basically sloping to a lesser or greater extent. The one exception was **Besom Hall**, which actually took advantage of a considerable slope in the surrounding field by having a two-storey section at one end of the building and a three-storey section at the other. **Besom Hall**, so named because special farmers' brooms, or besoms, were made and sold there, was built right up next to the Sharples-Hoghton Turnpike (the A675), "hutched up to it" as we would say in Lancashire, near Roddlesworth and Cliffe Fold. You could walk from the road straight into its kitchen/living room, I am told. At the other, or field-slope, end there was a shippon, stable and pigsty on the level below the living room. (The building was at right angles to the road.) Besom-making, practised in other farms nearer Brinscall too, was a useful extra earner, like handloom weaving, picker-making or quarrying, of course.

Among all the 48 I can think of only one other farm where the longhouse gable wall was, like **Besom Hall**'s, right next to a road and its passing traffic (occasional, and horse-drawn, in the nineteenth century). All the remaining 46 had their own tracks – short, in some cases, but more often covering quite a long distance – leading up to their farm yard and main outer doorway from a road. **Hatch Place** and **Heaton House**, for instance, or **Liptrot's** or **Marsden's** or **Fir Farm** had their own track leading from another track. The one other farm whose domestic-end gable wall was only a few feet, a metre, say, from passing carts and carriages was also abutting the Sharples-Hoghton Turnpike. This was **Lower Calf Hey**. You can hurtle now in your car immediately past the remaining part of the gable wall – but without knowing so, initially, for the gable wall is now less than half its original height. You can, however, easily see the gable wall of the barn, even while hurtling, for this is a good 40ft (circa 12m) in from the road.

At **Besom Hall** you can simply see the routine, tell-tale sycamore tree as you pass it (while still in hurtle-mode) but you can then park your car some distance away and walk back to find the familiar sad heap of stone on the slope by the tree. You can also – while your car remains parked – find the only other farm at all near to a road (and it is again the A675 Sharples-Hoghton Turnpike). This is **Rake**, now under relatively recently planted trees, about 60ft (say 18m) in from the road near the quite sharp (and potentially dangerous) Rake Reservoir bend. There are two separate heaps of stone, presumably the house and the barn, in addition to the remains of field-walls. Passing fishermen might wonder why you are more interested in stones than in the fish below the reservoir's surface.

h) Missing Member

There is one other farm that deserves individual attention at this stage – because, unlike all the rest, there were two of it (but not at the same time) and now there is nothing left of it at all. This is the unfortunate **Richmond's**. If you seek the remains of the eighteenth-century **Richmond's** that lasted almost until 1888, you will have to stand quietly on the track that leads up to **Botany Bay** and glance briefly at Withnell Villa. The Liverpool Corporation Waterworks Committee decided to demolish **Richmond's** and to build in its place, more or less on top of the foundations of the farm, a smart new residence, in a semi-Scottish style, for its local engineer. This is the Withnell Villa at which you are briefly looking, until, noting the surviving Ramsden's (now a row of cottages) along the track to your left, you politely press ahead, cross the stile and rise up with the path on to the moor and find yourself eventually at **Botany Bay**.

By the time the new Ordnance Survey map of 1894 was issued there was a new **Richmond's** about 300m to the west, with its own new track leading up from the

Butterworth Brow-Twist Moor Lane road. It appears, on the map, to be a longhouse, but with three separate yard or garden areas, each with a small (lavatory?) block away from the house, as if it was actually a short terrace of cottages. The principal resident was a Joseph Billington, however, and the building was also known as 'Billington's' as well as 'Richmond's'. Billington himself, mind you, was not a farmer but a quarryman! Could he be said to have dug, not his own grave, but that of his house? The house had, alas, a short life if not a merry one, for by 1901 it was already on the edge of the expanding Withnell (now Brinscall) quarry. In that year it was, as local residents say, "pulled down". This is the farm that I invite you to imagine in your mind as a ghost house hanging in mid-air, for the quarry has now not only engulfed the site of the farm but has dug deep into and under the fields that once surrounded it.

i) More Different Plans

Not so much a mystery in terms of their structure and appearance as **Botany Bay** and **Solomon's Temple**, but two farms in the Twist Moor group, **The Oaks** and **Tower View**, have ground floor plans that are nearer to a square than a long, narrow rectangle. They were probably the last of our 48 to be built, for on an 1831 map of the area, which shows **Scott Hall**, **Grouse Cottage** (actually then called 'Twist Moor'), **Aushaw's**, **Deal** (for **Dale**) **Fold**, **Keck**, **Mosscrop's**, **Pope's** (then called 'Clough') and **Snape's**, there is no **The Oaks** and no **Tower View**, and no sign of their field walls. By 1891 both farms are on the map, together with their new, largely straight-edged fields.

The Oaks in 1891 contained Stephen Miller, a general labourer and farmer, and his wife Ellen, aged 37 and 38 respectively, plus their six children (four girls and two boys) aged 12, 10, 8, 5, 2, and, in the case of their recently born daughter, just a few months. Mr. Miller's widowed mother Mary, aged 71, was their resident 'housekeeper'. The 12-year-old daughter Mary was a cotton weaver and part-time 'scholar', and was the only family member bringing in a little extra income, of course. Presumably Stephen Miller needed to do quite a bit of general labouring! **The Oaks** had been a farm of only three acres in 1881 when 66 year old William Miller, father of Stephen, had been tenant, and his 60 year old wife Mary, the 'housekeeper' of 1891, had been the only other resident. Likewise, **Tower View** was a farm of no more than five acres. Its tenant in 1881 was a 67-year-old widow, Margaret Culshaw, with her two unmarried daughters, 38-year-old Elizabeth and 34-year-old Mary, both of whom were cotton winders. All three were 'refugees' from Ormskirk.

The house (**The Oaks**) the Millers of 1891 lived in appears, when you stand next to it, to have an original section (two rooms deep, one about 10 ft by 18, the other about 14 ft by 18) on a more or less north-south axis. There is a fine fireplace, still with smoke-blackened stone and mortar, in the larger of the two downstairs rooms. There is a central doorway on the south side and sturdy quoins on the four original corners. Attached to the east side of this original section, however, is an even larger section, with the broken remains of a well-shaped stone window ledge on the south side. Was this the barn? On the west side of the original two-roomed section has been added a further, narrower (perhaps lean-to?) building. Separate from the main block, at the west end of the farmyard, was a small two-roomed building. A lavatory and a store room?

A clear track ran up to the farm from **Grouse Cottage** and **Scott Hall**. It continued past **The Oaks** and on up to the nearby **Tower View**. The view from **The Oaks**, meanwhile, on a crisp, breezy, blue-skied autumn day, is truly glorious, the sheep-fields (full of munching ewes) sloping down to the Roddlesworth Valley, with the distant Bleasdale Fells, Pendle Hill and the even more distant Black Combe and Coniston mountains all bathed in sunshine. Did the Miller family have time to notice and rejoice in this? Did the 10-, 8- and 5-year-olds run and play in the fields here? Did young Mary, the 12-year-old, plod wearily, hopefully and hungrily up the track from her several hours at the power looms in Abbey Mill? Was old Mary, her granny, hanging out the washing? Did they wave to each other as young Mary passed the **Scott Hall** gateway on her way home?

There is a good deal of upright stonework left in place, or lying significantly around, at **The Oaks**. There is also a curious and interesting series of humps and hollows (the remains of a type of 'opencast' quarrying, the source of building stone for the two farms?) if you walk up the track to take a look at the **Tower View** ruins. And the particular tower you are viewing, by the way, once you reach these ruins, is obviously the one that belongs to the former great landowner here, that is, Hoghton Tower, on its tree-clad hill four miles away. Neither of the other two possibilities, the Blackpool Tower of 1894 or the Darwen Tower of 1898, was even thought of, let alone erected, when **Tower View** farm was built (in, presumably, the 1870s at latest).

As with the plan of **The Oaks**, **Tower View**'s plan is by no means that of an orthodox longhouse. Quite long it is, some 55ft (17m), but also wide, some 25ft (8m) indeed. It appears to have three distinct sections, the western-most one having an internal dividing wall, as if separating shippon from barn. There are two upright but slender stone slabs near the interior wall of the central section. There is also an extensive and separate outer building (lavatory and storage, again?) at the west end of the farm yard. One small sloping, half-height gatepost survives at the southern entrance to the farm yard. And if you look carefully at the rubble in the western section of the house (or barn) you will see a pleasingly shaped block of stone that looks like a survivor from a window or door lintel, or from a piece of stonework running round the building where top of wall met base of roof. The Nowell family in 1891 would have known exactly where it was from.

It was, however, an intriguing first name that the head of the Nowell family had at this time. Though he appears as 'Thomas' Nowell on a short list of local farmers printed in the 1960s, he is clearly dignified as 'Doctor' Nowell on the census returns of 1891 – and yet, by profession, he was not a medic but a 'Quarryman'. The local history list calls him both 'Doctor' and 'Thomas', just to be on the safe side. But either he had withdrawn from the medical profession, or he was a serious former university academic, or rather more probably, like some rough or aspiring North American dwellers who boldly used the first names 'Duke' or 'Earl', he had been ambitiously christened 'Doctor' as well as 'Thomas'. Whatever his former way of life, the quarryman Nowell of 1891 was 35 years of age, he had a wife, Alice, also 35, and he had five children of 11, 6, 4, 3 and 1 – Martha, Robert, Aaron, John and Nancy. There was not one 'Doctor' among them.

j) Winds and Shelter

Thinking of wide, exciting vistas and the almost entirely open-to-four-winds locations of **The Oaks** and **Tower View** – and of **Scott Hall**, with its single sycamore tree, too – it would probably be unfortunate and inappropriate to dare to have favourites among the ruined farms in terms of the quality of their siting. It would be equally wrong to have less-than-favourites whose sites might be considered dull, unimaginative, bleak … Nevertheless, for me, four particular farms do stand out for the visually 'nestling' quality of their physical position in an otherwise particularly lofty or exposed landscape. You may well be willing to supply other (and possibly even better?) candidates, but I repeat now three names and sites that I have offered previously in a similar context as providing the appearance of especial shelter in high places. I recommend **Great Hill**, **Drinkwater's** and **Pimm's**, and I now add a fourth: **Pope's**, in its own little clough. (No wonder the farm was originally called 'Clough' – a clough being a narrow valley, a depression, a ravine.)

Great Hill Farm, at 329m (1,070ft) the highest of all the 48, is neatly positioned on an almost level piece of land, with raised terrace on the south side, the whole comfortably tucked into the south-facing slope of Great Hill itself. All the fiercest blasts from the north, the north-east and north-west would have passed high above the farm, hardly disturbing a chimney or the surrounding stand of trees. The hill is a benign protector; its summit is 180ft above the farm. Only an occasional – really a very rare – south-easter would dare to affront **Great Hill Farm**. Far more frequently, sun from the south and west would warm, as it still does warm, the hillside slopes above and below, down the fields to the Dean Black Brook, which has its own charming and lengthy stand of trees. One could pause – or sit, indeed – for lazy minutes, an hour even, marvelling at the ingenuity of a seventeenth-/eighteenth-century builder who chose this site. What an excellent site for a picnic, one could find oneself adding. But, of course, this was a workplace, a guarantee of subsistence and survival, a refuge, a proud and busy home for the Counsell family in 1881 and the Gaskells in 1891 – seven people and more at any one time for two centuries at least, whatever the weather. There were two main blocks at right angles, a house-building with porch, and a separate barn. There was one small outhouse and a cart track that climbed up from White Coppice and from **Drinkwater's**, and then dropped gently, smoothly down over the high summit slopes and into the farm yard on Great Hill's flank. It is a delectable spot.

Rivalling it in ingenuity, in charm, in shelter and in bosky security and strength is **Drinkwater's**, some one third of a mile to the west and about 50ft lower at 1020ft. In its later days, in the 1930s when it was still habitable and much used during large-scale sheep-shearings (see the photographs of Harold Mayor on page 169), it was an impressively large single structure, 100ft (30m) long more or less. There was a sizeable (wide and high as well as long) barn at the east end, and at the west end not only a house but a cottage too. The whole was distinctly larger than the combined size of **Great Hill's** separate house and barn blocks. Apart from overall size, **Drinkwater's** also has five memorable features.

It has, immediately to the south of the buildings, an impressively high terrace with a row of five large trees grandly overlooking the Dean Black Brook valley. It has a separate but ostentatiously fenced plantation of tall mixed deciduous (mainly beech) and evergreen conifer trees, about 25 of each type, 100 metres to the White Coppice side of the farm – a plantation that makes the position of the farm instantly recognisable even from distant Chorley and the far plains of West Lancashire. It has a famous spring, a smooth pool of clear, fresh water welling up below the terrace in a sort of stone-lined sump.

Above it, the broad track from White Coppice to Great Hill, **Pimm's** and the Belmont Road passes right along the terrace, and the gates and gateposts at each end plainly and purposefully marked the extent of the farm yard section. You still feel, almost, that you should ask permission from ghostly former residents before presuming to pass along that terrace. (We could try the shades of Joseph and Elizabeth Jackson living there in 1851, for example, or William and Mary Bibby who lived there in 1881. Mind you, Joseph and Elizabeth, by then aged 76 and 59, were still there in 1881, although living with their granddaughter Elizabeth Smith in the **Drinkwater's Cottage**, not in the main house with William and Mary and their 14- and 4-year-old sons Frederick and Arthur.) Finally, as at **Great Hill Farm**, the buildings, above and to the north of the terrace, are splendidly comfortably set against the rising land behind, to provide the protection that both farms enjoy from the coldest northerly winds. On a late November afternoon, with a piercingly cool air scything in from the palest blue skies over Ingleborough and the Coniston Fells, there was hardly a stirring of a twig in the trees of **Great Hill** and **Drinkwater's**, though out on the main Brinscall Moors below, all was a cold, wild buffeting.

Pimm's, at 1002ft (305m) high, is also most comfortingly placed against, in this case, the north-east shoulder of Great Hill, and especially well protected from north or north-west winds. Though just visible from the A675, it is actually rather more isolated than, say, **Drinkwater's**, being a good 20 minutes' brisk walk from its nearest neighbour. It can be exposed to easterly winds, but there is a reassurance, as one

Drinkwater's in ruins, 1966. Great Hill and the trees of Great Hill farm in the distance.

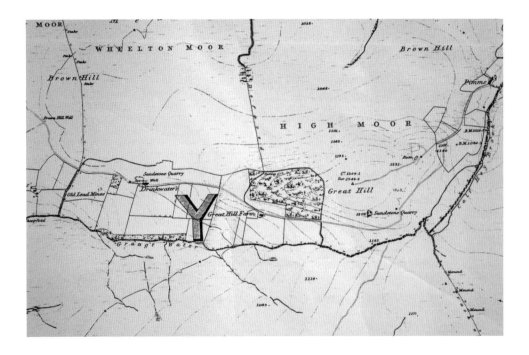

Peter Mayor by the Drinkwater's porch, circa 1930.

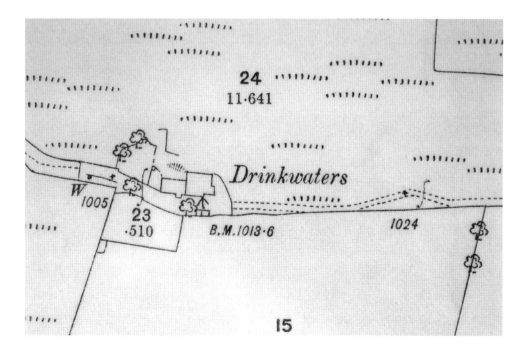

approaches it, in the height and spread and familiarity of its four large protecting trees. These give it a civilised, welcoming, domestic quality. There is no formal high terrace of the **Drinkwater's** kind, but there is, immediately south of the building, a charming grassy slope that steepens beyond the line of trees down to the nearby Calf Hey Brook. Chattering agreeably very close (but not too close) to the western end of the building is a small tributary of the Calf Hey. **Pimm's** (Pims) is very clearly shown on a Lancashire area map of the 1790s.

The single farm-with-barn building is large, almost as long as **Drinkwater's** (about 90ft – 27m), and a good 20ft wide. There are excellent quoins (but not too sophisticated) on the north-west corner, and an indication of exterior doorways on both sides and also of internal communicating doorways (pairs of upright stone slabs) within the house. It has been yet another fine example of the longhouse type. The eastern end (a barn section?) appears to have been slightly wider than the rest of the building. Again, one can feel that it is an ideal place, now, for a picnic and, in its day, for a happy working farm – for the Brownlow family in 1881 and 1891. It is high enough up the south-eastern slopes of Great Hill still to receive good sunlight even on a late November afternoon. Though protected from most storms, it does not find itself in a winter sun-shadow cast by those same protecting slopes. Full marks again to its original builder-surveyor.

The three farms whose virtues I have just been extolling are not only the highest of all the 48 but are also on the south-facing sides of what one might describe as the 'Great Hill Massif'. Their special protection is from northerly winds. My fourth example of unusual shelter in high places – **Pope's Farm** on 'Withnell Moor' – is, by contrast, well protected from the west and east and, to an extent, from the south, but not at all from the north. Indeed, as one discovers on a cold and breezy winter's day, its little clough is entirely open to northerly airs. On the other hand it stands (or it used to stand!) at 'only' 775ft (240m).

The clough in which it hides (and indeed you cannot see the ruins until you are almost upon them) has been formed by the swiftly flowing 'Rushy' brook. This cuts its way downwards from Ferney Slacks and Old Man's Hill past **New Temple** and **Botany Bay** until it flows energetically under Twist Moor Lane and into the Rake reservoir. On its route it has scooped out a special, short, sheltering hollow just at a convenient point where an important footpath from **Ratten Clough** to **Aushaw's** and **Keck** needs to cross it. There are certainly 'Stepping Stones' next to **Pope's Farm**, but, more, now, of an improvised, casual type than of the formal, official type suggested by the OS map designation. If you approach **Pope's** from the east, however, there is a fine stile on which to stand for a first surprise sighting of the farm ruins just below you, with the brook and the ongoing path on the far side of the clough to entertain you further.

It was again a traditional longhouse, as you can rapidly tell. Comparatively modest in size; about 50ft (15m) long by the usual 20ft wide; probably three bays or sections; a porch on the 'brook' side; certainly an obvious 'containing' wall extending northwards from the house to hold back the valley sides below the farm and near the position of the present stile.

When you stand to look at these things, do think of the tenant, William Dewhurst, living there apparently alone in his sheltered homestead in 1858, three double 'boosts' or stalls for cattle in his shippon at the top end, plenty of handloom-woven cloth emerging from his solitary hours' labours according to one record; and the same William Dewhurst still living there alone at age 69, farming his 10 acres in 1881. By 1890 it was Ellen Marsden who was living there alone. By 1891 **Pope's Farm** was 'unoccupied'. By 1960 (and probably a good deal earlier) it was 'a heap of stones' according to a local record. The 'Rushy' brook rushes heedlessly on however.

k) 'Lost' in the Woods

Most accessible, easiest to find in theory among all our 'lost' farms, are those quite close to familiar tracks that run round or through the Brinscall Woods. Yet in practice they are, for more than half the year, the easiest to overlook, the easiest to walk right past without realising. Not only are their tumbled walls thickly covered in rich, damp green moss (an excellent disguise in itself) but once, by May, brambles, bracken, saplings and burgeoning undergrowth generally have joined holly bushes in full leaf, the ruins can hide behind a thick canopy of stems and foliage. Not quite a tropical jungle but certainly a barrier to instant recognition. Nevertheless, all except two sets of cottages follow the traditional, venerable, longhouse plan, and have design features most worthy of your attention. In any case, the sheer delight of finding them, of successfully searching them out in their leafy concealment, brings its own smiles and satisfaction. Between May and October, however, eyes do need to be specially peeled.

Recognisable as a small longhouse with its porch, modest extension and separate store house, **Ripping**, under its trees, is one of the more easily spotted and explored of the Brinscall Woods farms. To see it, just turn aside by a simple stile near the Well Lane-Edge Gate Lane junction shortly before the waterfall. Seven people lived there in 1851, four in 1881, and two in 1891. Similarly, once you have taken the track to the right through the gateway at the junction and then turned left up another and formerly cobbled track (most of the cobbles rather buried by grass) just beyond the waterfall, the extensive ruins of **Heaton House**, with its well, its horse trough, its rough-hewn pairs of gateposts and cobbled yard, are soon visible beneath the trees. The visibility is even better now that many of the mature conifers in the immediate area have been felled.

Hatch Place is then less than 100m to the east, with the parallel walls of a short, curving track connecting the farm to Edge Gate Lane. There is a pair of early gateposts at the lane end, but it is wise and necessary to respect the barbed wire fence that links them. There are 2 other gateposts to inspect just beyond the rectangular pile of stones that were once the **Hatch** longhouse. Field enclosure walls that belonged to **Heaton** and **Hatch** abound, some of them still upright. You can then walk slightly uphill a further 200m to the east to find that particular tree-clothed heap of mossy stones that used to be the **White Hall Cottages**, next to a ladder stile over the open moor's boundary wall. These cottages, two of them evidently making a single block of roughly 30 by 20ft (9m by 6m), form the one obvious non-longhouse of the woods. (I suppose one could classify the **New Ground** row of five cottages as a multi-occupancy long longhouse.)

If you then walk south next to and inside the boundary wall where wood now meets moor, you will eventually, having passed a pair of ancient gateposts, find yourself stumbling, almost, over the porch (or dairy?) and then the main longhouse building of **Liptrot's Farm**. A typical example of its kind, with a small outhouse just beyond it (to the south), and evidence of a cobbled yard and trackway there too. It was a small establishment altogether, of six or seven acres, with just three residents (the Taylors) in 1851, three (the Briggs) in 1881, and four in 1891 (a 44-year-old widow, Sophia Bradbury, with her two middle-aged sisters – one of them born in Russia – and a brother). Quite near at hand, as you stand at **Liptrot's**, are three more longhouse farms: **Leigh Place**, **Top o'th'Wood** and **Marsden's**.

Just a little way downhill, one small field away from **Liptrot's** in fact, is **Leigh Place**. A good longhouse, with a projection at the north end, a west porch and a separate (lavatory?) block at the south end, it also had a splendid stone-lined, square well just across the track where the track makes a double right angle bend. Some good gateposts too. Continuing west and downhill in a more or less straight line from **Liptrot's** (following the signs of the walled track) you will quickly arrive at that extraordinary combination of country house site and farm site that is Blackhurst and **Top o'th'Wood**. Blackhurst, along with the familiar and slightly later Heather Lea, will deserve its own separate attention in due course, neither of them ever being working farms. For the time being our attention is on **Top o'th'Wood**.

This eighteenth-century longhouse was built on a level site just where the steepest slope on our Ice Age edge temporarily relents and before it resumes its climb at a less abrupt angle. **Top o'th'Wood** was, and in a way still is, served by the track which runs right from Edge Gate Lane, past the waterfall and **New Ground** to pass Heather Lea and Blackhurst (to which it became a sort of carriage drive) and continues down to the far end of the present woods by **Goose Green**. **Top o'th'Wood** is right up against and alongside this track. There is an obvious, fairly rough-and-ready, barn and then the house with what appears to be a small garden and a pair of garden gateposts. A drive had run off the track to finish behind the farm. Once Blackhurst was built, a second drive ran behind the **Top o'th'Wood** drive to finish higher up and in front of the Blackhurst entrance and lawn area. Below the main track are the enigmatic (if not unique) underground stables and a small complexity of paths and gateways. **Top o'th'Wood** was a sizeable farm of 20 acres with eight inhabitants in 1851, eight, six and eight in three separate households in 1881 and four and 10 in two separate households in 1891.

There used to be a special track leading from **Top o'th'Wood** to **Marsden's**. This is impossible to follow now, the conifer plantation having obliterated it. The alternatives are: to plunge boldly through the conifer and brushwood mass, keeping at roughly the **Top o'th'Wood**/Blackhurst height (contour height 200m.), and making for the southern edge of the wood where the moorland slope is suddenly visible and **Marsden's** is plainly revealed; to return almost to the **Leigh Place** site and follow a wall and alternative track which crosses Sour Milk Brook on stepping stones (formerly on a wooden bridge) and makes directly for **Marsden's**; to give up adventurousness and walk down almost to **Goose Green** and then walk up a clear but unofficial path on the inside edge of the wood, bringing you unerringly to the prominent surviving gable of **Marsden's**.

This farm, like **Liptrot's**, is certainly, now, by the edge of Brinscall Woods, though the former boundary walls of its fields are more obvious. There is also a good deal more of it left. It was a narrow longhouse, comparatively, but of quite a length (60ft or 18m including barn and lavatory/attached shed at the north end). It has an almost complete south gable end, with bedroom window, internal blue-brick chimneys, internal slots for bedroom joists, two excellent (eastern) ground-floor window ledges, carefully laid courses of dressed stonework on the eastern wall, external steps down to the kitchen door, a probable well and a walled garden area to the west.

Undoubtedly the most extraordinary building development in the whole of the Brinscall Woods area was the large and long two-building main farm of **New Ground**, with the separate row of five cottages (**New Ground Cottages**) nearly 100m to the south. The main longhouse blocks, though now beneath an almost impenetrable cover of brambles, nettles, saplings and massed tree-roots (the latter the result of the emergency clearing of huge windfallen oaks and birches) are immediately next to and just below the Edge Gate Lane-Heather Lea-Blackhurst 'carriage drive' after its passing of the waterfall. There you can see the track coming up from the Bakehouse Lane bridge, with two gateposts still standing, and suddenly there are the low remains of the two **New Ground** longhouses, with just one section left up to shoulder-height. Next to these two on the lower side was a large artificially flattened yard area raised up on a high terraced stone wall structure that still, just about, survives. Notice, also, two upright stone slabs of a not entirely obvious purpose. Within this first main part of the **New Ground** 'complex' were at least four separate households in 1851. There are at least two, possibly four, lavatory structures by the yard wall too.

Proceeding southwards and slightly uphill along the 'carriage drive', passing a roofless barn on the right and the beginnings of the long parallel walled lane (now signposted as a public footpath) that runs down to the lower parts of Brinscall Woods, you shortly should see the remaining one of two gateposts on your right. This is about adult hip-height, but it is totally ivy-covered and therefore, in this environment, effectively camouflaged. Supposing that you spot it, you, with determination, will notice that there is another track, now well tree-covered, leading fairly steeply downhill. It led to another terrace along which were built five cottages in one long row. Their roofs and chimneys must have been about the height that the 'carriage drive' has now reached as it passes along and above them. On the lower side of the cottages was an open space terminating in another wall overlooking the lower woods. There were at least three lavatory blocks along this wall. At the far (south) end of the open space was a narrow pedestrian gateway by means of which one could reach what until the twentieth century were sloping open fields. It is an intriguing scene.

The cottages must have been no more than two-up-two-down in size. Of the total of seven **New Ground** households (with two cottages unoccupied) in 1851 – including longhouses as well as cottages – six households contained, respectively, five, six, seven, eight, six and seven persons. One household contained just one person, the 17-year-old unmarried Esther Neville. This solitary girl, born in Livesey (towards Blackburn), spent her lonely days – earning her modest living, no doubt – as a handloom weaver. Of the 40 **New Ground**-dwellers in 1851, excluding the 18 who were either housewives or 'scholars', or too young to go to school, seven were farmers or farm-labourers, but 15 were weavers. **New Ground** was an industrious little village on its own. It was, however, entirely 'pulled down' in 1908.

CHAPTER THREE

The People and Their
Way of Life

THOSE WHO INHABITED our moorland farms in the nineteenth century seem in many cases to have lived particularly healthy and lengthy lives – by comparison with nineteenth-century urban dwellers at any rate. The number of Brinscall Moors farmers and their wives who lived at least through to their 60s and 70s is not small. Similarly the size of their families – the frequency and regularity of the births of their children up to a total of five and six, and even to nine or more on occasion – is especially notable.

But then the pure moorland air, the pure and plentiful water supply, the home-cooking of home-produced food, the efficient siting – and spacing – of lavatories, and the regular, varied and unavoidable physical exercise for both men and women provided an environment conducive to good health. It was very different, for instance, from that of the cramped, concentrated back-to-back or cellar dwelling populations by the river Irwell in Manchester, the Croal in Bolton or the Brun and Calder in Burnley. And the tenant-farmers on the moors, though never cash-rich, did have a considerable independence and scope for initiative, and a certain pride therefore in achievement and in decent survival.

For a balanced awareness of the numbers and general character of persons living in the moorland farms it will be helpful to get to know the surnames of several of the families and of the particular farms they lived in at one time or another. You will probably begin to know people even better, as individuals, once you also know their Christian names, their ages and their occupations where they were old enough to have these. I hope you would soon like to meet, firstly, several of the more remarkable among the long-lived farmers (male and female), and then, subsequently, several of the larger family groups followed by a selection of the smaller ones – most of these details relating to the period from the 1840s to the 1890s, being chiefly derived from census returns between 1851 and 1891.

When you do read the forthcoming statistics, however, the names, the ages, places of birth and occupations, please be sure to see the people not the mere words, the lively faces not inanimate lists on a page. I would profoundly regret it if I buried, in a mass of information, the once-living reality, the flesh and blood humanity of those who lived in closer contact with the earth and the seasons than most of us now need to do. And if, as you afterwards walk the hills, you also touch with boot or hand the moorland stones, please touch especially gently any whole or fallen walls, field walls or house walls or barn walls, any still squared foundation blocks, any rough or any smooth stone gateposts, any surviving iron hinge-pins protruding from their posts, any posts with gouged-out holes or slots, incised to receive a field-closing pole by way of gate. Touch them when you do with some reverence for those who made them and had to leave them here, and with a warm respect for their efforts and their skills.

I also ask you please to tread carefully, metaphorically as well as literally, when you walk and stand in places where, 100 or 200 years ago and more, fine people, our predecessors, have also stood, have delved and spun, have lifted and carried, built and sheltered, loved and comforted, have slept, given birth, laughed and wept, argued and striven, run, instructed, sweated and shivered, sown and reaped, gathered and scattered, consumed and wasted, woven and unravelled, fashioned, fettled and refurbished … The moors are curiously quiet now at nights except when sheep gather with their lambs.

a) Some Mature Characters

The 'retired' farmer Thomas Miller of **Dale Fold** was 85 years-old in 1881 when he was living with a branch of his extended family in a houseful of seven further persons with ages ranging from 32 years to five months. Gabriel Taylor, 70 in 1881, and farming then with his 70-year-old wife Jane at the 28-acre **Calico Hall**, was still alive at age 80 in 1891 having become a greengrocer and moved to **New Ground**, though his wife, sadly, was no longer with him. He, apparently, had been responsible for much dry stone wall building and repairing on the moors. Ann Pilkington, aged 43 and the wife of 42-year-old Miles Pilkington at **Great Hill** in 1851, was still living at **Great Hill**, but now with her daughter, son-in-law and their four children, when she was 72 in 1881. By 1891, when she was 82, she had moved with them to **Cocker's Folly** and was living comfortably there "on her own means". George Brindle, a besom (broom) maker aged 63 at **New Ground** in 1881, was still there, besom-making, 10 years later. He had been at **New Ground** in 1851 with his widowed, 64-year-old head of household mother Ellen, when he'd been nobbut a young-ish farm labourer. He had not moved very far but his besoms were evidently well liked.

Mary Miller, at age 60 farming with her 66-year-old husband William at **The Oaks** in 1881, was, at age 70, housekeeper to her son, daughter-in-law and six grandchildren, still at **The Oaks**, in 1891. Margaret Shorrock, aged 65, was farming at **Ripping** with her 66-year-old husband Thomas, an ex-hand loom weaver and expert picker-maker, in 1881. (A picker was the wooden stick with leather strap that controlled movement of the shuttle on the loom in the cotton weaving process.) As a 75-year-old widow and head of household she was still farming at **Ripping** in 1891, and members of the Shorrock family were still picker-making at the nearby **Hatch Place** and **Whittle's**, for instance.

William Rossall, a 72-year-old widower in 1881, was farming the 36-acre **Solomon's Temple** then and was still doing that at age 82 in 1891. William Dewhurst, aged 69, was farming and living alone at **Pope's** in 1881. By 1891, at 80, he had moved, probably most sensibly, to live with his widowed sister, the 75-year-old Mary Smith, at **Stake Hill**, where she was clearly in charge, although assisted by her 43-year-old unmarried daughter Margaret. A realistic and viable solution for all three, evidently.

Joseph and Elizabeth Jackson, once in charge of **Drinkwater's** as man and wife (aged 45 and 29) in 1851, were still, at age 75 and 59 in 1881, helping the 46- and 47-year-old William and Mary Bibby to run the 48-acre **Drinkwater's**. They were also caring for their own eight-year-old granddaughter Elizabeth. George and Mary Southworth, at 72 and 70, were farming at **Snape's** in 1881, aided occasionally perhaps by their lodger, an Irish-born 23-year-old Liverpool Corporation Water Works labourer, Bernard Foy.

Slightly oddly, bearing in mind the number of Irish labourers involved in Goit-building and adjacent railway-building in the 1850s and 60s, and the transformation of some farms, notably **New Ground Cottages** and **Goose Green**, into temporary alehouses, there seem to have been hardly any Irishmen resident in the farms longer term. But that was probably because a successful farm tenancy depended on women as much as men, upon a recognised effective married partnership at any rate, with well-learned, well-understood, reliably carried out, housewifely domestic duty-routines combined with agreed and shared farming responsibilities at appropriate times of the day and the year. A successful team benefited from several generations-worth of joint activity, with the young naturally learning good practice from their elders, including on occasion their grandparents.

For instance, Miles Brownlow's widowed 70-year-old mother Lucy was living with him, his wife Alice and his two-year-old son at **Pimm's** in 1881. John Kershaw, a 69-year-old widower, was working as a farm labourer, and lodging at the **Greenlands** household of Agnes Clarkson. The unmarried 66-year-old Smalley Briggs, previously living with the Hoggs at **Goose Green**, was now a lodger with the Shorrocks at **Hatch Place**. He was still working patiently as a labourer at the Brinscall Print Works, as he seems to have done, day after day, for much of his life. More dynamically, the 68-year-old, Wheelton-born and now widowed Isabella Heald (once a young wife at **New Ground** in 1851) was head of a two-person household in 1891 at the large **Drinkwater's Farm**, her partner being exactly half her age, the 34-year-old widowed labourer Richard Fisher from Preston. At nearby **Great Hill Farm** the 76-year-old Sarah Gaskell from Stockport, mother of quarryman and farmer John Gaskell (born in Chorley) was living with him, his wife Jane (born in Manchester) and their three young children (born in Chorley) at this, the highest of all our 48 farms. Plenty of exchange of generational wisdoms there no doubt.

Among all those fine people who at one time or another have occupied and farmed **Ratten Clough**, a particular and distinctive trio was in charge in the 1840s and 50s. Two brothers and a sister, all unmarried, Withnell-born and proud 'freeholders' (not tenants) farmed the 19 acres. Nominally head of household was the 57-year-old Richard Bennett, but assisting him were his 65-year-old brother James and his 61-year-old sister Nancy. One can perhaps begin to imagine how they managed to spend their dark and quiet

Ratten Clough, circa 1950, showing the two porches. The Shorrocks' cottage is on the left, the Mayors' cottage on the right.

winter evenings together, with, unlike almost every other farming household on these moors, no sounds of youngsters at work or play. (Interestingly, on an early Ordnance Survey map of 1831, the whole of the **Ratten Clough** 'estate' was designated 'James Bennett's land', i.e. not belonging at this time to either the de Hoghtons or the Parkes.)

Outperforming the Bennetts in maturity and self-control, however, it is probably fair to say, was a slightly later resident at **Ratten Clough**, the formidable 90-year-old (in 1929) Mrs Sarah Shorrock. Her ankle-length dark skirt, almost ankle-length white (very white) pinafore, tight white cap with ribbons, shoulder-covering shawl and uncompromising clogs mark her out as a representative character for the whole of the nineteenth century on the moors. Certainly a 'survivor' well into the twentieth century, she was. Her bespectacled glance at the camera seems to suggest irritation, at least, that her feeding of her nearby poultry should have been thus rudely and unnecessarily interrupted by a photographer. There's more important work to be getting on with, clearly, than celebrating a 90th birthday! (See photo on page 4.)

b) Some Large Families in 1851

If we now consider evidence of the typical working activities in some of the larger families in the 1840s and 50s (via the 1851 census returns) we shall ultimately be able to compare the general way of life on Brinscall Moors in mid-century with what appears in later sections of this chapter covering family activity in the 1880s and 90s. It is possible that we shall see that life is subtly changing before our eyes, and this well in advance of the apparently sudden abandonment of many farms after 1898.

Coming originally from Heapey and Chorley respectively, William and Jane Baxendale at **Calico Hall** in 1851 had nine children between the ages of 25 and 5 years – six boys and three girls. Four were handloom weavers at home and three were farm labourers. **Calico Hall** is high on the moors, remote from the steam-powered mills of the valleys. It controlled 18 acres of rough grassland.

Originally from Tockholes and Wheelton, Thomas and Alice Snape at **Cocker's Folly** in 1851 had seven children between 26 and 10 – three boys and four girls. Six were power-loom weavers in the valley. **Cocker's Folly** is on the edge of the moors relatively close to Withnell Mill.

Originally from Entwistle, John Rosthorn, a widower at **Goose Green** in 1851, had six children between 29 and 5 years – three boys and three girls. Four were handloom weavers. One was an errand boy. **Goose Green** is in the valley but quite distant from the large spinning and weaving facilities of Withnell Mill.

Originally from Wheelton and Hoghton, Henry and Elizabeth Grime at **Hatch Place** in 1851 had seven children, all of them daughters. Five of these were power-loom weavers. **Hatch** is a quick walk down to and back up from Withnell Mill via Edge Gate Lane and Well Lane – and via other farm tracks in the valley, there being no thought as yet in 1851 of a Railway Road to walk along, let alone a railway.

Alice Heys, a widow at **New Ground** in 1851 and born in Wheelton where she still lived of course, had seven children from age 20 to just one year – three boys and four girls, Alice herself being 44 years old. As usual at the **New Ground** farms and cottages there was a mixture of handloom and power-loom weavers among the young workers.

Both of them originally from Mellor, Thomas and Margaret Shorrock at **Solomon's Temple** in 1851 had six children between age 15 and a newly born girl of one month. There were four boys (including an Abram and a Bartholomew inspired, perhaps, by the thought of a Solomon) and two girls (a Nancy and a very young Mary Ellen). The two elder boys, James and George, born in Blackburn and Mellor, not in the perhaps greater freedom of Wheelton and Withnell like their younger siblings, were handloom weavers, as was their father. **Solomon's Temple** is stoutly and remotely set, mid-moor.

Originally from Darwen and Wheelton, Thomas and Peggy Wilkinson at **Top o'th'Wood** in 1851 had six children between 15 years and one year – two boys and four girls. Two of these were already power-loom weavers in the valley.

Both originally from Wheelton, Richard and Margaret Briers at **Whittle's** had seven children between 28 and 6 – three boys and four girls. They also had two granddaughters living at the farm. Their eldest son, 24-year-old James, was a farm labourer, helping his father manage the 16-acre holding. Two of his sisters and two other brothers were power-loom weavers, however.

Given the number of persons in these eight farms said to have been born in Wheelton – including all 11 of the occupants of **Whittle's** – I should perhaps remind readers that Wheelton is not and was not a tight, separate, single, small, centralised village but a widespread, dispersed, extensive and mainly rural area, even though it was sometimes referred to by the archaic term 'township'. So, for instance, **Whittle's Farm** was and is firmly in Wheelton. So is **New Ground**. So is **Hatch**. So is **Heaton's**. So is **Top o'th'Wood**. I have probably made this point even more laboriously here than was either necessary or desirable! But the same general understanding does apply to both Withnell and Heapey, of course: large rural areas or regions (parishes or townships) they are, not single villages.

Pausing at this point in our consideration of 1851 statistics, we can begin to draw some conclusions before moving on to 1881, by which time cotton mills were larger and the Brinscall railway was firmly established. In 1851, the average size of a family throughout the whole range of our farms is two parents plus five (actually 5.3) children. Almost all children aged 12 and above are in paid employment. Some children under 12 are half-time 'scholars' and half-time factory workers. Marginally more children are handloom weavers working at home (and earning income for their parents) than power-loom weavers in a factory, but the critical issue here appears to be the distance for walking between farm and factory. More generally, in Lancashire and Yorkshire by the 1850s, handloom weaving was in rapid decline. It commanded only a low wage by comparison with the prosperous times of the 1820s.

Farmers' sons occasionally (but not routinely) became farm labourers before eventually taking over fuller responsibility, this depending on whether the farm was small (say five acres) or large (say 25-plus acres). Overall there were more weavers than spinners among the farm workers. There were comparatively few quarrymen or mechanics in 1851. Only in some small cottages at **New Ground** and in one household at **Richmond's** were there heads of family who were not primarily or exclusively 'farmers'. The farms of Brinscall Moors were still chiefly agricultural enterprises (in terms of care of livestock and provision of food, clothing and shelter for the children) with a subordinate but numerous young workforce of cloth-weavers. Whether a new birth in a family was a potential problem (i.e. an extra mouth to feed) or an opportunity (i.e. a future additional wage-earner) depended, no doubt, on a delicate balance of cotton trade fluctuations and climate and soil conditions, in addition to the extent of love and energy available and flowing happily from parents to children.

c) Some Large Families in 1881

We find that in 1881 there are still several large families living on the moors. Yet, taking the moors as a whole, it is clear that the average family size had already been significantly declining. What had been an average of over five (5.3) children per family in 1851 had fallen to fewer than four (3.8 in fact) by 1881. There is also a greater variety in the types of occupation that younger persons, and even some heads of family, had been taking up.

One particular farm, **Rake**, near Twist Moor and Abbey Village, housed the largest single number of youngsters in one family in 1881. Richard and Elizabeth Waring had four boys and six girls with an age range stretching from 20 years to one year. Richard Waring had been born in Preston in 1831 and his wife in Kendal in 1835. One wonders, as one does with several couples between the 1850s and the 1890s, how and where they might have met, given some of the restraints on long distance travel (even though a railway network was now in existence, and Preston and Kendal had been linked by canal from 1819). Mrs Waring had been 26 when her first child was born. She was 45 when her youngest child, named Richard after his father, was born in 1880.

What further information is available on the quietly eloquent census page? Of the 10 Waring children in 1881, four were already earning their own living – Elizabeth (20), James (14), and Jane (11) as cotton weavers (quite probably in Abbey Mill) and William (15) as a carter. The four who were aged five, six, eight and nine – Sarah, Martha, Betty, and Edward – were classified under the general and by now routine description: 'scholar'. One-year-old Richard and three-year-old Margaret were not yet allowed, or encumbered by, any formal occupation!

With 13 acres of land to attend to at **Rake**, Richard Waring must surely have welcomed a little part-time assistance now and then from his 'scholars' if not from his wage-earning weaving and carting children. It would be some comfort to know that at **Rake** there was also a little extra income coming in from rent paid by a 'boarder', the 22-year-old unmarried Ellen Power born in Blackburn, working locally as a cotton machine tenter. **Rake** held 13 persons then, all told, in that one household in 1881.

At **Aushaw's**, across the A675 (as it now is), a little higher and to the south of **Rake**, the Blackburn and Walton-le-Dale-born James and Ellen Southworth had seven children from age 21 to just 11 months, all of them born in Withnell. James Southworth himself, farming only six acres, was also a cotton weaver as were his daughter Mary and his son Enoch. Another son, Alfred, was a cotton spinner. Abbey Mill was their likely workplace. Four other children were still too young for paid work, and were looked after at home by their mother, Ellen.

At **Beardsworth's** the head of family, Hoghton-born Sarah Cotton, was a 44-year-old widow, obviously recently bereaved. Of her nine children (spanning the typical range 19 years to 4 months) two were farm labourers and one was a railway porter (at nearby Brinscall Station, presumably). One 11-year-old son was already working half-time at Brinscall Print Works. Three were still 'scholars'. The two youngest children had been born in Withnell (at **Beardsworth's** itself, very probably) but the seven oldest were originally from Whittle-le-Woods. The serious impact of widowhood on the mother of two particularly young children (one aged one year, one aged four months) can be imagined. Can you visualise the gathering of the family on their return to the farm after their father's funeral? By their mother's side were John, Hugh, William, Esther, Thomas, Sarah, Susannah, Margaret and Lucy. With how much hope had they been named? What was to be their future?

When you visit the site of **Beardsworth's** with its tight fields, its hawthorn trees and its view over Brinscall village, you might also imagine the sympathetic help pouring in from several near-neighbourhood farms – **Greenlands**, **Ripping**, **New Ground**, **Heaton's** and **Hatch** – all of them within 300m or so of **Beardsworth's**. (**Cocker's Folly**, 100m away, was temporarily unoccupied in 1881.) Sarah Cotton must surely have deserved the most kindly assistance.

Forty-six-year-old Richard Cookson and his 41-year-old wife Margaret had evidently come from their own birthplace in Tarleton to run a farm in Withnell over 20 years earlier, for all nine of their children had been born in Withnell. However, though the Cooksons were now working the 41-acre **Higher Calf Hey**, a considerable responsibility, all three of their eldest children, Elizabeth (21), Jane (19), and John (16), were working elsewhere while still living overnight at the farm – Elizabeth and Jane in a cotton factory and John as a quarryman. Ellen (12), Margaret (10) and Ann (8) were 'scholars' while Richard (5), Ruth (3) and Hugh (1) had not yet begun their formal education. It is not clear that any members of that large family would be able to assist their father day by day let alone expect to succeed him in managing a large farm. We shall soon meet the Cooksons again, however.

At five of the **New Ground** houses in 1881, employment trends (and some marriage trends) tell a clear tale. In the household of Wheelton-born John and Ellen Heyes,

John Heyes himself was a (non-agricultural) general labourer and his eldest daughters Jane (19), Alice (17) and Mary (15) were cotton mill weavers, probably at Bury Lane (Withnell Mill), while James (14) was a cotton creeler. Isabella (11), Jacob (9) and Sarah (4) were 'scholars', of course.

In the Samuel Pilkington family household, 47-year-old Samuel (born in Whittle-le-Woods) was an engineer at the Brinscall Print Works, his sons Samuel (20), James (16) and Alfred (13) were Print Works labourers while his daughter Alice (12) was a cotton mill weaver. His son Miles (9) was the sole remaining 'scholar' in the family.

In the **New Ground** house of Richard Sumner, farmer and general labourer, it is interesting to see that 66-year-old Richard, born in Withnell, had earlier married a wife, Elizabeth, 11 years his junior and from Newtown in Montgomeryshire. Their children Richard (22), William (20) and Elizabeth (16) were respectively, a general labourer, a stonemason and a dressmaker. There were also two boarders in the house, Luke Rawcliffe and William Walsh from Heath Charnock and Bolton, both of them mature quarrymen.

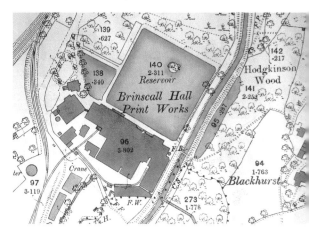

In the nearby house of Withnell-born Thomas Sumner, quarryman, aged 50 and married to 43-year-old Mary Ann from Birmingham, were not only their three children Thomas (4), Mary Ann (7) and Elizabeth (1) but also a 50-year-old unmarried lodger from Wheelton, John Baxendale, a stonemason. (As a 20-year-old, John had been living with his parents at mid-moor **Calico Hall** in 1851.)

The two Sumner gentlemen from Withnell must presumably have displayed some initiative in meeting and then marrying ladies from Newtown and Birmingham. Railways are likely to have helped them in their travels. (Marriage thanks to Brinscall Station, then?) Trains may also have been a feature in the lives of **New Ground**-dwellers 24-year-old millwright John Longton, born in Warrington, and his 32-year-old wife Eliza, born in Castleton, Rochdale. Presumably Warrington Station did not ban discreetly amorous greetings on the platforms in the 1870s as it seems to have tried to do in 2009.

At **Richmonds** in 1881, 51-year-old Bolton-born James Hull, farmer of 24 acres, was married to a 44-year-old wife from as far away as Scotland (precise location unspecified). Their one son, 21-year-old James, was a book-keeper, while daughters Mary (17) and Eliza (15) were a farm worker and a cotton mill weaver, respectively. Of the four further daughters, Christina (11) and Isabella (7) were 'scholars', and both Martha and Margery had so far reached the age of two. James junior had

The Brinscall Print Works circa 1870. Photograph taken from Hodgkinson Wood on the hillside.

been born in Scotland, but all six of the girls had been born in a variety of villages in the Ribble Valley in Lancashire. After at least two decades of housing mobility, presumably the Hull family was not yet aware that their farmhouse in Withnell was about to be demolished.

When considering **Sharrock's**, the valley farm in Heapey in 1881, there are several special features to notice. Heath Charnock-born 37-year-old Abel Pilkington, for instance, was a quarryman as well as a farmer of 19 acres. His two Heath Charnock-born sons Thomas (18) and Joseph (16) were also quarrymen, not farm labourers. His Heapey-born wife Sarah (mother of Thomas and Joseph?) was 32 years of age. Two other children, Samuel (11) and George (9) had been born in Anglezarke and Wheelton, respectively, while the youngest three children, Isaac (4), Jane (3) and Mary (6 months) had all been born in Heapey (at **Sharrock's** perhaps). There was also at **Sharrock's** a 14-year-old Ann (surname unconfirmed but born in Anglezarke) who was conveniently a 'general servant' in the house. There are times when one admires the common-sense practicality of the inhabitants of our farms.

It is slightly disappointing, however, to find that Abel and Sarah Pilkington were no longer at **Sharrock's** in 1891, having been replaced by another quarryman, Adam Hindley (42), his wife Dinah (35) and their young five-year-old son Harold. There was also living at **Sharrock's**, intriguingly to relate, a 12-year-old adopted son, Richard Brocklehurst, who was a half-time worker at the Brinscall Print Works, and … there was a boarder, the now 28-year-old but unmarried Thomas Pilkington who, alone among members of his own family, still lived where he had lived 10 years earlier. And he was still a quarryman. There may be those among twenty-first century walkers who, while surveying the ruins of **Sharrock's**, might wish that the stones could speak. Such tales to tell! The nearby Goit, meanwhile, glides impassively on.

Top o'th'Wood, divided at the time into three households, had become by 1881 scarcely an agricultural establishment at all. One of its heads of family, the Welshman (born in Brecon) James Thomas (44), was undeniably a blacksmith (either of the 'village' kind, or of the Print Works kind, or both). His wife Alice (47) and all six of his children were Wheelton-born (though his eldest son had been given the perhaps appropriate name 'David') but so far none of them had escaped the 'scholar' status, being of age 12, 11, 9, 7, 5 and 2. It was not likely, however, that any of them would mature into the farm labourer lifestyle rather than the paid factory hand role. Four of the six were girls.

John Bury, 59, a Wheelton man at **Top o'th'Wood** with a Hoghton wife Alice (58), had one son, William, aged 30 and two adopted children from Wheelton, Rebecca Beesley (17) and her brother Andrew (8). John himself was a watchman at the Print Works, William was a mechanic there, and not only was Rebecca employed at the Print Works (as a 'sticker') but so was their lodger, 55-year-old Wheelton bachelor John Haworth (as a labourer). There was, and still is, a special narrow path leading steeply downhill from **Top o'th'Wood** and Blackhurst, which was a Wood family house, across the Goit to the Print Works, also owned by the Woods, you will recall.

In the third **Top o'th'Wood** household, 48-year-old John Knight from Great Sutton in Cheshire really was an agricultural labourer (and his wife Ann was from Scotland) but four of his six children were already cotton mill operatives (two weavers, one warper and one spinner).

In 1873–74, thereabouts, there arrived in Withnell all the way from Dorset (by train or by the simple exercise of walking?) three bold farming or ex-farming families: the Joys, the Mastersons and the Vachres. From a 'Wessex' that was beginning to experience what Thomas Hardy was to know well – an increasingly grim agricultural depression – came families seeking a home in a farmhouse but a weekly income in a cotton factory – or in a quarry if necessary (stone masonry being an established craft in Dorset, as Hardy also knew well).

In the very year of publication of 'Far from the Madding Crowd' (1874) the young Maria Vachre was born in **Whave Gate Farm**, Withnell. Her older sister Ellen had been born just two years earlier (1872) in Milton Abbas (Hardy's 'Middleton Abbey') where her father and all five of her elder brothers and sisters had been born. Maria's mother Martha had been born in Winterborne in 1837, her father in Milton Abbas in 1833.

In 1875, at the latest, the young Edith Joy was born in **Dale Fold Cottage**, Withnell. Her father John had been born in Hinton-Martell in 1849, her mother Mary in Edmondsham in 1848 and her step-sister Mary Cookman in Blandford in 1865.

Although the Mastersons chose to settle in Lower East View Farm (off Bury Lane, Withnell, on the western side of the Goit) their story is equally worthy of the attention offered already to the Joys and the Vachres. They must have arrived in Withnell in 1878 at the latest, for young Annie Masterson was born then in Withnell, though her sister Lydia, five years older, was born in Thorny Down, west of Blandford, in 1873. Their father, 48-year-old Cornelius Masterson, was born in Shapwick, Dorset, as was his eldest son George. Their mother, Harriet, was born in 1839 in Bere Regis (or, as the 1881 census enumerator spells it, 'Bearages' – which surely tells us how it was pronounced).

It is a truth tentatively advanced that any persons at least loosely attached to the names 'Harriet' and 'Lydia' are more likely than not to have a nodding acquaintance with Jane Austen if not yet with Thomas Hardy. But what one is to make of a farmer called 'Cornelius' is another matter. And it is not only Cornelius. The Mastersons' eldest daughter had been christened 'Alma' following her birth in 1863 – a name which might have been taken either from a river or a battle site (of 1854) in the Crimea, but could also simply be a reference to the village of 'Almer', 4 miles east of Bere Regis in Dorset and 3 miles west of Shapwick. On the other hand, and more seriously, the name Alma probably referred to a moral virtue that it was hoped the young lady would aspire to as she grew up – in the way that nineteenth-century ladies more frequently found themselves striving to justify being called Patience or Faith or Mercy or Prudence. Alma, as in 'Alma Mater', means 'bounteous' or 'bountiful', of course. While it is comforting to know that Alma was joined quite soon by the brothers Walter and Charles, born, like she was, in Charlton Marshall, Dorset, I have to reveal that the youngest of the Mastersons, born in Withnell and just six months old in 1881, had been named 'Rosina'. A small rose in Bury Lane is a pleasing idea.

As to the principal objectives of the grand transfer in the 1870s from Dorset to Lancashire it is plain that in 1881 the erstwhile farmer Cornelius Masterson was quite simply a labourer in a cotton mill (Withnell Mill?), that George was a cotton grinder, Alma a cotton rover and both Walter and Charles were cotton piecers. Lydia and Annie were still scholars. The Mastersons might now have been more prosperous than they had been on the perhaps bitter edge of 'Egdon Heath'. Certainly they do not appear to have been anxious to compare the farming demands of a Dorset moor with those of Withnell, Wheelton or Heapey Moor.

Similarly, although the **Dale Fold** Joys had three young or very young children (Edith, Charles and Elizabeth, aged six, one and six months in 1881) it is quite clear that their likely future was not a career in farming. John Joy, the head of family, was now, at 32, a quarryman (at one of two quarries close to **Dale Fold**, presumably) and his wife's daughter Mary Cookman was already, at 16, a cotton creeler (most probably at the nearby Abbey Mill).

The new Lancashire life of the Vachres was almost, but not quite, a similar story. John Vachre, the head of a family who had originally been refugees in Dorset from

Withnell Mill, circa 1900, the weaving
shed in the foreground next to Railway
Road, the spinning mill to the right,
beyond the engine house.

France, had accepted that at **Whave Gate**, close to both Ramsden's and **Richmond's** and just above Norcross Brow, he was principally 'a farmer of nine acres'. However, his Milton Abbas-born eldest children, Charles (23), William (21), Beatrice (17), Elizabeth (15) and Edith (12) were, respectively, a cotton catching tenter, a cotton spinner, a cotton cardroom hand, another cotton cardroom hand and a cotton weaver. Logically, all five of these would work (with a 6am start, of course) at Withnell Mill, just 200m down the special path from **Whave Gate** on to Norcross Brow and into Bury Lane or Railway Road.

Whave Gate was no longer the Vachre family home in 1891 (too small for all 10 of them, perhaps; they had been replaced by a family of three – two farming parents and a quarryman son). But there was one ex-Dorset resident and his wife, just the two of them, in a **New Ground** cottage in 1891: George Lewis, a general labourer of 61, and Fanny, his Scottish wife aged 53. It is said that there was until quite recently an elderly widower with the surname of Vachre (pronounced Vayker) still living in the village of Brinscall into the twenty-first century.

d) Some Large Families in 1891

The census statistics from 1891 tell us that the general trend towards smaller families was continuing. The average number of children per family has fallen again – from four (3.8) in 1881 to just three (3.09) in 1891. There were, nevertheless, still some quite substantial individual families with four, five or six children, and two families, indeed, with eight children each. The largest 1891 family, however, was still one occupying **Rake Farm**, but this time it was no longer the Warings but another local family, the Marsdens.

Richard and Elizabeth Marsden (and, the senior Marsdens did have exactly the same Christian names as their Waring predecessors) had six boys and five girls between the ages of 18 years and just two months in 1891. Richard Marsden had been born in Withnell in 1850 and his wife in Walton-le-Dale in 1851. Mrs Marsden had been 22 when her first child, George, was born in 1873. It will be interesting to compare the 'domestic economy' at **Rake** in 1891 with the Waring family practices of 10 years earlier, where six people were making some contribution to income via wages or rent or produce including foodstuffs.

Of the 1891 Marsdens, 18-year-old George was regularly helping his father to work the farm, while the 17- and 13-year-olds, Hannah and Winifred, were fully employed cotton weavers (at Abbey Mill again?). However, Richard (12), William (11), Elizabeth (9), Dorothy (7) and Robert (5) were all 'scholars'. Thomas (3), John (2) and Margaret (just a few months old) did not enjoy the dignity of an occupation, of course. There were just four income-providers, then, at this stage.

Can you imagine the scene in the Marsden family kitchen at mealtimes, the eight 'under-12s' gathering hungrily round the big table, being made to sit down on the benches as tidily as they could, while the two senior farm-workers, their father and their brother, eased themselves carefully into their seats and Hannah and Winifred, tired by the hours of weaving in the mill, did their best to help their mother dish up and serve the food? Then, as this scene unfolds, allow yourself to consider the working day for that mother: the sink, the makeshift cradle, the oven, the table, the farmyard, the milk-parlour and the sheep pasture.

Meanwhile, what we also find at **Rake** in 1891 is that an entirely separate family had taken up residence in what was regarded as an attached 'Rake Cottage'. Interestingly this was a younger branch of the Waring family: 28-year-old Joseph Waring and his 29-year-old wife Deborah, with their two-year-old daughter, also Deborah, and her newly born brother Richard. Young Mrs Waring was not only a mother but also an employed cotton weaver (at Abbey Mill, as usual?). How did she cope? Which members of the Marsden family looked after little Deborah and even smaller Richard during the day? Perhaps nine- and seven-year-old 'scholars' Elizabeth and Dorothy? They would quite probably have enjoyed this, under the general supervision of their own mother. And given the **Rake** household's financial exigencies it begins to make some sort of sense.

Not only was Mrs Deborah Waring earning a wage but her husband Joseph was not a farmer but a wage-earning quarryman. And the possibility is that he was related to the 33-year-old Robert Waring who was also a quarryman and was now living in one of the two **Aushaw's** houses with his wife Fanny (31) and sons Harry (4) and Daniel (1). You will find in your Twist Moor walkings that it is easy to see from the site of **Aushaw's** down over the sheep fields to the site of **Rake's**, just beyond the A675. And what is there also down the slopes and just a little to your right? The craggy remains of the very considerable Birch Clough Quarry. Beware its mouldering hummocks and shaggy precipices!

Mrs Fanny Waring, by the way, did not have an additional job beyond her **Aushaw's** responsibilities. She had come to Lancashire for her marriage from her original birthplace in Worcestershire. Her husband Robert, on the other hand, had transferred to Withnell all the way from Tarleton.

There is little doubt that the 1891 Cookson family of **Hillock Farm** were almost entirely committed to wage-earning in the textile industry. In that year seven of their children in the house were rather fully engaged: just one in quarrying, and six in a cotton factory. But we have already met the Cooksons at **Higher Calf Hey** in 1881 when the three eldest children at home – Elizabeth, Jane and John – were working away from the farm during the day though returning there at nights. Jane and John have married by 1891, but one can see why **Hillock**, far nearer to mills and quarries than **Higher Calf Hey** had been, was a more convenient base for the family, including the married Jane.

Richard Cookson himself (aged 56 in 1891 and born in Tarleton like his 51-year-old wife Peggy – previously known politely as 'Margaret') was by now a general (wage-earning) labourer as well as a farmer. One of their sons, Richard (aged 15) was indeed employed – like his elder brother John – as a quarryman, but of their other children Elizabeth (30) was a cotton winder, Ellen (22) was a cotton weaver, Margaret (20) was another cotton winder, and 2 younger ones, Ruth (13) and Hugh (11) were cotton weavers. James (8) was the sole scholar. That left the 18-year-old Ann, who for reasons undefined, was a 'farm assistant' and not a cotton worker. The house did also contain a three-year-old grandson, young Richard, whose mother might well have been the farm assistant Ann, of course.

It should come as no surprise to any reader to learn that the married 29-year-old 'boarder' Jane Mosscrop was employed as a cotton weaver. As the 19-year-old Jane Cookson of 1881, before she married in 1886 and became Mrs Mosscrop, she had already been a cotton weaver. Eight of the 12 persons living in the house were bringing in a wage. One might suppose that this was a more prosperous household than it might have been if still resident in the Tarleton district of agricultural West Lancashire. The two parents had left Tarleton in 1859 at the latest. **Hillock**, very different from **Higher Calf Hey**, is roughly half-way between Withnell Mill and Abbey Mill. It is also close to Central Quarry. Ideally placed, therefore? At least its residents could enjoy their night's sleep in comparative rural serenity. Mind you, a family containing no fewer than three Richards might suffer some disturbance at night when the wrong Richard responded to an urgent call for help, say. **Hillock's** modest ruins can be found near a small former mill reservoir above Dole Lane.

The six children of Brecon-born blacksmith James Thomas, whom we met at **Top o'th'Wood** in 1881, had become seven children by 1891. A further newcomer to **Top o'th'Wood**'s Thomas household, however, was not, as might be thought, a young Thomas daughter but a 21-year-old niece, Grace Harvey (presumably James' sister's daughter) born in Bath and working in Wheelton as a dressmaker. James and his wife Alice did have a new son of their own meanwhile, the five-year-old William, already a young scholar in 1891. But what is of particular interest to us just now is to find out what the six Thomas children of 1881, all of them then being scholars apart from two-year-old Alice, were doing 10 years later. Any farm labourers among them, perhaps, given that their father was a blacksmith? There were some decent if rather sloping fields within easy reach of the farm.

We find as follows. David, the eldest, now 22, had followed in his father's footsteps and become a blacksmith. We do not know, alas, whether he was shoeing horses in a modest smithy (there were at least two of these in the Brinscall village area) or creating or repairing machinery in a forge in, say, the Print Works. David's 21-year-old sister Sarah certainly was employed at the Print Works, as a stitcher. All the rest were equally engaged in textile production. Elizabeth (19), Margaret (17), James (15) and Alice (12) were all cotton weavers, Alice only part-time as yet, but the career pattern was obvious. What we had reasonably predicted when viewing the 1881 statistics had come to pass. **Top o'th'Wood** was not really a farmhouse any longer.

The only other household in the **Top o'th'Wood** building in 1891, the small family of 24-year-olds Isaiah and Alice Moss with their two children Herbert (3) and Ruby (11 months), had no overtly agricultural connections. Isaiah himself was a coachman and domestic servant, almost certainly working with and for the neighbouring branch of the Wood family in their 'superior' stone villa of Blackhurst. It seemed likely that the Woods' elegant coach would be kept in the then new building (now demolished) that stood above (literally on top of) the still extant underground stables just across the carriage drive from **Top o'th'Wood**.

The **Dale Fold** family of John and Sarah Miller (43 and 42 years-old in 1891 and both born in Withnell) had already sent the three eldest of their six children to work in the mill while their father worked the farm on his own apart from the assistance that his already busy wife could provide. Thomas (18), Nancy (17) and William (15) were all cotton weavers. It seems very probable that the two scholars John (12) and Elizabeth (10) would be joining them shortly. Would the two-year-old Joseph inevitably follow suit? If so would **Dale Fold** by 1901 become yet another nominal farmhouse peopled largely by young factory workers? Could it survive as a farmhouse?

The example of **Mosscrop's Farm** in 1891 is not auspicious. There the 47-year-old

Thomas Miller, with his Withnell-born wife Mary (also 47), was undoubtedly a farmer, but their eldest son Henry (22) was a cotton spinner, 19-year-old daughter Margaret was a cotton weaver, Esther (15) was a cardroom hand and Alice (14) was a cotton winder. Margery (10), a scholar, would be waiting to join them. Like the Cooksons at **Higher Calf Hey** in 1881, it is almost certain that the young mill-workers at the 1891 **Mosscrop's** would have to undertake long walks in the mornings to their nearest cotton factory at Abbey Mill or Withnell Mill, and what might seem even longer walks in the evenings to return to their moorland home for mere food and sleep. And this would be their regular way of life for six days a week.

At least at **Beardsworth's** in 1891, the Sarah Cotton family of 1881 having departed, there was the possibility of a career or two involving some connection with the land. James Eastham (56), born in Longridge like his 51-year-old wife Jane, was a farmer and produce merchant. While his eldest son John (21) was a general labourer, the second son, Albert (15), was undisguisedly a farm labourer. (Both these lads were born in Preston.) The remaining four children, Thomas (11) and William (9), born in Penwortham, plus Lucy (7) and Lily (5), born in Withnell, were scholars. The fact that there is still, in the twenty-first century, a company of specialist florists known as Eastham's, said to be descended from the Easthams of **Beardsworth's** and operating now in Blackburn and Chorley, suggests that for them the connection with the land, with horticulture if not agriculture, remained significant.

At **Heapey Moor Farm**, a fine large set of buildings in the midst of a high wide sweep of rough grassland, it would be interesting to see what the relatively recently arrived Scambler family would make of their agricultural opportunity. Christopher Scambler, aged 51, had arrived from Tatham (a remote rural village near Hornby in the Lune Valley) no earlier than the middle 1880s. His youngest child, Edith, aged six in 1891, was born in Roeburndale, not far from Tatham, in 1885. Christopher himself, his 30-year-old wife Margaret, and all three of their other children, had been born in Tatham (or in Margaret's case slightly nearer to Bentham). Edith, like Christopher (11) and Edwin (9), was a scholar.

The 17-year-old eldest child, Joseph (was he Margaret's son?) was already working, but not as a farm labourer. He was, instead, a quarryman – and there were two quarries below Heapey Moor near to White Coppice, where there was also a small textile mill to tempt other Scambler children if quarrying was not to their taste. They would not be staying at home as handloom weavers like the Baxendale children of nearby **Calico Hall** in 1851. And the farm-labouring that attracted others of the Baxendales in 1851 would perhaps not be their first priority either, or that of their parents for them. Another nearby moorland farm, **Sour Milk Hall**, was unoccupied and perhaps already abandoned by 1891.

At **Botany Bay**, high on the northern wilds of Withnell Moor, the head of household, James Robinson (54), with a 66-year-old wife Mary, was undoubtedly still a farmer, but all three of his daughters – Alice, Mary and Dinah – and three of his five grandchildren were equally undoubtedly cotton mill workers. They would have had quite a long walk each morning and evening, apart from their one day of rest on Sundays.

The analysis over the last few pages of some eight of the larger 1891 families confirms a clear picture of farms that were changing their function, and this across wide areas of our grand moorland triangle. Though still outwardly following the way of life of animal husbandry and human self-sufficiency, with heads of household who were primarily farmers, whose wives cared for the feeding, clothing and well-being of their offspring, the bulk of the inhabitants of the farms were actually, as soon as they reached the age of 11 or 12, forming an important proportion of the workforce of the surrounding cotton mills and quarries. These younger 'industrial' workers were in practice using the farms as slightly inconveniently sited but otherwise comparatively healthy and essentially supportive dormitory units.

The fathers and mothers – the farmers and their wives – most of them still working 'at home' for most of most days, would of course have welcomed the 'industrial' wages handed over by their children at the end of each week. As a means of counteracting what was happening from the 1870s onwards not only in Dorset but nationally – a permanent agricultural downturn (in the face of cheap foreign imports of food) which fairly rapidly ended mass employment in farming – the wage contributions of the young mill and quarry workers were a means by which the moorland farms could be kept going a little longer.

Quite obviously, also, there was an endless (and virtuous?) economic cycle at work here. Who in the nineteenth century (until 1898) owned the Withnell and Wheelton moors and the farms built on them? The Parke family. To whom did the tenant farmers on the moors pay their rents therefore? The Parke family. Who had set up and for most of the century operated both the Withnell Mill and the Abbey Mill? The Parke family. Who paid wages to the young textile workers at Withnell Mill and Abbey Mill? The Parke family. The Parkes, as we have already seen, were benevolent and public-spirited owners and employers. So were their successors, Marriages and Pinnocks at Withnell Mill, and the Birtwistles at Abbey Mill.

e) Some Smaller Families in 1891

Besides presenting evidence of widespread economic changes and of the family responses and adjustments to these, both the 1851 and the 1881 and 1891 census statistics have also, I very much hope, supplied insights and awarenesses on a personal level too. You now know more about the typical Christian name choices of Brinscall parents in the nineteenth century, and about the ages of marriage and patterns of child-bearing, as well as about geographical mobility among would-be farmers and would-be farmers' wives (who were now willing to travel longer distances in search of jobs, homes and marriage partners). You surely are now able to stand by, and even on, the ruins of moorland farms and to know not only who was once there before you but what it was like to be them in time past. To develop this a little further I present over the next few pages some distinctive news items from other, and sometimes rather smaller, family units.

Please as usual enjoy gradually getting to know these families, one or two at a time, say, rather than trying to take in all the information at once. (A blur of massed names and facts is not what you want.) In this way you can happily build up your own private and selective archive of personal detail and activity when you are wishing to make clear – to yourself and others – what life in the 1880s and 1890s on Brinscall Moors was really like.

While, as we know, the quarryman Robert Waring was head of one of the **Aushaw's** households in 1891, at the other, the larger of the two, 36-year-old Richard Fazackerly and his wife Ellen (31), with six children (all Leyland born) between the ages of 10 and one, also had no apparent link with farming. Richard was employed at Brinscall Print Works as a 'fireman'. That is to say he kept up steam pressures in the boiler house by feeding coal regularly into the furnaces – a rather continuous and exhausting endeavour. The quality of dark smoke emerging from a Print Works chimney in one of our photographs shows the effect of his work. Meanwhile there is little point in pretending that **Aushaw's** by the end of the century was still a working farm.

Supporting Richard Fazackerly in the boiler house was the 16-year-old David Shorrock, a stoker at the Print Works, who was the only young worker living at **Hatch Place**. That farm which in 1851 contained 10 persons contained only three in 1891, David and his parents George and Sarah Shorrock (aged 52 and 50). George was still the farmer and picker-maker he had been in 1881. He and his wife had had no more children after David. Sarah it was whom you met earlier – as a 90-year-old living at **Ratten Clough**!

At **Greenlands**, Coleburn Hall (25) from Church, Lancashire was an engineer at the Print Works working, presumably, in the engine house there. His 26-year-old wife Mary from Accrington was a cotton weaver with two children, William (2) and Bertha (1). In the three **Greenlands** households there seems to be one person, Agnes Clarkson (32) from Manchester, housekeeper and mother of Gertrude (2) and Herbert (7 months), who would be able to look after the young William and Bertha Hall while their mother was at work.

Two of the three **Greenlands** households contained a remarkable mixture of lodgers and relations who worked as weavers, quarrymen and labourers. Among others, there was one farm labourer, one labourer at the Print Works and an overlooker at the Print Works who had an 11-year-old grandson with no named father but with a cotton weaver mother who was also the Print Works overlooker's married daughter. **Greenlands**, a rather crowded farmhouse with attached cottage and separate barn, was just off Well Lane on the steep slopes overlooking Brinscall's School Lane, and

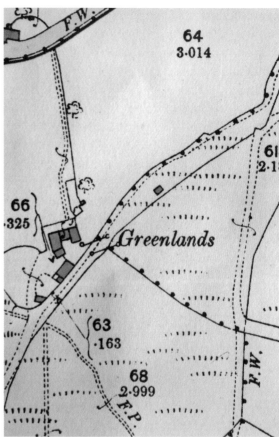

Greenlands on the hillside above and beyond the "new" houses and St Luke's church on Quarry Road. The unculverted Goit in the foreground, circa 1900.

just below **Cocker's Folly** and **Beardsworth's**. Trees grow now through its heaps of tumbled stone. There are some good firm gateposts.

Even at the large and venerable **Ratten Clough** in 1891, the 25-year-old head of household William Catlow (born in Whittle-le-Woods) was both a farmer on the moors and a general labourer at the Print Works. Significantly he and his 28-year-old wife Margaret (from Longridge) had four children aged 9, 3, 2 and 6 months. The nine-year-old (born in Longridge) must be Margaret's son from an earlier marriage, for he is known as Edward Bibby, while the three youngest are John, Catherine and William Catlow. To help look after them William and Margaret employed a 16-year-old live-in nurse and domestic servant from Scotland, Mary Beattock. No wonder William (the elder) did two jobs, one at the farm and one at the Print Works. You should please remember this sympathetically when walking round the extensive ruins of **Ratten Clough**.

It is the case, too, that the Twist Moor Lane area provides three telling examples of the changing way of life in the early 1890s. At **Grouse Cottage** 34-year-old Joseph Snape, with a 28-year-old wife Margaret and three young children aged four, two and one, was not at all a farmer but a full-time cotton spinner. The Snapes also had a lodger, 26-year-old William Waring, who was not a farm labourer but a blacksmith. All these were born in Withnell except Joseph himself who had come from Whittle-le-Woods.

At the nearby **Snape's Farm**, just two fields away, downhill and across the "Rushy" brook, 36-year-old William Bolton with a 47-year-old wife Alice and four children aged 13, 11, 10 and 7 was, like the Joseph Snape we have just met, a full-time cotton spinner. His eldest daughter, Jane, was already a cotton weaver. All were born in Withnell except Mrs Bolton who was from over the hills in Darwen.

At **Scott Hall**, also nearby (two fields up the gentle slopes to the south of **Grouse Cottage**, in the direction of **The Oaks** and **Mosscrop's**), 32-year-old Thomas Gregory, with a 32-year-old wife Ellen and four young children aged five, four, two and one month, was, almost unusually for his time and place, a farmer – but only a part-time one, for he was also a part-time cotton weaver. For him, as for Joseph Snape and William and Jane Bolton, Abbey Mill was temptingly close at hand. **Scott Hall** was a farm of only four acres when John Moss (28), his wife Betsy (29) and daughter Mary Ann (1), lived there in 1881. All the members of the Gregory family had been born in Withnell and must have known the realities when they took over from John and Betsy Moss. **Aushaw's** and **Dale Fold** were close by, and it seems likely that the equally close **Twist Moor House** was already empty.

Living in one of the smaller **New Ground** cottages, 29-year-old Samuel Pilkington was an 'engine driver', but not of a steam locomotive on the railway, rather of a stationary steam engine in one of the local factories – an almost equally responsible position, since the profits of his employers and the jobs of hundreds of his fellow workers would depend on his maintenance of the engine. His wife, Bolton-born 28-year-old Ellen, was confidently 'living on her own means', as was 55-year-old widow Esther Pilkington, not only head of household in a neighbouring cottage but also Samuel's mother and Ellen's mother-in-law. Samuel's younger brothers included former Print Works labourer now printer/compositor Alfred, and fitter/machine-maker Miles (named after his **Great Hill** grandfather) both of whom, at ages 25 and 17, were still living with their mother.

Samuel and Ellen, at 29 and 28 in 1891, had an 11-year-old son, William. They had not so far had any further children. A decade of enforced restraint? It is probable that Mrs Esther Pilkington had become a lady of some authority, influence and determination in the light of her grandson's birth and her husband's death. You might have enjoyed meeting her, or at least listening to her? She might well have had the support, should she have needed it, of her own mother-in-law and neighbour, the 82-year-old Ann Pilkington once of **Great Hill** and now of **Cocker's Folly**, also 'living on her own means'. You can in 2011 stroll past the site of **New Ground** cottages and hear nothing but birdsong – and the occasional roaring of the Hatch Brook waterfall.

James Heyes ('John Heys', originally, in the 1881 census returns), 55 years old and a widower (his wife Ellen having died since 1881), was a farm labourer living in one of the larger **New Ground** households. His 29-year-old daughter Jane, a cotton weaver in 1881, had taken her mother's place as housekeeper by 1891. His daughters Alice, Isabella and Sarah were still at home but working in the mill as cotton weavers. Daughter Mary and sons James and Jacob had evidently left home since 1881. Mary was a cotton weaver in 1881 when James was a cotton creeler and Jacob was still a scholar. No one had followed the senior James into a career of labouring on a farm.

At **Leigh Place** and **Marsden's**, two farms whose remains now lie in the southern boskinesses of Brinscall Woods, there were apparently no farmers to be seen in the 1891 census returns.

At **Leigh Place** Robert Grundy, born in 1844 on Monk's Hill (Munsell), Wheelton, was by 1891 a quarryman. His two working-age daughters, Jane and Alice (Monk's Hill-born in 1872 and 1876) were cotton weavers. Of his two younger daughters Ann (9) was still a scholar while Isabella (11) was at the half-time scholar/half-time weaver stage. Robert and his Chorley-born wife Jane (44) had no further children. A son, if they had had one, would have been a quarryman like his father?

Meanwhile at **Marsden's**, 32-year-old Thomas Dixon, born in Kendal, and his 35-year-old wife Elizabeth, born in Shalford, Essex (where did they meet?) had four young children, Annie, William, Henry and Thomas (7, 6, 4 and 2), the latter two certainly born in Heapey and almost certainly at **Marsden's Farm** itself. Annie and William were Wheelton-born – i.e. across and on the northern side of Sour Milk Brook at least. The senior Thomas Dixon's daily occupation came at the end of each day. He was a night-watchman, just down the hill, conveniently, and across the Goit,

William Isles (left), formerly of Solomon's Temple, with Alfred and Ellen Rossall, circa 1940.

at the Print Works. As he walked there he might see the sun setting in the west over Monk's Hill and the cottage where quarryman Robert Grundy had been born.

As to where the Dixons originally met: it is now apparent that, having been a lady-in-waiting to a pupil or pupils at Harlow School in Essex, Elizabeth Jane Wyatt had become a governess to a Westmorland family. Near Kendal she had met the young farmer Thomas Dixon, two years and four months her junior. They were married at All Saints' Church Underbarrow on 12 November 1881. (See Part Two, Chapter Six for details of their further children and of family life at Marsden's Farm until 1910 and afterwards as recorded in Elizabeth's extraordinary daily journal. They had lived at Marsden's since 1886.)

Farming did continue in 1891 at four sites off Edge Gate Lane, in addition to **Hatch Place** and **Ratten Clough**, of course. At **Solomon's Temple** both the head of household William Rossall and his daughter Ellen Isles have freely admitted to being full-time farmers, but then both originally came from agricultural communities in the Fylde District, William from Great Eccleston and Ellen from Pilling. Grandson William Isles (22), born in Sowerby, Yorkshire, was a general labourer at the farm. At **Whittle's**, James Shorrock, who had grown up at **Solomon's Temple** just three fields away, was also content to be defined as a farmer, though he continued to make pickers (for looms) as well. The two of his daughters who still lived at home, Mary and Rachel, were both cotton winders in a valley mill, however. Even at the impressive **Heaton's (Heaton House)**, a little further down Edge Gate Lane, where Thomas Heyes was a determined farmer with the support of his wife Martha, his one child, Alice (16), was a cotton winder in the valley too. Alice perhaps joined Mary and Rachel from **Whittle's** for the daily walk down and then back up Edge Gate Lane and Well Lane? Think of the three of them next time you try to walk quickly up Well Lane and Edge Gate Lane even without a day's work in the mill beforehand. Remember that they did this walk in all weathers (with shawls over their heads if need be) and in dark winter mornings and very dark evenings. They very probably carried a lantern.

Back on the higher stretch of Edge Gate Lane again, at **White Hall Farm**, Ashworth Howarth (59) from Bury, with his wife Ann (63), from Ribchester, and with no children, was a farmer pure, entire and undistracted, presumably. However, his neighbour at the almost next-door **White Hall Cottage**, James Bolton (39) from Brinscall, was equally entirely a quarryman. Unusually, his Birkenhead-born wife Mary, nine years older than her husband, was given a rather precise occupation on the census form (instead of none at all as was more common). Was she employed day by day in a neighbouring household? Or had she a closely defined role in her own home? One does wonder. Whatever is the case she was described exactly – or bleakly – in the census as a 'personal domestic servant'.

Were older wives thought likely to be overbearing in 1891, unless thus artificially defined and constrained? It is a noticeable fact, to be sure, that in all the marriages recorded in Brinscall Moors farms for 1891 no fewer than 20 out of 41 wives (i.e. almost

One man and his dogs: John Dixon of High Bullough (the Manor House, Anglezarke) circa 1930.

half) were of the same age as, or actually older than, their husbands. That might be thought a rather progressive position even in the twenty-first century. Perhaps it was simply another case of sheer common-sense practicality, a getting-on-with-it realism, in a community with few false dreams.

One way to avoid having an older or even an overbearing wife might be to avoid having a wife at all. At **Higher Calf Hey** in 1891 there were just two persons, an uncle and his nephew, both of them named James Park, one aged 42 and the other aged 21. Both, quite credibly, claimed to be farmers. What else was there to be up to at **Higher Calf Hey**, as the Cookson family had found a decade earlier?

Wives there certainly were, as it happens, at the only two farms whose gable-ends stood firmly next to the A675 Belmont Road, as we noticed earlier. And these two actually had a special characteristic in common. Margaret Bateson (52) at **Besom Hall**, wife of Robert from Brindle, and Agnes Nelson (36) at **Lower Calf Hey**, wife of John from Kendal, were both born, although 16 years apart, in the same remote and special valley in the east of the Lake District. Both Margaret and Agnes came from the delightful Mardale, site of the future Haweswater. From Riggindale Beck to Roddlesworth River, indeed. An odd coincidence.

We also find a distinctive character in the young lady of the farmhouse in cosily sited **Goose Green** in 1891. No dressmaker, no spinner, no weaver was she, no general servant either. Sarah, the 21-year-old daughter of farmer Henry Hogg and Rachel his wife, was, uniquely among inhabitants of our farms in 1881 and 1891, an elementary school teacher.

f) Farming Practice – and Food and Drink

Anyone who has spent an hour in a moors farm kitchen, with mug of tea and cheerful, chatting host, knows why farmers do the job they do. There is with them a calm, unhurried confidence, an at-ease understanding, and an expertise and a warm concern for the proper use of land and the well-being of animals including their essential partners the sheepdogs. There is a realistic acceptance of the limited soil-qualities of both past and present moorland fields – the shallowness, the stoniness ("a nightmare to plough"), the acidity, the fact that only in the three summer months is it worth letting sheep roam freely on the highest parts of the open moor, for otherwise the grass lacks nourishment.

In the Tithe Map records for the 1840s it is clear that on the moors the amount of 'tillage' was nil. Even in the lower, non-moorland parts of Heapey, for example, the area of tillage was minimal. Such land there as was ploughed was expected to produce oats, certainly not wheat and probably not barley. Hay-making – for winter animal feed – did happen, of course, though not on the high, rough, open moorland. The hay-making was a grand family activity, labour-intensive, with horse-drawn mowing machines and carts, plus rakes and pitch-forks ….. and it continued in this traditional fashion into the 1930s, 40s and 50s, as seen in photographs supplied by the Mayor family formerly of Higher Healey, **Drinkwater's** and **Ratten Clough**.

Besides the sheep (chiefly Swaledales) with all the lambing and the shearing, most farms did keep a small number of cattle (for the milk and the consequent home-made butter and cheese) plus poultry (for the egg supply); several also kept a few pigs (for the ham/bacon). In the mid 1800s, before the railway came, the Robinsons of **Botany Bay** (the **Summer House**) used to take a horse and cart into Chorley or Blackburn both to "buy in" food items not available at home, and also to sell their own ham, eggs and butter in the markets. In the early twentieth century the Mayors sold their butter at a grocery store off Eaves Lane in Chorley. Some farms packed and sold their own honey produced by bees that "worked" the moorland heather.

Government pressure during the Second World War (in line with the Dig for Victory campaign) did encourage remaining farmers on the moors to take up ploughing and sowing, in an effort to produce oats at least, but the quality of the crop was desperately dependent on decent weather, unreliable as that was and is. A walker might find it an unexpected surprise, these days, to see, following a light snowfall in winter in the Twist Moor area, the unmistakable ridge and furrow signs of former ploughing. Several fields in the neighbourhood of **Grouse Cottage** and **Scott Hall**, for instance, had obviously been ploughed 60 or more years ago. The long parallel lines of snow-filled hollows tell no lies. But that does not mean that ploughing and harvesting in high places had ever been the norm.

Far more common in the nineteenth and early twentieth centuries was cattle droving. This, an activity successfully practised by members of the Smith family in

A hay-making party at White Coppice, circa 1930. Harold Mayor is on the left, in cap. On the back row, wearing a trilby, is John Smith. His son E. I. Smith is also on the back row, wearing a cap.

particular, involved purchases of young beef cattle at, for instance, auctions in North Wales and a bringing them by rail to Brinscall station. This would be followed by several months of 'fattening', usually in the high fields of the Twist Moor-Roddlesworth area, and then, ultimately, by a grand walking expedition in search of sales. Long walks for man and beast these were. A spectacular mass progress. Most often the target was Clitheroe Market. The route involved Tockholes and Mill Hill, on the southern outskirts of Blackburn, and then Whalley. A large field would be used for an overnight stop prior to a sale next morning. Beasts that were not sold would have to be walked back all the way to Roddlesworth, say. That might be followed, after some days' pause, by a fresh attempt at a sale involving another long expedition, this time on the route via the **Calf Hey** farms and Piccadilly to Belmont, and then over Scout Road to Smithills on the north side of Bolton.

The amount of walking considered normal or acceptable for persons living on the moors in the nineteenth century was quite extraordinary by modern standards. Young farm-dwelling persons in particular were obliged to take long daily walks to and from school (the 1870 Act had made elementary education compulsory as well as desirable) and then, as they matured, to and from their place of employment in spinning mill or weaving shed, bleach works or print works, railway yard or quarry. Their fathers, too, after long days of working with the sheep or repairing the dry stone walls, or besom- or picker-making, or hay-making or ditch-clearing, would often walk miles to earn a few extra shillings by assisting fellow farmers – lending a hand with muck-spreading, as Harold Mayor did, or with calving or lambing or hay-making or general labouring and fetching and carrying.

The farmer's working day had normal, accepted and uncomplicated limits throughout the year. No carefully timed schedules. Just "dawn to dusk", a simple but formidable expectation. Farmers were physically fit, not surprisingly; their way of life was, in a sense, self-imposed, even if throughout the eighteenth and much of the nineteenth century, it was largely a complying with tradition and seemingly unavoidable.

Farmers' wives did not, on the whole, take part in the long walkings, but the variety and continuous nature of their labours was at least equally demanding. They certainly carried in the fresh water from well or brook to the kitchen, they fed and cared for the poultry, they often milked (hand-milked, of course) the cows, they helped with the lambing, they made, mended and washed everyone's clothes, they looked after the small but significant vegetable garden, they quite simply ran the household and they presided as central characters over all aspects and stages of their own and others' child-bearing and child-rearing. Above all, perhaps, in day to day activities, they did the cooking.

Cutting the hay at White Coppice, circa 1930.

Harold Mayor with a faithful companion at Higher Healey, circa 1935.

It is quite clear that, by 1898–1900, several specialist shops had sprung up along School Lane and Railway Road, shops that sold groceries and confectionery, and shops offering meat, fruit and vegetables, hardware, clothing, clogs, boots and shoes, sweets and tobacco – and, eventually, ice-cream. But these shops catered chiefly for that increasingly large proportion of Brinscall's population that was living in the terraced cottages of School Lane and Railway Road (including South View, 1883, and Salisbury, Hartington and Churchill Roads named after leading politicians of the mid-1880s – Lord Randolph, Winston's father, in the case of Churchill, of course). On the moors, however, the tradition continued that farmers' wives baked their own bread every day and made their own cakes. "Never once bought a shop cake" was a proud boast from a grandparent that was still being equally proudly reported in 2009.

Certainly the main kitchen of the Mayor family at **Ratten Clough** as recently as the 1930s contained a large flour bin that was kept well topped-up and was in daily use. Home-baking ruled okay! There was also much bottling of fruit, and much jam-making – chiefly but not exclusively involving locally picked raspberries, blackberries, whinberries/bilberries and apples. If you know where to look you can still find raspberries on wild 'canes' near **Hatch Place** on Edge Gate Lane. There was also home-brewing – of blackberry wine, elderberry wine, dandelion and burdock, and nettle beer. The kitchen table at **Ratten Clough** "always", I am told, displayed a jug containing some recommended healthy but imprecisely defined home-brew (possibly based on yarrow – the herb not the river), a dark liquid lying temptingly within. Possibly, or possibly not, even more health-giving was a jug of home-made buttermilk.

The **Ratten Clough** sitting room was well furnished, too, with rocking chair, sofa (under the window), sideboard (bearing two black wooden elephants), whatnot, sewing-machine and a section of old iron bedstead to stop cows peering in through an open window. All this, plus the cooking, continued into the 1950s, with outside loo, oil lamps, peat (and some coal) fires, and water carried in in pails from the Hatch Brook. Fred Mayor, the last resident at **Ratten Clough**, did not leave until June 6 1960. Farmers and their lads, but not their women-folk on the whole, did like their beer in an evening down in the village pubs, of course, or even in the neighbouring towns. Fred Mayor in 1960 found that his new residence on Butterworth Brow left him with fewer miles to walk home at nights. Still a hill to climb, but a smaller one.

Meanwhile, plenty of tea, with plenty of milk and sugar, was drunk on the moors while the farms were still occupied. At many of the farms tea was actually offered to, and gladly accepted by, passing walkers, single walkers as well as groups, in a continuing of an age-old tradition of hospitality. Payment for the tea was naturally accepted, too. Sadly, walkers must these days carry their own refreshment as they explore the thoroughly de-populated moorlands. **Ratten Clough**, as one of the last three farms out of the 48 to be inhabited, became especially well known for its offering of tea.

g) Family Surnames

(Lists based on census returns from Withnell, Wheelton and Heapey for 1851, 1881, and 1891.)

Seventeen surnames appear most frequently. They are:
Bibby, Blackledge/Blacklidge, Briggs, Brindle, Bury, Fowler, Heys/Heyes, Miller, Moss, Pilkington, Shorrock, Smith, Snape, Taylor, Thomas, Warburton. Wareing/ Waring.

Other surnames appearing at least once:
Ainscough, Ainsworth, Allsop, Bateson, Baxendale, Baxenden, Beardsworth, Beardwood, Beesley, Bennett, Benson, Berry, Billington, Blackburn, Bolton, Bradbury, Briers, Brocklehurst, Brownlow, Butler, Catlow, Clarkson, Collinson, Cookson, Cooper, Cotton, Coulston, Counsell, Culshaw, Cureton, Dewhurst, Dixon, Duckworth, Duxbury, Eastham, Farnworth, Fazackerley, Fisher, Fish, Foy, Gaskell, Gorman, Gregory, Grime, Grundy, Hall, Haworth, Heald, Hindley, Hodkinson, Hogg, Howarth, Hull, Isles, Jackson, Jonston, Joy, Kershaw, Kirby, Knight, Lang, Lewis, Longton, Loyd, Marsden, Masterson, Mayor, Moulden, Nelson, Neville, Nowell, Park, Parker, Phipp, Power, Rawcliffe, Robinson, Rossall, Rosthorn, Scambler, Simpson, Singleton, Southworth, Stalter, Sumner, Talbot, Thompson, Turner, Vachre, Walmesley, Walsh, Walton, Whalley, Wilkinson, Worsley.

h) Christian names

(As shown on census returns from Withnell, Wheelton and Heapey for 1851, 1881 and 1891)

The eight most popular male names and the number of times they appear:

William	47	Richard	23
John	46	Joseph	20
Thomas	39	Henry	13
James	36	Robert	12

The eight most popular female names and the number of times they appear:

Elizabeth	44	Alice	27
Margaret	37	Jane	27
Mary	37	Sarah	26
Ann	29	Ellen	22

All other male names and the number of their appearances:
Aaron 1, Abel 2, Abram 1, Adam 2, Albert 1, Alfred 4, Andrew 7, Arthur 2, Ashworth 1, Bartholomew 4, Benjamin 1, Bennett 1, Bernard 1, Charles 1, Christopher 2, Daniel 2, David 6, Doctor 1, Edward 5, Edwin 1, Eli 1, Elisha 2, Enoch 1, Frederick 1, Gabriel 2, George 3, Harold 1, Harry 1, Herbert 2, Hugh 2, Ichabod 1, Isaac 1, Isaiah 1, Jacob 1, Job 1, Josiah 1, Lawrence 1, Luke 1, Mark 1, Miles 7, Moses 1, Nathan 1, Nicholas 2, Oliver 1, Ralph 1, Reuben 1, Roger 1, Rowlandson 1, Samuel 6, Stephen 1, Tom 1, Wilfred 1, Williamson 1.

The number of Biblical, especially Old Testament, names is noteworthy.

All other female names and the number of appearances:
Agnes 4, Alma 1, Beatrice 1, Bertha 1, Betsy 1, Betty 1, Catherine 3, Charlotta 1, Christina 1, Clara 1, Clementina 3, Deborah 2, Dinah 2, Dorothy 2, Edith 3, Eliza 4, Emily 1, Emma 1, Esther 3, Ethel 1, Fanny 1, Gertrude 1, Grace 2, Hannah 3, Harriet 2, Jessie 1, Letitia 1, Lettice 1, Lilian 1, Lily 1, Lizzie 1, Lucy 5, Malvena 1, Maria 1, Mariah 1, Marion 1, Marjory 3, Martha 4, Minnie 1, Miranda 1, Nancy 5, Peggy 1, Rachel 1, Rebecca 1, Rose 1, Rosina 1, Ruby 1, Ruth 3, Sally 1, Selina 1, Sophia 1, Susannah 1, Violet 1, Winifred 1.

Again, Biblical, especially Old Testament, influence is apparent, but there is also what might be called a 'literary' element, too.

CHAPTER FOUR

The Liverpool Purchase and the Decline of the Farms

T HE EVENTUAL COMPULSORY PURCHASING by Liverpool Corporation of the Brinscall (Withnell, Wheelton and Heapey) Moors and adjacent water-gathering ground seems not seriously to have been considered when reservoir building was first planned in 1847 and completed in 1857. Simply it was the actual surface areas of the reservoirs and the Goit that were put under Liverpool's ownership by the 1847 Act, with their boundaries being defined by newly built stone walls. All the evidence suggests that farming and farm-dwelling on the moors remained a steady and relatively thriving way of life in the nineteenth century up to at least 1870 or so, as it had been in the eighteenth century. After all, it was the 1800 to 1870 period which saw the establishment of **Botany Bay** (the **Summer House**), the doubling in size of **Solomon's Temple**, the more than doubling of **Ratten Clough** and its barn, and the building from scratch of **The Oaks**, **Tower View** and the two-cottage (semi-detached) **Twist Moor House**. There did continue to be a demand for well-produced hand-woven cloth until the 1850s, thereabouts, and there certainly was a sale for good-quality woollen fleeces on into the twentieth century.

A significant problem, however, was that the size of families – the sheer number of children born and surviving – in many of the farms was greater than the managing of sheep and the production of wool for sale actually required; the imbalance was emphasised once domestic handloom weaving collapsed as an additional earner. Families in the 1880s and 90s increasingly had to find, and wanted to find, employment in the developing factories and quarries of the area rather than in the farms themselves. Indeed employment for young persons in factories or quarries began to be the reason why some families came to live in the area's moorland farms. Even a male head of household – a 'retired' farmer – might look for work in factory or quarry alongside his children. The original sheep farming activity began to be concentrated in fewer and fewer farms.

In 2011 it now requires not 48 or 49 but only two main farms – Baron's Fold and Anglezarke's Manor House – with their machinery and efficient workforce to manage the still quite large flocks of sheep kept on the moors between Anglezarke and Abbey Village. In the nineteenth century moorland-dwellers had to earn their living as best they could, by whatever means was available, by factory or quarry work if picker-making or besom-making did not suffice and handloom weaving had gone. There were no government or EU-agreed subsidies to help preserve a way of life and promote care of the countryside. Nor, for that matter, were there designated Open Access areas for the benefit of walkers and ramblers! But the days of the economically viable and self-sufficient three or five or 10 acre moorland sheep farm were gone forever by 1900.

To be sure, we now understand a good deal more about economic change and the inexorable and often cruel and 'undeserved' social consequences of this. We can see that from at least the fourteenth-century Black Death and the decline of classic feudalism onwards, economic change and social disruption has become the norm, though the pace of change has been variable and to an extent unpredictable. The fluctuating fortunes of British ports, fishing towns, resorts, ship-building towns and railway towns, plus textile areas, mining areas, iron and steel areas, potteries and motor trades areas have all been well documented. We cannot be surprised that Brinscall Moors were not immune to this process of rising, thriving and declining. Indeed, the industrialised Brinscall Valley, prospering in 1900, fell upon disastrously hard times with the closure of the Bleach Works and the Print Works in 1928 and Withnell Mill in 1930. It was "the valley of desolation" in the MP Douglas Hacking's dramatic phrase.

To sum up, so far, the fact is that there had been a major change in the use made of our moorland farm buildings in the short period from the 1870s to the 1890s. By the 1890s the majority of the 48 farms (49 including the now invisible **Richmond's**) were no longer so much directly concerned with sheep-farming and the care of cattle and poultry as with the housing of a mainly young industrial workforce that happened to live on the moors rather than in the comparatively close-knit housing conditions of the valley, on or about School Lane, Railway Road, Bury Lane and Abbey Village.

The logical conclusion, forgetting sentiment perhaps, was that moorland farm dwellers would, or even should, swiftly or gradually abandon their tenancies and their comparatively rural remoteness, and come down to live in terraced cottages where there was the convenience of gas lighting (for streets as well as houses), piped indoor water, mains sewage disposal, cheaply available coal for cooking and heating, shops for every need, banks, chapels and churches, council offices and a railway station providing easy access (via special early morning trains) to factories in Chorley or Blackburn or their outskirts. Terraced cottages in the valley provided at least as much accommodation (in terms of size and number of rooms) for a family as had the moorland farms. They just had a backyard where the farm houses had had their barns and fields, of course.

It is not surprising that during the 1890s several of the 48/49 farms began to be unoccupied, to fall empty and to fall into disrepair. In 1891, **Calico Hall**, **Fir Farm** (beautifully sited but remote), **Grime's**, **New Temple**, **Pope's**, **Sour Milk Hall** and **Twist Moor House** were already unoccupied. With the exception of **Twist Moor House**, all these had at least two things in common. They lacked easy, or short, cart-track access, and they were rather on the 'exposed' side. They were not alone in this. Several others, equally 'exposed' or remote, were still occupied and even engaged in 1891 in sheep-farming, but, for the afore-mentioned six, their site was hardly an advantage if access to paid employment in the valley was important to a potential tenant.

Meanwhile, in spite of being, like nearby **Twist Moor House** and **Grouse Cottage**, very close to a good track, **Dale Fold**, still fully occupied in 1891 (as in the photograph) is not shown at all on an 1894 Ordnance Survey map. It must have been very thoroughly demolished as early as 1892–93. 'Delenda est Dale Fold', some latter-day Scipio might have said. The destruction was even more thorough than the job the Romans did on Carthage. The occupations of its inhabitants did not augur well on the 1891 census form, and **Dale Fold** did not survive to 1901 as a farmhouse or anything else.

Next to what is still a public footpath (across the slopes and streams from Lower Roddlesworth to Norcross Brow), all that can be seen of **Dale Fold** in 2011 is a smooth, flat field with a trace of two slight ridges and the extensive walled enclosure that formerly surrounded the buildings and farmyard. Of the house, cottage and barn not the slightest piece of stonework survives above ground. Though one can be confident about exactly where it stood, it is, apart from the two versions of **Richmond's**, the most thoroughly vanished of the 49 abandoned farms. Even the flattened and occasional car-and-lorry-park that marks the site of **White Hall** (on Edge Gate Lane) does reveal some significant stone slabs if you know where to look for them.

In the early years of the twentieth century, abandonment and demolition of farms seems to have continued at an increasing pace. A member of the Whalley family of Lower Roddlesworth calculated in 1976 that, by 1914, in addition to **Calico Hall**, **Fir Farm**, **Grime's**, **New Temple**, **Pope's**, **Sour Milk Hall** and **Twist Moor House**, the following 10, at least, soon lay in ruins: **Aushaw's**, **Higher Calf Hey**, **Hillock**, **Keck**, **Mosscrop's**, **The Oaks**, **Pimm's**, **Rake**, **Scott Hall**, and **Tower View**. To this number should be added **Besom Hall** and **Stake Hill**, and in due course the great avalanche of a list that contains another 19: **Beardsworth's**, **Cocker's Folly**, **Coppice Stile**, **Great Hill**, **Greenlands**, **Hatch**, **Heapey Moor**, **Heaton's**, **Leigh Place**, **Liptrot's**, **Marsden's**, **New Ground** and its cottages, **Ripping**, **Sharrock's**, **Snape's**, **Top o'th'Wood** (and Blackhurst, its non-farm neighbour), **Whave Gate**, **White Hall** and its cottages, and **Whittle's**. It seems that none of these survived beyond the 1920s, if so far. **New Ground** was 'pulled down' in 1908 and **Top o'th Wood** in 1910, for example. **Drinkwater's** and **Solomon's Temple** perhaps lasted till 1940, but there are persistent rumours that, once vacated, both were used as targets by the Army in artillery practice sessions during the Second World War. Certainly, by 1945 there appear to

Happy in the sunshine: Sarah, Dorothy and James Bennett at Grouse Cottage, 1952.

have been just three of our now (2011) abandoned farms that were still inhabited: **Grouse Cottage**, **Ratten Clough** and **Goose Green**.

Goose Green seems to have been demolished (reduced to a low, roughly rectangular heap of stones and foundation blocks among the summer bracken) in the late 1950s or early 60s. At **Grouse Cottage**, James (Jimmy) Bennett, the Liverpool Corporation employee who, by agreement, had fitted piped water and a wind-generated electricity supply in the modernised house, was obliged to participate in the demolition of his own former home in the early 1960s. He and his wife and daughter (Sarah and Dorothy) look perfectly happy as they sit in the sun in front of **Grouse Cottage** in 1952. Finally, **Ratten Clough** has been allowed to fall down gradually as wind and rain have done their destructive work, once roof flags were removed in the 1960s. It still remains as an impressive relic, a token of former long-term hopes and endeavour, a sign of what once was, as well as what could still have been.

But ... (and it is a big 'but') there seems to be an inconclusive, or inconsistent, element to the tale of the 'lost' farms and to the reality of the survival of significant others – 10 others, to be exact – within our well-defined triangle. Of the 10, four – Baron's Fold, Watson's and the two Roddlesworths – survive, still, as working farms; two – Pickering's and Wood's Fold – survive as refurbished houses with an alternative business use; three – Ramsden's, Norcross and Cliff Fold – survive as fine, partly reconstructed country residences, each large enough to be divided into more than a single unit; and one – Crosby's – survives as a totally rebuilt barn-house now named Butterworth Barn. The question is sometimes asked: why, if 10 farms could be preserved, upgraded and modified, could not the same have happened to **Ratten Clough**, **Grouse Cottage** and **Goose Green**, at least? Well, the 10 survivors are all on main roads (in four cases) or good side-roads (in six cases) where mains water and overhead power lines (if not mains sewerage) could relatively easily be provided. But are not **Ratten Clough**, **Grouse Cottage** and **Goose Green** quite similarly sited, fairly close to potentially easily improved side roads? Twentieth-century, certainly second-half twentieth-century, techniques of building and infrastructure provision could surely have been capable of providing service connections, it might be said.

Grouse Cottage in snow, circa 1950.

There are, it is claimed, two sets of examples among others, one in Lancashire and one in Yorkshire, which show how redundant but impressively sited and stone-built moorland farms have readily been modified and transformed into valuable and much-sought-after properties. A journey in North Bolton along Walker Fold Road and the Scout Road between the B6226 at Bob's Smithy and the A675 reveals at least 10 fairly remote moorland farms, very like those that once flourished on Brinscall Moors, farms that are now most desirable and characterful residences on Smithills Moor. Alternatively, a walk in Yorkshire along the Calderdale Way on the hills between Todmorden and Hebden Bridge allows one to pass very closely next to restored, tastefully reconstructed farmhouses of exactly the familiar type.

The answer to the big 'but' question, and to the 'why' and 'why not' questions lies entirely in the character of the 1898–1902 take-over of Brinscall Moors by the Liverpool Corporation Waterworks Department, a wholly well-intentioned and humane authority at the time, but motivated by a most pressing and serious matter concerning public health. I did say earlier that the Goit is very largely the reason why there are 48 abandoned and dismantled farms on Brinscall Moors. It is now time to provide the full explanation.

A considerable outbreak of typhoid at Maidstone, Kent, in 1895 was the critical event. Accidental contamination of the public water supply was held to be responsible. The relevant government department, the Local Government Board of the time, wrote to all suppliers of drinking water throughout the country, including Liverpool Corporation, urging the need for every possible care and precaution in maintaining the purity of water supply and preventing any contamination of water gathering grounds. Avoiding further outbreaks of the disease was a priority.

For Liverpool, this meant the compulsory purchase in 1898–1902 of the Rivington and Anglezarke Moors west of the watershed boundary line, which ran from Winter Hill northwards along Spitlers' Edge and Redmond's Edge, plus the valleys of the Calf Hey Brook and the Roddlesworth River and the whole of the Withnell, Wheelton and Heapey Moors. From our point of view that means all land to the east of the Goit that could possibly contribute water to the Roddlesworth and Rake reservoirs and then via the Goit, (with its extra contributions from the Hatch, Sour Milk and Dean Black Brooks) to the Anglezarke and Rivington reservoirs. (This was all confirmed by the Liverpool Corporation Act of 8 August, 1902.)

The main objective of the compulsory land purchase was the removing as far as possible from the moors of both animal and human life, and therefore of potential contamination by animal or human sewage. That the moors should be de-populated – the farms emptied – was clearly the theoretical ideal. But it is important to emphasise that Liverpool's policy was not an immediate and ruthless set of enforced 'clearances'. There was no intention of repeating the Scottish Highlands' experience. The primary motive was enhanced public health not economic advantage. The prevention of typhoid outbreaks among the people of Liverpool and in the transatlantic ships which also used 'Rivington's' water was the predominant intention. Given nineteenth-century assumptions about the efficacy and the limitations of water treatment plants (the Filter Beds at Rivington/Dryfield Lane for example), the eventual emptying of the moors seemed a wise and prudent measure, though it did go a good deal further than Bolton's policy of protecting the feeders of its reservoirs in the Belmont area, it is fair to add.

The coinciding by 1898, then, of two factors, the need to guarantee as far as possible the purity of water supplies, and the increased readiness of many farm-dwelling families to leave their moorland homes and move down to the valley where employment was mainly to be found, led to a new policy on tenancies once Liverpool had taken over. The Liverpool policy was not to force tenants out of their farmhouses but, rather, not to renew tenancies when these expired and the farm buildings had become vacant. This seemed conveniently to be in line with economic reality, with the cycle of decline which was affecting agriculture nationally from circa 1875 onwards.

From the point of view of a Liverpool rate payer, income from agricultural rents was set to decline, money could be saved by not spending on maintenance of, or improvements to, moorland farm buildings, and more money could incidentally be made from, say, forestry than from sheep-farming (still rather labour-intensive at the time). There was an economic case as well, then, albeit of a secondary kind. Farms that seemed in the eyes of determined tenants to be still viable might survive for a while, even for a century and more as it turned out, in some cases; but a future, generally, for the moors involving abandoned and empty farm buildings and new plantings of trees – e.g. the so-called Wheelton and Withnell plantations – seemed the most likely one.

A little extra money might be made, periodically, by the use of the moors for organised shooting, grouse-shooting in particular. The **Botany Bay** buildings, or a temporarily preserved section of them, could be used as an occasional base and shelter for grouse-shooters, whose refreshments could also be served there. **Grouse Cottage** could be used as a residence for a gamekeeper.

The growth of woodlands, meanwhile, had the added benefit of restricting surface water run-off (and with it possible sheep-dropping contamination) from the moors down to the valley, to the Goit particularly. As the century progressed, new-grown conifers could stand tall and ready to serve as the pit-props that in the 1920s it was thought British coal mines might desperately need but now never will. Thus, we eventually have the splendid Brinscall Woods as they have become by the twenty-first century, almost a nature reserve in practice though not in original intention. Within them are the hidden farm ruins and crumbled field-boundary walls; outside them, of course, the splendidly sad ruins of **Ratten Clough** and **Solomon's Temple** and, along the track to Great Hill, the later shooting butts. **Botany Bay** and **Grouse Cottage** have become little more than untidy heaps of broken foundation wall.

However, here at last comes almost the final 'but' question, almost the final question to be asked about the ruined farms. It is here that regret, not so much resentment as

Richard Robinson at a semi-derelict Botany Bay, circa 1945. He lived there as a boy.

regret, is at its most persistent locally. No one among local people can be surprised that the 48 have not survived as farms. Clearly, no owner, not the Parkes, not Liverpool Corporation, not the North West Water Authority, not United Utilities with its positive publicity, its well-meant information notices and country wardens could have preserved many, if any, of the 48 farms as working units with a genuine economic function. But the regret, the hurt even, the sadness over the loss of houses that were once so sturdy and so full of life comes down to one question: why did Liverpool not only preside over the emptying of the farms but also actively organise the subsequent demolition of almost all of them? There seem to be two main answers.

The first might be thought nowadays to display an excess of caution, though in the context of the twentieth century up to 1970 or so perhaps it was no more than wise and responsible; but the demolition programme was certainly intended to ensure that once a farm was left empty and abandoned it could never again be occupied, and could therefore never again be a potential threat to the purity of water supplies. There was an air of finality about it. Demolition was a final statement, an ideal conclusion from a bureaucratic efficiency point of view. (And bureaucracies after all do have to be efficient, or at least appear to aim at efficiency.)

The second answer is an early and in its way wise application of what has now become the notorious Health and Safety outlook. An empty farm and barn are, always were, as empty factories also have been, an attraction to adventure-seeking lads. The lure of high walls to climb and walk on is almost irresistible. The presence of windows, especially upper windows, to break, and roofs to slide on or jump down from, could hardly be ignored by the foolhardy. In these circumstances the danger of serious injury was considerable, and landowners do quite reasonably like to avoid accusations of being carelessly at fault. A demolished farm is far less likely to attract the wrong sort of notice. A sprained or broken ankle is the worst calamity likely to result from unwise attention to a heap of stones. Strolling round the moors nowadays is surely at one's own risk.

All this leads to a subsidiary 'What if?' issue, a question of the counter-factual kind which is worth serious if brief consideration. It is this. If the Roddlesworth and Rake reservoirs had never been built, and if therefore the Goit had never been built, the Anglezarke reservoir must surely have been a much smaller affair, being almost entirely dependent on waters contributed by the River Yarrow and the Limestone Brook (with or without an eventual Yarrow reservoir). Not only that but, significantly, the Brinscall (Withnell, Wheelton and Heapey) Moors must surely have been left in the hands of their existing owners and tenants, with no Liverpool Corporation involvement at all? In that case, might several of the now-demolished farms still be inhabited, in original or modified or reconstructed form? I leave the question hanging there, for your further thought.

This chapter is now almost at an end, but before we move on I have one further question to address. It may stir positive thoughts in you too. It concerns a mere fantasy, an indulgence in happy day-dreams, but I have been asked the question and therefore I ought to answer it, in spite of the claim to neutrality I made earlier. The

A rare view of Grouse Cottage from the south, amid wide snowfields.

question is this. If I had the choice of one of the 48 farms to restore and live in, which would it be?

After much thought, much going-over of all the walks and visitings of every one of the farms, I do have a first choice, but, perversely, I also have a close second choice, just in case. My first choice would be **Fir Farm**, if Trigg Lane could be extended again beyond Old Withnell's to **Goose Green** and then up the 'sunken track' to the **Fir Farm** site. I have no idea of the external appearance of **Fir Farm** but I know very well its foundation plan, and I know that the site took up one rood and two perches for the house, outbuildings, yard, access track and garden, and that its tenant (with 39 acres to look after) in 1845 was Jane Simon. It was built on a convenient natural ledge a good 10m wide and 60m long, half-way up the Brinscall Fault/ Ice Age Edge hillside. It is backed by rising slopes to the east which provide good shelter. The farm also has a pleasing line of adjacent sycamores, hawthorns and hazels. It has a glorious view down to White Coppice, Grey Heights and Healey Nab, across to the Harbour Lane ridge as well, and then beyond to the sea coast near Southport, the Ribble estuary and Blackpool. On many days the mountains of North Wales are easily visible, as are, to the north, the higher slopes of the Bleasdale Fells. Its one deficiency is that the Lake District mountains are hidden by the Harbour Lane ridge. A quick canter up the rise towards **Sour Milk Hall** soon reveals them, however. The refurbished and extended Old Withnell's farm is below and has happily survived because it is on the western side of the Goit (though very close to it) whereas **Goose Green**, also just below, is on the Goit's eastern (water-gathering) side.

My second choice, **Grouse Cottage**, is almost equally splendidly sited. It stands above Twist Moor Lane, with its own short access track rising gently from the lane and being quite capable in the 1950s of taking an Armstrong Siddeley car. It has sheltering sycamore trees, a further couple of refined trees (laburnums) planted by Jimmy Bennett, and a wonderful view not only of the moors to the east and south (Darwen Tower and Great Hill included) but also of the landscape north to the Bleasdale Fells, the Lake District, Ingleborough and Pendle. You can still see the metal bracket-supports which held the sink, allowing anyone who happened to be washing up in the kitchen to gaze through the window at a most inspiring vista. The same view was available from the two bedrooms at the front of the house. **Grouse Cottage** would have easy access to the A675 without suffering its twice a day traffic noise. The M65 is also distantly visible (two miles away) near to Junction 3. **Fir Farm**, on the other hand, would involve a motorist in a necessarily leisurely drive through narrow lanes for nearly three miles before reaching the A674 and then eventually the M61 at Junction 8 a further mile away.

But, away now with these practical or impractical imaginings. My third choice, however (if you were to ask), would be **Ratten Clough**, my fourth **Keck**, my fifth …

CHAPTER FIVE

The Older Cottages of Brinscall's School Lane

THERE IS GREAT VARIETY and character among the terraced cottages and houses on both sides of School Lane. They tell a worthy story, being at least as thoroughly and smartly maintained now as at any time in their history. The gardens and the particular architectural details of the newer (post-1880) and several of the older (pre-1830) terraces are especially pleasing. Doorway and window lintels of the later stone and brick terraces often received special attention from their builders, with refined architraves and simple but stylish (square Doric) capitals, for example.

However, for the time being I want to concentrate mainly on the older cottages of School Lane, those that are entirely stone-built and that date from as early as 1800–1820 thereabouts. These are the obviously vernacular but very attractive and efficient houses that are in many cases almost contemporaries of the moorland farms. While many have had extra rooms added at the rear in more recent times, the originals were very much a two-up, two-down design. That means, nevertheless, that they initially began life with twice as much space for a family as **Coppice Stile** or **Sour Milk Hall** or the first version of **Ratten Clough**, for instance.

The North Side

If we begin a survey of School Lane on its northern side at the bottom of the hill, we start with the then unusual terrace of five (or perhaps it was really seven) cottages known on early maps as Brinscall Row. Terraces even of this length were very rare nationally for most of the eighteenth century, except particularly in London and Bath. They were rare even in towns let alone in villages.

Brinscall Row was quite a departure from the normal village practice of building single cottages or groups of two or three at the most. That this terrace should have been built as early as 1805 was part of the establishing of a new tradition. That these cottages with their charming and cosy character, should still be happily occupied more

School Lane, Brinscall, circa 1900.

The Ordnance Survey Map of 1848 (2nd edition) includes the Goit (River Cut) of 1857 but not yet the railway of 1869.

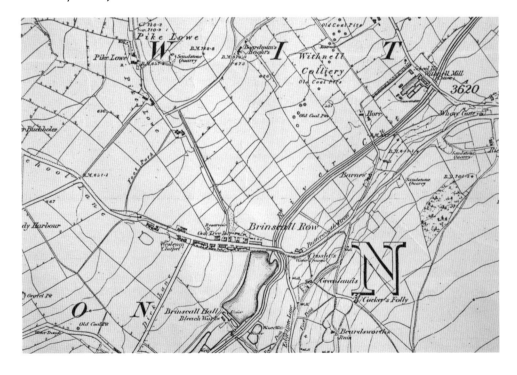

than 200 years later, is heart-warming indeed. Their façades were not random-built but carefully constructed using squared stone laid neatly in courses. Looking in detail at these courses reveals an intriguing fact about Brinscall Row. The row of five cottages now numbered 12 to 20 School Lane share a common roof-line, and might be thought to be the original Brinscall Row, as mentioned prominently on a map of 1848. Numbers 22 and 24 by contrast, have a raised roof-line and might be thought to be of slightly later date. However, when you carefully examine the courses of all the façades, it is apparent that the courses of number 20 are fully integrated, or bonded, into the courses of number 22. Therefore it seems that numbers 22 and 24 were built at the same time as numbers 12 to 20, so that this was a row of seven, not five, cottages, evidently. Yet the question arises as to why it was that numbers 22 and 24 were given the higher roof-line. Was this just because the ground level was rising at that end of the terrace? Or is there a possibility of a slight difference in status among tenants?

A quick consideration of window types gives a possible clue. Obviously numbers 12 to 20 have always had the traditional casement-type windows. Numbers 22 and 24 on the other hand seem to have had the newly fashionable sash windows from the start, even though there have been changes to the frames more recently. (*Fashions changed slowly in the north. Sash windows had become fashionable in the south of England a hundred years earlier.*) Perhaps numbers 22 and 24 were built for slightly wealthier tenants, for the families of overseers or foremen in a local 'sandstone quarry' or 'coal pit' (both of which occur frequently in early maps of the area). That seems quite possible. Herein lies a subject for further research on some future occasion.

Walking on now, beyond number 24, we come to an area where at one time there were more shops than straightforward cottages (just one shop still survives there now) but the area's principal feature is the gap between buildings where, from 1869 till 1967, a steel girder overbridge carried the railway across School Lane. The shop buildings are mainly mid to late-Victorian. Two of them reveal aspirational and decorative quoins. One of the former shops was a baker's. One used to sell ice-cream (especially to home-coming passengers who had walked down the ramp from the railway station). One former shop has a decidedly random stone façade from which rendering has been 'experimentally' removed. Between the shops there is one pair of pre-Victorian (probably) sash-windowed cottages, numbers 32 and 34. The numbering of School Lane properties in this area is obviously post- rather than pre-railway, of course.

The higher part of what is now St Joseph's Club (the former Printers' Arms) has one infilled doorway with a semi-circular arch which might once have contained a fanlight over the actual door. (Compare with cottages number 90, 92 and 96 higher up School Lane.) The lower part of the Club is a later insert. 'Printers' Arms', by the way, is no doubt a reference to textile workers, to calico printers specifically, and perhaps in this case to workers at the Brinscall Print Works beyond Brinscall Hall.

Between St Joseph's Club and the current Post Office lies the ancient route known as Withnell Fold Old Road which used to lead not to modern housing developments as it now does, but over Pike Lowe to the farms on the near and far sides of the hill – the Pike Lowe hill itself being a rising continuation of the Harbour Lane ridge.

Above the Post Office (with its modern and extended brick and glass frontage) and one more be-quoined mid-Victorian era house, we come to the Oak Tree Inn. With small sash windows and a comfortingly low, early nineteenth-century roofline, the Oak Tree looks rather like a particularly well-made moorland longhouse. There are different proportions as to plan and function, however: two thirds of its length had obviously always been domestic, while one third was formerly devoted to stabling or accommodation for horse-drawn coaches. The front elevation has orderly courses of dressed stone. The east gable end and the rear premises have walls of random stonework. The gable end contains an infilled but well shaped archway that once enclosed a coach or stable entrance. There was quite a large yard (for a small village) behind the inn.

Next, the brick-built Victorian school (a Methodist establishment from 1876 to 1968) is followed, as one continues uphill, by 'South View', the smart brick terrace of 1883 with its 11 houses, each one with front garden and sitting room bay window. These were the first bay windows on School Lane. You have to go almost to the top of the School Lane slope to see any others, two others in fact, on the smooth brick semi-detached houses of 'Hillside'. Meanwhile, living now, in 2011, towards the centre of 'South View' is 96-year old Jack Murray who, among his many memories of village life, remembers seeing David Shorrock in the 1920s regularly carrying sacks of coal from the railway yard up Well Lane to his home at **Hatch Place**. He carried these on his back.

After 'South View' come 4 'superior' stone properties of the late Victorian era, with elegant details and refined and graded stone courses. Well-dressed, indeed. The last of these four, number 88, was formerly a greengrocer's shop. Above these are numbers 90, 92 and 94, two small and older cottages (with gardens) and an inn, the Cricketers' Arms. All three of these have very similar random stone façades – with signs of alteration here and there. It seems quite likely that the three were constructed at roughly the same time, even though the inn is a considerably taller building with much larger sash windows. Numbers 90 and 92 do have the semi-circular arched doorways and appropriately small sash windows. Then, one might notice, the Cricketers' Arms also has a semi-circular arched doorway, now infilled, beyond its larger main door. The Cricketers' is a former coaching inn (like the Oak Tree) which used to have stables, as well as fields, behind both inn and cottages And then number 96, a cottage attached to the inn, also has a semi-circular arched doorway. Can it be that its stone façade, tastefully hidden behind a smooth rendering, has a random stone construction? Certainly numbers 98 and 100, the last stone cottages on the north side of School Lane, do have façades with solid courses of dressed stone, quite different from numbers 90, 92 and 94. They also have square-topped doorways. And number 98, in particular, has a charmingly bijou character.

Apart from the stone-built Methodist Chapel of 1899, all is brick above number 100 on the north side of School Lane, including the village store (the former Co-operative grocery) and its attached house, and then, beyond Chapel Street, the end-of-nineteenth-century row of five stylish houses whose stone lintels include a version of traditional drip-stones as a decorative feature over the doorways.

Now it is time to look closely at the cottages on School Lane's south side, starting again at the bottom of the hill.

The South Side

A semi-detached pair of dignified stone-fronted houses, followed by a firm stone terrace made up of private houses and one surviving shop, are the first sights to greet one at the foot of School Lane on the south side. All these properties, which include former shops and a former bank, clearly date from the later years of the nineteenth century. Before they (and a now-demolished chapel) were built there was nothing for the inhabitants of Brinscall Row to look across to other than the Bleach Works lodge. This seems to have reached almost as far as School Lane in the middle years of the nineteenth century.

The first early nineteenth-century structure we would meet beyond Lodge Bank (Croft Bottoms) as School Lane begins to climb would be the cottage which had once been a cobbler and clog maker's workplace and shop. This became a fine specialist grocery store and house before being largely rebuilt in recent times and becoming a pair of cottages, numbered 23 and 25. The façade is sympathetic though modern. The same could be said of the two wholly new houses – sympathetic though modern – that now occupy the space previously taken up by the railway bridge and embankment.

Another re-build, replacing a former ladies' hairdresser's, is the new, stone-fronted and very welcome number 25A, the Cottage Tea Room. This should be a major asset for Brinscall. However, after the Tea Room we at last come to the start of a series of older and original structures that, with some obvious interruptions, we can now follow almost all the way to the top of School Lane. Neat courses of well-cut stone make up the façades of almost all of these.

Numbers 27 and 29 are a characterful pair of early nineteenth-century cottages of modest height and great charm, the higher of the two proudly announcing that it was 'The Old Post Office'. These two originally stood alone and separate as a pair, not attached to any other immediate neighbours, a typical arrangement on some sections of School Lane. Their upper, and attached (but not integrated) neighbour now is the former inn, the mid-nineteenth-century 'Bull's Head', most of whose structure has been transformed into 'Topps Cottages'.

Beyond Topps Cottages, however, we come to another old, attractive and mostly original set of buildings, numbers 37 and 39 School Lane (number 41 being incorporated into number 39). I am told that number 37 was initially – by 1805 – a farmhouse, with the entirely pre-railway age designation 'Number One Brinscall', and that number 39 was originally its barn. (Number 41 has at one time been a separate cottage with a lower roof line than it now enjoys.) The space in front of these cottages, now turned into cheerful gardens, survives because of the original farming requirements, but also partly because number 37, at least, became for a time a smithy. Horses always did need shoes.

Moving on up School Lane as far as The Square, it is clear that there were originally just three groups of cottages in this area and that there were open spaces (unbuilt-on) between the three. The three groups were, according to present numberings: the pair of cottages numbered 45 and 47, built in 1804, the pair numbered 51 and 53, built in 1810 and the three cottages numbered 61, 63 and 65, built in 1805.

Numbers 45 and 47 have had their doorway lintels significantly raised to take account of the greater height of householders in the twentieth century compared with the original occupants. Their window sizes have also been adjusted.

Numbers 51 and 53 have apparently always had casement windows on the first floor, and their ground floor windows are large enough to make one wonder if these houses were mainly built to accommodate handloom weavers. Perhaps handloom weaving was carried on from time to time in most of the early cottages on School Lane?

The three cottages in the group numbered 61, 63 and 65 seem always to have had sash windows, but there was handloom weaving in farms on the moors, like **Whittle's**, where there were similarly sized sash windows. Perhaps handloom weaving happened in numbers 61, 63 and 65 too.

The intriguing process of 'reading a building' now allows us to notice what evidently happened a little later in the nineteenth century to the open spaces that had remained between the earlier groups of cottages in the area up to The Square.

Firstly the single cottage now numbered 49 has clearly been inserted in the space between number 47 and number 51. Likewise, the small but solidly built number 43 has been added – attached to the east gable end of number 45. And then, above number 53 and below number 61, three houses have been inserted, a pair of later Victorian houses (houses rather than cottages in style), numbers 55 and 57, and one very similar house, number 59. All three of these have a touch of late-Victorian grandeur, with rather fine entrance doorway lintels, for example.

Above The Square, we come to a remarkable development, a terraced row of 10 cottages (11 originally) dating from as early as 1815. (A 999-year lease on the land for the cottages had been agreed on March 2 1815.) This was easily the longest terrace in Brinscall when it was built. It is almost twice the length of the 1805 Brinscall Row, and is roughly the same length as the much later (1883) 'South View' opposite, and the 1880s/1890s stone-fronted terrace of houses (numbers 99 to 117) higher up School Lane.

Our 1815 terrace, now numbered 69 to 85, has a series of stepped roofs (one step per cottage) to take account of the steepness of School Lane. At each end there is an extra cottage "round the corner", as it were. At the Dick Lane end, the last cottage has its entrance doorway on Dick Lane rather than on School Lane, and the extra cottage is then number 3 on Dick Lane. At the end next to The Square, the first cottage (number 67 it would have been) has been demolished, and the extra cottage "round the corner" has an address on The Square.

Manifestly the whole row was a single concept, with construction going on more or less simultaneously. The general style, the quality of stone courses and the size and shape of window spaces tell one this. It is interesting to allow oneself to think that the Duke of Wellington was defeating the Emperor Napoleon at Waterloo (June 18 1815) while these cottages were being built. Equally, Admiral Nelson was defeating the Franco-Spanish fleet at Trafalgar (21 October 1805) while the cottages of Brinscall Row were being built. So why were these cottages built between The Square and Dick Lane?

There seems to be strong reason to suppose that what were almost certainly the earliest cottages to be built on School Lane, numbers 119 to 125, built 1798–1800, were, from time to time if not continuously, handloom weavers' cottages. There is surviving talk of a workshop area in at least one section. This fact, and the comparatively large-sized casement windows of the stepped-roof 1815 row, suggests that handloom weaving might well have been the main occupation of the Dick Lane to The Square-dwellers too, at least until the 1840s/50s.

As the nineteenth century progressed it is likely that other occupations took over, of course. We know, for instance, that by 1870 and thereafter some of the 1815 row's cottages became shops. It was on July 6 1870, indeed, that the grocer George Whittaker bought (for £100) the shop and the rest of the premises at number 71 School Lane from the yeoman-landowner Ephraim Warburton. All the row's shops have, by now, like almost every other shop on School Lane, reverted to the dwelling house rôle.

Above Dick Lane we come first to the former mid-Victorian Wesleyan Methodist Chapel, a dignified but plain stone structure which was replaced in 1899 by the new and larger and more ornate chapel higher up on the opposite side of School Lane. Since 1899 the smaller building has enjoyed a variety of uses. From 1900 onwards until 1974 it was the Council Offices for the Withnell Urban District Council. From 1974 to 2008 it was home to a major picture-framing enterprise. At present it serves as a base for a sophisticated medical-dentistry manufacturing firm. In some respects the building and its immediate environs are still regarded as representing the centre of Brinscall on account of its apparent guardianship of the area's main War Memorial and official flag pole and on account of its appearing to have the area's most substantial bus shelter.

Beyond the former chapel there used to be a minister's residence (Bethel House) and beyond that a small but distinctive village petrol station. Both these have recently been replaced by a stone-fronted, semi-ecclesiastically styled group of four smart 'town houses' (Bethel Terrace, 1993). Beyond these is the long row of late-Victorian, sound, sensible, stone-fronted (with graded courses) terraced houses, numbered 99 to 117. I should point out that these seem to have been constructed in two phases. Numbers 99 to 107 have single sash sitting room and bedroom windows. Numbers 109 to 117 have double-width sashes (and central mullions) to their sitting room and front bedroom windows. The front doors are also differently set.

I should further point out that number 99 is the house from which the young Frank Halliwell left in 1914–15 to fight in the Great War. He lies now in a most peaceful, deeply rural, flower-decked, meticulously lawned cemetery in France, near to Beaumont-Hamel in the Somme Valley where he fell on the first day of the four month struggle in 1916 to capture a quarter of a mile of no-man's land. I found Frank's grave quite by chance when briefly visiting the Somme battlefields on my way home from a walking holiday in the French Alps. Frank had no chance of such a holiday.

The cemetery is just south of the famous 'Sunken Road' and near to the Hawthorn Ridge site of the explosion under German lines (often seen in film sequences) which signalled (at 6.30 a.m.) the start of the Somme offensive on July 1 1916. Over 19,000 British soldiers were killed on that first day. Frank was a member of the First Battalion of the Lancashire Fusiliers and was 20 years-old when he died. His parents were Frank and Sarah Halliwell of 99 School Lane, Brinscall, as is carefully recorded in the memorial book in the cemetery in France. In Frank's case, "there's some corner of a foreign field that is forever England". His name – as HALLIWELL F. – is of course on the Brinscall War Memorial at the Dick Lane-School Lane junction some 50m from where he had lived.

Beyond house number 117 we come to the characterful and probably earliest and now most recently refurbished cottages on School Lane, the small terrace of four cottages that are numbered 119 to 125. These stand back from the road behind what are now orderly driveways and gardens but were probably originally food-producing plots serving a little community of handloom weavers. The cottage façades are of random stone. The number, shape and size of their windows suggests weavers' houses, with stone mullions dividing and supporting the glazing on the ground floor at least. They were built in 1798, 1799 and 1800.

Beyond number 125 and rather nearer to the road are three neighbouring groups, each of two cottages with, on the whole, rather smaller windows and with smaller gardens (especially colourful in Spring and Summer). Number 129 (with its semi-detached partner number 127) was built in 1800. Number 137 (and therefore numbers 131, 133 and 135 almost certainly) was built in 1801. In the case of number 137 it was rebuilt and pleasingly extended in 1981.

Just before concluding this review of School Lane cottages we should return briefly to the garden area of cottage number 119, the 1798 weavers' cottage. It was there, right against School Lane, and close to number 117, that a strange, squat, square, low-roofed detached cottage stood defiantly until it was demolished in 1948. This was the singular little building known as 'Salt Pie Cottage'. No one locally is currently able to explain the 'Salt Pie' title, though there are Salt Pie Cottages in Bolton-le-Sands and Kirkby

Lonsdale. (Perhaps a pie made in Spring using over-wintered salted meat, and not the most delicious or attractive of pies, therefore?)

My object now, however, is not to explain the Salt Pie derivation so much as to propose one possible reason why Brinscall's main street – its only street for much of its time – is known as School Lane. This may have been puzzling many of my readers as it has also puzzled me. Salt Pie is not the answer, however!

The fact that Salt Pie Cottage was once a school has been offered as an explanation for the use of School Lane as the name of the street leading to it. A nice idea this, but quite false, alas. Salt Pie was a school for only 11 months, from February 1874 to January 1875. Maps of 1860 show the name School Lane in use at least 14 years before Salt Pie received its first pupils. Furthermore, the name applied to the whole road from its junction with Butterworth Brow in the Brinscall valley right up the hill and on to the west down 'Buckholes' as far as Wheelton Stocks – what we now call Higher Wheelton.

So, if the Brinscall Methodist School on School Lane dates only from 1876 and its Anglican-Methodist replacement (St. John's) from 1968, what other school could have been in mind prior to 1860?

'National' (i.e. Anglican) Schools began to be established (by Parliamentary permission) from 1833. At Higher Wheelton, and still there in situ, though now as an attractive house by the A674, there is a former National School dating from 1842. It therefore, at first sight, seems likely that from 1842 onwards, 'School Lane' is an appropriate name for a road running all the way from the valley over to the new National School at Higher Wheelton.

This is especially so when one remembers that all land and buildings on the south side of School Lane were in Wheelton until 1899. At least half of Brinscall's inhabitants belonged to Wheelton rather than Withnell until 1899, therefore. The idea of sending children from Brinscall down to a school at Higher Wheelton is not a strange one.

Sadly, however, this neat explanation for the use of the name 'School Lane' from 1842 is no better than the false Salt Pie suggestion. Authentic legal documents, the surviving Deeds recording the sale of building plots and the erection of dwelling houses in Brinscall from 1805 onwards refer to these plots and dwelling houses as being on 'School Lane'. The name was in general use as early as 1805. The puzzle remains, therefore, and the date has to be earlier now. What other school could have been in mind prior to 1805? Further research is required. New evidence will have to be sought.

Finally, if you would like to imagine in your own mind what School Lane must have looked like in the 1800–1830 period and also what the views might have been from the windows of the early cottages, perhaps you would now like to re-read my descriptions of the north and south sides. It should be possible to work out what was there and what was not there by, say, 1825–30. I now offer the occasional helpful reminder, and I will of course use modern numberings in order to identify particular buildings.

Brinscall Row Cottages (numbers 12 to 24) had a completely clear view to the south. Not even a bleach works lodge was there at that early stage. Meanwhile, Numbers 32 and 34 and numbers 27 and 29 must have looked directly across the road towards each other as they do now. The cottages – but not their front doors – really are absolutely opposite each other, as you will find if you stand next to them.

Numbers 37 and 39, 45 and 47, 51 and 53, and 61 to 65 had almost completely open views of fields to the north to look out upon, apart, of course, from the Oak Tree Inn and perhaps the Printers' Arms (or a predecessor building). They would have a view of the Withnell Fold Old Road as it rose up the hill towards Pike Lowe.

Moving up School Lane, numbers 67 to 85 had a completely clear view of the fields opposite and probably of the buildings of Drinkwater's Farm (the Brinscall, not the Great Hill Drinkwater's that is), the nearest of the Pike Lowe farms.

Numbers 90 to 100 had entirely open views to the south. Numbers 119 to 137 had an equally open view to the north, including Drinkwater's buildings and possibly Pike Lowe Farm itself and its cottages, plus the distant Boardman's Heights. From their rear windows they might well have been able to see the original low buildings of Windy Harbour Farm.

Of course, by turning to the east, the inhabitants of School Lane's cottages in 1825–30, even those living at the foot of the hill, would have been able to see from their own front doors, some, at least, of our familiar moorland and hillside farms. **Cocker's Folly**, **Beardsworth's**, **Greenlands** and Crosby's would have been completely visible.

From half way up the School Lane hill it must have been possible to see another half-dozen or so of the farms. From the highest cottages, those now numbered 119 to 137, a whole range of farms must have been visible, including **Ratten Clough**, **Solomon's Temple**, **Whittle's**, **White Hall**, **Hatch Place**, **Heaton's**, **Ripping** and **New Ground**, and very probably **Liptrot's**, **Leigh Place** and **Top o'th' Wood** too. A fine sight that could have been and not only in daylight hours. You will recall that in 1800–30 School Lane would have had no street lamps at all. Now think of the effect of oil lamps shining from the distant windows of 15 farms across the moor at 6 o'clock on a dark December evening. Magical!

CHAPTER SIX

The Dixons of Marsden's Farm and the Elizabeth Jane Dixon Journal

I T HAS BEEN A REMARKABLE and wholly unexpected privilege to be offered such a splendid source of original documentary evidence as the journal of Elizabeth Jane Dixon, ex-governess and then farmer's wife of exceptional quality. The journal has recently been loaned to me by Harold Gomersall of Brinscall, grandson of the Mrs. Dixon who actually wrote it. For the critical period 1908–1910 particularly, it has been most helpfully informative and revealing.

The precious (and large and heavy) volume, with its careful copperplate script, has been both a stimulus and a delight. It is a means of confirming exactly why forty-nine farms have been lost on Brinscall Moors, and it is a proof of the precise observation-powers, resilience, devotion and good humour of members of the farming community and of one of its finest farmer's wives in particular. I am deeply grateful to Dorothy Gomersall (née Dixon) and to her son Harold for their careful preservation of their mother's, and grandmother's, writings, and to Harold for his temporarily entrusting them to my care.

Following their marriage at All Saints' Church, Underbarrow (Kendal) on 12 November 1881, Thomas and Elizabeth Jane Dixon eventually came to live and work at **Marsden's Farm** Heapey in May 1886. They led long, full, productive lives. Thomas, born in Westmorland on 11 June 1858, died on 12 June 1938. Elizabeth, born in Essex on 17 February 1856, died on 1 November 1938. They died within less than five months of each other, and in the same small cottage on Brinscall's School Lane to which they had moved in 1928. It was a relationship of much affection, as their grandchildren happily affirm.

Besides writing a regular daily journal until at least 1932, Elizabeth wrote much poetry, especially during and after the First World War where they lost two of their

Elizabeth Jane Dixon, 1856–1938.

Thomas Dixon, 1858–1938.

sons, Jack, aged 17, on the Somme in 1916 (on the first day of the battle, just like Frank Halliwell), and Herbert, aged 23, near Ypres in 1917. Her poems, as with the many letters and post cards she sent throughout her married life, went frequently to her numerous children, sisters, brothers, cousins and friends. She maintained a correspondence with relations in Australia and New Zealand also. She delighted in keeping her extended family together.

The census returns of 1891 show that Thomas and Elizabeth had four children at that stage: Annie (b. 27 November 1883), William (b. 21 March 1885), Henry (b. 3 October 1886) and Thomas (b. 3 September 1888). Eight more were to be born by 1902: Nathan (b. 15 April 1891), the twins Christopher and Ellen (b. 22 and 23 February 1893), Herbert (b. 19 July 1894), Elizabeth (b. 1 April 1896), Dorothy (b. 26 May 1897), John (b. 6 October 1898) and James (b. 23 January 1902).

Elizabeth Dixon's journal makes it quite clear that until 10 October 1910 **Marsden's** was both a flourishing mixed farm (with horses, cattle and poultry in significant numbers, but no sheep) and also the home of young factory workers. The majority of the children worked down in the valley from the age of twelve either in Withnell Mill or in the (calico) Print Works (and occasionally the Bleach Works). Thomas ('Father', as Elizabeth normally referred to her husband in the journal) also occasionally worked in the Print Works when not fully engaged by the multitude of tasks on his farm.

The 1805 Brinscall Row in 2010. Left to right, numbers 24, 22, 20, 18, 16, 14, 12.

The journal emphasises the outdoor physical duties that 'Father' regularly undertook: the managing, feeding, purchasing and selling of cattle, horses and poultry, the repairing and improvement of structures and the land, the carrying-in of water from the wells, the hay-making and rick-building, and the carting (literally by horse- or pony-drawn cart) from the village of heavy loads – of coal or potatoes, for example. The selling of eggs, however, was usually in the hands of Elizabeth or the children.

What is quite admirable, indeed, is the extent to which the children were encouraged to learn and practise the knowledge and skills involved in animal husbandry and routine household duties. The children assisted in the buying-in process where they could, going down to Brinscall village or accompanying their mother to help carry items from Chorley or Blackburn.

Above all, and most obviously, the rôle of wife and mother was a huge and constant one, as demonstrated here in Elizabeth's meticulous recording of her own actions, duties and responsibilities. Weeks are characterised by the routine of (clothes) Washing Days, Baking Days, Cleaning Days and Churning (butter-making) Days. To these were added what must often have been several hours of clothes-making and repairing (usually by sewing machine), plus the caring for children or husband or self during times of illness (as in the case of Chris in March-April 1910). Journeys, by train, to Chorley or Blackburn were fairly frequent for the purpose of "buying-in" foodstuffs not produced on the farm, and also for the buying of special clothing and footwear for special occasions including Sunday-best wear. Not infrequently Elizabeth showed that she was quite capable of walking the five miles back to **Marsden's** Farm from Chorley, or the five miles to and back from Brinscall or Heapey or Withnell centres, as were her husband and children. She does occasionally admit to being "very tired", however, and not surprisingly.

Nevertheless there were hours or even days of relaxation and recreation for Elizabeth and for the rest of the Dixons. There were visits by train to the seaside and to organised race meetings, as well as to local fairs (or even farm sales) and to local church services. There were brief stays in the homes of relations. A walk on the moors or "down Buckholes" was not unusual. There was an interested awareness of political processes, even before the 1918 partial emancipation of women. There was an awareness, as recorded in later sections of the journal, of professional football matches. There was a spirited willingness to compete in crossword and other similar challenges in the newspapers.

One particularly attractive trait, in Elizabeth and in Thomas her husband, was an eagerness, chiefly when they had left **Marsden's** for Harbour Lane and more especially Calender House/Hall/Cottage, to grow from seed and/or buy as seedlings and then carefully to plant out, garden flowers as well as their normal fruit and vegetables. Besides rhubarb, raspberries and strawberries, besides cabbages and turnips there appear, especially after 1910, wallflowers, lily-of-the-valley, primroses, sweet peas, sweet Williams, lilac… A watering can was newly bought in May 1911.

Elizabeth had an interest in music and in musical instruments, at least of the concertina and harmonica kind, as reported by her grandson, Harold Gomersall (Dorothy's son, born in 1928). As a youngster he was advised by his grandmother to remember always to play 'Home, sweet home' whenever he visited her.

Home for the two senior Dixons meant three different houses after their departure from **Marsden's** in October 1910. A house on Harbour Lane (well away from the Goit and Liverpool Corporation land) was theirs for the next three years. It must have become obvious to them by 1910 that with the impending loss – to brand-new Liverpool timber-growing plantations – of **Marsden's** (and other nearby) pasture and hay-making meadows there was no future on the hillsides for cattle-farming and milk and butter production, to say nothing of free-range poultry-feeding and egg production. **Leigh Place**, **Top o'th Wood**, Blackhurst and **Fir Farm** had already been abandoned, as had the more distant **New Ground**.

From 1913 to 1928 the Dixons occupied a most suitable house, with appropriate land and garden, on the boundary between Wheelton and Heapey, in the gentle valley of the Brinscall Brook. The house lay just where there was, and is, a lodge feeding both a stream and a leat, the leat taking water to drive the wheel of the original Brinscall Mill. The recently re-built version of the house is now known as Blue Dye House; it was known in 1913–28 as Calender House (or in some correspondence as Calender Hall or Calender Cottage, depending on the perceptions of the correspondent).

It was to Calender House that a letter from Buckingham Palace was addressed in December 1914, when King George V instructed his Keeper of the Privy Seal, F. W. Ponsonby, to congratulate Mr. Dixon on the fact that no fewer than five of his sons had volunteered to serve in Britain's armed forces. Nathan, already serving in the regular army from 1908, had been joined in the first four months of the war by Henry, Christopher, Herbert and Jack.

Possibly this letter commending the Dixons' spirit of patriotism and loyalty to sovereign and empire may have offered some comfort to Elizabeth in 1916 and 1917 when John died in France and Herbert in Belgium. Herbert died in a field hospital from wounds suffered not far from Ypres and Passchendaele. John is one of those whose name appears among the 73,000 who are remembered on the Lutyens Thiepval Memorial as having no known grave. In other words, nothing remained of his body after his participation in the opening attack near the Ancre and Somme rivers on 1 July 1916. Both brothers served in the Loyal North Lancashire Regiment. Their names are inscribed on the Wheelton Clock Tower War Memorial.

'Poor Jack' is how Elizabeth regularly and gently refers to her 17-year-old in her 1916 journal entries. She did receive incongruously in the post a small parcel from France, sent by Herbert, and arriving at Calender House on 21 August 1916. The parcel contained Jack's watch. 'Poor Jack' she writes again.

By 1928, needing a house for two persons rather than fourteen, Thomas and Elizabeth finally decided, and with some regret initially, it appears, to leave Calender and to move into a cottage on Brinscall's main street. Their home until both died there in 1938 was at number 14 School Lane. So it was that after 52 years in the Brinscall area – or, technically, in Heapey, Wheelton and finally Withnell – Thomas and Elizabeth, natives of Westmorland and Essex, completed their lives together in one of those especially cosy and charming cottages of the 1805 Brinscall Row.

THE ELIZABETH JANE DIXON JOURNAL

(Extracts from entries written at Marsden's Farm between 1908 and 1910)

1908

Jan. 14:   Commenced to sew a poppy quilt.

Jan. 15:   Baking. Finished the quilt.

Jan. 17:   Bought Annie two pairs of stockings. Went to Chorley. Nat helped me. Late home [by train]. A beautiful night.

Jan. 18:   Chris's wages for the week, 12s 9d. Nellie's 13s 6d. Herbert's 10s 3d. [Their ages 14, 14 and 13 respectively.]

Jan. 20:   Jimmie [aged 5] ill. He gave me a locket wish. [Elizabeth's locket, on a necklace, contained family photographs. A child seeing it and touching it, might hope to be made better from illness.]

Jan. 21:   Started Father's gloves.

Feb. 3:   Cut father's hair. Much obliged. Washing day.

Feb. 4:   Baking day.Went to Chorley. Chris and Herbert came to meet me [at the station]. New moon. Frosty, starlit night. Nathan's wages 5s 1d. Tommy's 15s.

Feb. 13:   Father carting coals. Henry still out of work.

Feb. 17:   My birthday. 52 years of age.

Feb. 19:   Henry started at the Print Works.

Feb. 24:   Repaired Nellie's corsets. Also Tommy's pants, and finished James's stockings.

Mar. 9:   Letter from cousins in New South Wales.

Mar. 11:   Very fine weather. Busy sewing Lizzie's dress for factory. [Lizzie 12 years old on April 1, 1908.]

Mar. 14:   Herbert's wages 10s 9d. Nellie's wages 14s 1½d.

Mar. 25:   Busy knitting.

Mar. 26:   Baking day. Making pants for the two young nippers.

Mar. 28:   Got Lizzie's certificate for the factory [Withnell Mill].

April 4:   Gisburn and Kirkham Races.
April 6:   Lizzie started work at the factory.
April 18:   Went to Chorley and bought Chris and Willie some Saturday togs.
April 25:   Sat some goose eggs. Henry started work at breakfast-time [instead of overnight].

May 2:   Mrs. Hogg [at Goose Green] died in her 63rd year.
May 3:   Two hens sat [to hatch eggs]. Father bought a young heifer at N. Russell's.
May 19:   Walked home from Chorley. Started cleaning the dairy.
May 28:   Finished cleaning in the dairy.

June 2:   Made a mistake in the train [at Chorley] and went to Preston [instead of on the Blackburn train].
June 3:   Miss Smethurst came for 6 quarts of milk.
June 4:   Sewing Annie's, Nellie's and Lizzie's skirts. Tidied the drawer.
June 8:   Went to Cartmel [races] with Pa. Lucky day. Very tired.
June 10:   Father's birthday. 50 years of age. Washed and baked.
June 12:   Cleaning upstairs. Putting up curtains. Letter from Nat.
June 16:   Went to Chorley for medicine for the cow Daisy.
June 17:   Mended Tommy's pants, also Jack's shirt, and finished a pinny [pinafore] for Lizzie. Sent a letter to Nathan [who was going to join the regular army].
June 20:   Walking Day for St. Luke's [Brinscall].
June 21:   Went to Heapey Church in the evening with Mrs. Haywood and Mrs. Riding.
June 22:   Churning [butter-making] and Baking Day.
June 24:   Making a checked pinnie for Dolly [Dorothy]. Father went for coals. He got a new knife for the scythe. Commenced mowing in the meadow.

July 2:   [My] sister Kate arrived from Lancaster.
July 4:   Baking Day.
July 7:   I went to Chorley to buy in. Aunt Kate and Annie came to meet me [at the station].
July 9:   The joiner came to put up the staircase, and sister Kate went back to Settle [by train].
July 11:   Workmen finished staircase.
July 14:   Annie went to Chorley for stair carpet.
July 15:   St. Swithin's. Working hay in Bolton's meadow. Wet in the evening.
July 23:   [My sister] Lydia came on a visit.

Aug. 3:   Lydia went home.

Aug. 5:   Went to Morecambe with Ellen [by train].

Aug. 19:   Finished Dora's black frock.

Aug. 20:   Father erected some clothes posts. Dora cleaning up.

Aug. 24:   Father sold 3 heifers.

Aug. 26:   Father took a heifer to Schofields, Lower Lane.

Sept. 1:   Washing Day. Sent Dolly [Dorothy/Dora] to Chorley for the first time by herself [at age 11].

Sept. 3:   Thomas Dixon Junior's birthday. 20 years of age. "Happy Returns."

Sept. 24:   Sister Martha came over on a visit.

Sept. 26:   Sister Martha returned home. Went to the station with her.

Sept. 30:   Father went to Kendal to visit his father.

Oct. 3:   Father returned home.

Oct. 6:   Little Jack's Birthday [10 years old].

Oct. 7:   Received a letter from Kate. Also some photos from Settle sent from Australia.

Oct. 8:   Baking Day. Father cleaned out the calves' place. Began to make a pinafore.

Oct. 10:   Went to Chorley. Very tired.

Oct. 11:   Annie [aged 25] went out to tea.

Oct. 12:   Father went to Richardson's sale. Bought hay-forks. Sold his hens.

Oct. 14:   Father finished carrying [straw] bedding for cattle.

Oct. 19:   Sold Mr. Clare a goose. 8s 6d.

Oct. 20:   Henry got measured [in Chorley] for a suit for his wedding. Wrote to cousin Dorothy. Made oat cakes.

Oct. 24:   Brought Henry's clothes and hat home [from Chorley].

Oct. 26:   Churning Day.

Oct. 27:   Washing Day.

Oct. 28:   Baking Day.

Nov. 3:   Henry took some quilts to Chorley [to what will be his new home].

Nov. 4:   Bonfire at the farm. Started to make Nellie a blouse.

Nov. 7:   Henry's Wedding Day. Finished Nellie's blouse.

Nov. 9:   The King's Birthday, 67 years of age. Nat came home from [barracks at] Preston. He gave us a few yarns about his comrades which we did not believe.

Nov. 11:   Nat went back to join the Line for 7 years with 5 on The Reserve.

Nov. 15:   Father went for coals. Also flit the young pups into the kennel, James helping him in the flittings.

Nov. 19:   Commenced making Dad a pair of trousers.

Nov. 22:   Harry brought his wife, [Rose] up in the evening.

Dec. 14:   Baking and Sewing Day. Brinscall Print Works re-started, working from 8am to 5pm.

Dec. 29:   Severe snow storm, drifting. Ceiling dropped in our room.

1909

Jan. 4:   Making two bolster cases. Knitting and baking. Sent Dorothy for "Sunday Companion".

Jan. 5:   Washing. Went to Chorley, bought two save-alls for Lizzie and Dorothy. Also a toy piano for Dorothy, and slippers for myself.

Feb. 11:   Father went for coals [with pony and cart]. Confirmation service at Withnell [St. Paul's]. Chris, Nellie and Herbert candidates for same.

Feb. 13:   Nellie paid for Dora's clogs, 4s.

Feb. 16:   Letter from Liverpool [Corporation] concerning "right of way" through Blackhurst meadow.

Feb. 17:   My Birthday Anniversary, 53 years of age. Frosty.

Feb. 20:   Wrote to Kate. Took a cow to R. Bolton's.

Feb. 24:   Fine day. Father carting manure to Well Meadow.

Feb. 27:   Very cold. Snowing.

March 5:   Very rough weather. Snowing.

March 8:   Father went for provender [cattle feed].

March 17:   Herbert got work at the Print Works [having been found too young to join the Navy]. Mending quilt, also knitting Father's stockings.

March 22:   Went to Chorley. Bought a pair of boots for myself and a pair of stockings [socks] for Tommy.

March 24:   Baking Day. Chris went for two sitting hens. Cleaning our room.

March 26:   Churning etc. Sat the hens in Fir barn. Started to refoot Chris some stockings. Finished one pair of stockings for Father.

March 27:   Cut Chris's and James's hair. Swift impounded Bolton's two heifers for which Jim Bolton had to pay 2s to release them.

March 28:   White-washing the living kitchen.

March 29:   Baking Day. Putting curtains up and straightening up the kitchen. Father brushing the meadow. Lassie had pups. Sat a hen on eggs at Fir Farm. Boltons put up the flag for rejoicing on account of Blackhurst flitting. Father for coals and potatoes to Haywood's. Mail for Australia goes out.

April 1:   Lizzie's Birthday. Frosty weather.

April 11:   Went to church at Withnell [St. Paul's].

April 14:   Went to Blackburn. Repaired Ellen's skirt. Making Dora some pinafores.
             Father brushing the Well meadow.

April 17:   Brindle Races.

April 20:   Washing Day.

April 21:   Commenced cleaning the Dairy and Kitchen.

April 22:   Commenced cleaning the Boys' Room.

April 23:   Commenced cleaning the Girls' Room.

May 2:   Elizabeth, Ellen and I went to Heapey Church.

May 3:   Billy Barnes came across for pen and paper.

May 4:   Mr. Percival came about the land at Blackhurst.

May 5:   Went to Blackburn. Bought two blouses and cloth for a jacket for James.
             Father churned. 31 chickens at Fir Farm. Children went to be tried on
             for their navy blue dresses.

May 6:   Repaired Jimmie's jacket and John's pants. Started to refoot John's
             stockings. Father went up to Bolton's in the evening. Asked 3s. each for
             hens.

May 7:   Stephen Miller called to borrow the ladder for repairing at Heather Lea.

May 8:   Willie paid Horsefields for his clogs, 6s 6d. White cow calved, a nice
             roaned heifer calf. Henry came up for the table. Chris helped him with
             it to Chorley. Children went to the Fair in Brinscall. Late home at night.

May 9:   Letter from Liverpool Corporation asking for an offer for Blackhurst land.

May 10:   My first grandchild arrived in Tatton Street, Chorley, named Thomas
             Dixon. Schofield came up for the two heifers. Father helped him with
             them to Lower Lane.

May 11:   Washing and baking. Willie put his clogs on for the first time. Five young
             goslings hatched.

May 12:   Eight young goslings hatched. All eggs fertile.

May 14:   Father cashed the cheque from Schofield's for the two heifers.

May 15:   Bought some note paper at the door.

May 16:   Mr. And Mrs. Coleman and her sister met me on the moors. Mrs. Riding
             called but I was out.

May 17:   Sat two hens on geese eggs in pig cote at **Fir Farm**. Father carrying water
             from the well, filling up the tubs. 2 hen and 8 geese eggs, 9s. Mrs. Bolton
             came across for her scissors.

May 18:   Very cold weather. Repairing Herbert's pants, also baking pies and cakes.
             Putting lining into Chris's jacket. Went to Chorley and bought material
             for a factory frock for Elizabeth. Commenced to refoot James's stockings.
             Father bought provender from Brinscall.

May 19:   If the oak buds before the ash, there is sure to be a splash.

May 20:   A letter from Liverpool [Corporation] agreeing for us to have the land at Blackhurst, on the lower side of the road. To pay rates and taxes.

May 24:   Washing Day. Very tired. Father planted the last rows of cabbages and the last rows of strawberries. Father carrying water from the well, after washing finished. Dry weather.

May 25:   Harry came up. [He had been] working all night. Hen missing off duck eggs. Found it in the afternoon. Made Lizzie a factory frock with red stripes.

May 26:   Dora's birthday, 12 years of age. The cat brought its young one into the house. Father repairing road at Blackhurst.

May 28:   Churning Day, and cleaning upstairs. Received a letter from Nat. Three ducks hatched. Father finished repairing the road at Blackhurst. Received Dora's half-time papers.

May 29:   Very cold morning. Baking Day. Went to Chorley. Bought a waterproof and shirt.

May 31:   Went to Cartmel [Races?]. Got very wet. Got home at 12.30am. Annie went to Llandudno.

June 1:   Cut James's and Chris's hair. Found two geese eggs and one hen egg broken by some person unknown.

June 3:   Factory started working again. Dorothy started at the mill. John [10 years old] went for me to Brinscall. Father repairing the road at Knight's Brow by the well. [White] Coppice Mill stopped till further orders.

June 4:   Two gentlemen [called] seeking sheep.

June 5:   John Leigh came to ask Father to superintend Blackhurst premises.

June 6:   Went to St. Paul's, Withnell.

June 10:   Father hoeing turnips in the garden. Mr Whittle came for hot water from Blackhurst. Brought some wood to boil a kettle. Chris working at the Croft [the Bleach Works].

June 11:   Father went to buy in at the Stores [Brinscall]. Mr Ironfield came to put new rollers in the mangle. The old Basket Woman with white hair called. Tom got his shoes heeled, 1s.

June 14:   Washing. Willie took the red cow to R. Fowler's. Bad with indigestion. Sent Dora for bottle of Mother Seigel's.

June 15:   A [canal] boatman called at the door. Father cut ivy from the wall.

June 16:   Father hoeing and weeding in the garden. I cleaned the garden paths. Cut father's hair.

June 17:   Harry removed [from Chorley] to White Coppice. Father white-washing the shippon.

June 18:   Chris went with a chair for Rose to White Coppice. Dorothy took eggs down to Brinscall. Geese found their way home from Fir Farm.

June 19:   Went to the Show at Chorley. Wet day. Herbert off work, being ill.

June 20:   Went to Heapey Church. I fell and hurt my knee.

June 22:   Mr. Leigh gave Father some firewood from Blackhurst. Herbert started work after being ill.

June 24:   Father took the pony to be shod, and brought Willie some corn from Brinscall. He also went to the Quarterly Meeting at Withnell Mill.

June 25:   Churning. Cleaning upstairs. Father carting wood from Blackhurst.

June 30:   Stopped at the [Print]Works for taking stock. Annie went to a meeting at St.Luke's, Brinscall.

July 1:   Made Lizzie a skirt. Rabbit for dinner. Father took the white cow to Blackhurst. The boys carrying laths from Blackhurst [i.e. ceiling/roofing timber during the demolition].

July 3:   Chris got up and caught six rabbits.

July 4:   Harry had a walk up from the Coppice. I went to Heapey Church.

July 6:   The map-man and boy came up. Father ground his scythes ready for mowing grass.

July 7:   The Water Inspector called. Potato pie for dinner.

July 8:   Father started mowing grass in the meadow. I made a print bonnet for the hayfield.

July 9:   Stew and rice-pudding for dinner.

July 13:   Willie went to Chorley and had four teeth drawn.

July 14:   Father busy hay-working. The boy [John?Jimmie?] learning to mow in the meadow.

July 20:   Jimmie hurt his foot. A lorry [cart?] wheel pulled his nail off. Father carried him home.

July 23:   The poultry man called on us. The boys finished the croft at Blackhurst.

July 24:   Ordered a pair of stockings for Chris. Bought a pair of slippers for myself.

July 25:   Went to Flower Service at St. Luke's.

July 26;   Children gathering whimberries. Man came for 1s of eggs.

July 27:   Finished Dorothy's checked pinafore. Cutting out a shirt for Annie [for holidays].

July 28;   Got the hay in out of the croft at Fir Farm.

July 29:   Wet all day. Received a photo of Nat's Company.

Aug. 12:   Went to Morecambe [for the day, by train] with Ellen and Elizabeth. Chris went driving grouse.

Aug. 14:   Singleton's heifer got out. Annie returned from her holiday at Morecambe, from which she brought papa a pipe and myself some knives.

Aug. 27:   Finished a blouse for myself. John and I went to Chorley. Late home at night. Chris came to meet us [at the station – probably Heapey, or perhaps Brinscall].

Aug. 28:   Father finished hay. Nellie got three looms for regular [at Withnell Mill]. Herbert sent home for a week.

Aug. 29:   St. Luke's Anniversary Sermons.

Sept. 8:   Had a trip to Blackpool with Mrs. Bradley, Mrs. Barnes and Katie Barnes.

Sept. 9:   Father carting [i.e. in a cart] wood from Blackhurst.

Sept. 14:   Father went to a sale at Piccadilly [i.e. a farm on Belmont Road].

Sept. 16:   Father commenced thatching the haystack.

Sept. 19:   Harvest Festival at St. Paul's [Withnell].

Sept. 22:   Sent off the Puzzle papers [i.e. a competition, possibly crossword, sent by post to a newspaper].

Oct. 4:   Letter from Nat. He arrived at Tidworth [Wilts] on 25th of September.

Oct. 9:   Got some gaiters for Lizzie and Dora, also leggings for Father.

Oct. 11:   Father bought a young heifer at Pass's Sale, and a storm lamp.

Oct. 18:   Flying Week at Blackpool [i.e. early aeroplane displays].

Oct. 20:   Busy making black puddings.

Oct. 23:   Went to Chorley with John. Got Annie a cloak from Tattersall's, £1 2s.

Oct. 29:   Bennets came to [live at] Heather Lea.

Nov. 4:   Stopped for a week at the mill. [Withnell Mill].

Nov. 6:   Father busy making a settle.

Nov. 7:   Went to Withnell Church.

Nov. 17:   Father finished the settle. Father got a letter from Liverpool concerning the meadow land for planting trees [i.e. Liverpool Corporation Waterworks' intention to plant trees according to their plan of 1906 for creating Wheelton Plantation – the present Brinscall Woods, which now embrace **Marsden's** farm].

Nov. 22:   J. Bolton removed from **Leigh Place** [the last residents at that farm]. Father sawing wood.

Nov. 23:   Bought J. Bolton's hen-cabin, 8s.

Nov. 24:   Erected J. Bolton's hen-cabin at **Marsden's** Farm.

Nov. 25:   Children paid for a week's stoppage at the mill [i.e. Withnell Mill].

Nov. 27:   Nellie and John went to see our Harry [now living at White Coppice].

Nov. 29:   Nellie went to Mclean's for medicine for me, 2s.

Dec. 4:   Bought an alarm clock.

Dec. 5:   A second bottle of medicine, 2s. Not so well. Snowy weather.

Dec. 6:   Children started working at the factory [Withnell Mill] from 7am to 4pm.

Dec. 8:   Busy sewing chemises for the three youngest girls [i.e. Ellen, Elizabeth and Dorothy]. Chris started night work.

Dec. 10:   Nat came home [from his army base in Wiltshire] at 10.12pm.

Dec. 13:   Father carting coals.

Dec. 14:   Nat took dinners down to the factory. Tommy started working at nights. Went to Chorley for timber for hen cote.

Dec. 16:   Children started work at 6am.

Dec. 19:   Very stormy blizzard. Received Xmas card from Australia.

Dec. 22:   Very stormy. Children could not get to the mill for the snow storm. Went round by the [Print] Works at breakfast time.

Dec. 23:   Busy cleaning duck for Mrs. Guest. Also a duck and a chicken for **Marsden's** farm [i.e. for ourselves]. P.C from [my sister] Kate saying we must expect her on Christmas Eve.

Dec. 24:   Frosty morning. Nellie and Dora stayed [at home] from work, ill. [I] went to Chorley. Met with Aunt Kate.

Dec. 25:   Christmas Day. Rose, Harry and child came up. Also H. Bradley.

Dec. 26:   Fred Dobson and Edie came up for their tea.

Dec. 27:   Aunt Kate and little George went back via Settle. Children started working at 9am till 4.30pm.

Dec. 30:   Nat's [army] pay arrived.

Dec. 31:   Stopped for the New Year at noon at the [Print] Works.

Fir Farm from Marsden's. Looking up the zigzag 'Sunken Road' in 2010.

Sunset glow on Marsden's surviving gable, 2010. The upper window belonged to the Thomas and Elizabeth Jane Dixon bedroom.

1910

Jan. 1:	James Bennet came for hay [for cattle or horses].
Jan. 3:	Received papers from New Zealand.
Jan. 4:	Father went to the Tory meeting at St. Paul's School. Father went for meat and whisky for the wedding.
Jan. 5:	Annie's Wedding Day. She got a P.C. from Aunt Martha.
Jan. 6:	Very tired. John went for bread and mince meat. Dorothy went with Annie's belongings.
Jan. 7:	Father went to buy in [i.e. main grocery etc. shopping]. Nat went back to join his regiment at Salisbury Plain.
Jan. 8:	Father went for corn. Got a letter from cousin Suzie in New Zealand.
Jan. 9:	I won the Sweep at Riding's.
Jan. 10:	Received a letter from Nat.
Jan. 12:	Father and Chris took spotted heifer to Bill Wilson's.
Jan. 13:	Still short time at the factory.
Jan. 14:	Went to Chorley. Came back at 10pm. Children went to the Christmas Tree.
Jan. 19:	Polling Day [First 1910 General Election] in the Chorley Division.

Jan. 20:   Results of Polling: C. L. Balcarres 7,735 votes. L. Blease 5,523. Majority 2,212.

Jan. 21:   Busy sewing quilts [for warmth in January]. Dora ill in bed. Very frosty. Went to buy in. Herbert met me on the last train.

Jan. 25:   Went to Chorley. Started to make a hearth rug, also a cloth quilt. Very severe frost and snow.

Jan. 27:   Lizzie still at home. Chris still night-working.

Jan. 28:   Quite a blizzard. Very bad travelling. Father had difficulty in getting up the provisions. Willie late home from work.

Jan. 29:   Father took Bennet's milk. Chris went for me to Chorley to buy in.

Jan. 30:   Began to thaw in the evening.

Jan. 31:   Father went to Coleman's Sale. Got a letter from Ned.

Feb. 1:   Cut Herbert's hair. Went to Chorley. Very dirty underfoot. Sent notice in to the Corporation of Liverpool [about an intention to leave Marsden's].

Feb. 2:   Broke a sewing machine needle, sewing a quilt.

Feb. 4:   Finished Lizzie's dress. Frosty. Cleaning upstairs. Chris took Bennet's mule home.

Feb. 5:   Dora and Lizzie went to buy in . Raining hard. John went to meet them with their cloaks. Father got a bad cough.

Feb. 7:   Chris bought some wood for his hen cote from J. Leigh.

Feb. 9:   Tommy started night work. Withnell Mill started full time.

Feb. 12:   Ellen and Lizzie went to buy in. Father and Willie took the roaned heifer from **Fir Farm** to Bill Wilson's.

Feb. 17:   My Birthday Anniversary. 54 years. The wind today blew over Chris's hen cote into Hogg's pasture [down from Fir Farm to Goose Green].

Feb. 22:   Eggs, 10 for a shilling. Father clearing hen cotes out. I started to wash bedding. Lizzie started on one loom [at Withnell Mill].

March 2:   The red cow calved a heifer calf. Baking Day. Finished Herbert's pants. Chris stayed at home tonight, ill.

March 3:   The doctor came up to see Chris, ill with rheumatism. [Chris aged 17.] Father went down for medicine and liniment. Brought Chris's bed downstairs for warmth.

March 5:   The new [Doctor's] Assistant called to see Chris. 6s 6d for eggs at 10 for 1s. Herbert went for Chris's medicine. John went for oil [for lamps].

March 6:   Dr. Maclean came up to see Chris. A Liverpool Corporation man and boy came up seeking sheep to impound them.

March 7:   Dr. Taylor came up.

March 8: Father repaired road coming up the wood. Baking, sewing and other duties. Willie shunting in Jim Lowe's place on account of his illness. [This on the railway, either in the Print Works sidings or on Brinscall Station yard.]

March 11: Two men taking slates off **Fir Farm** pig cotes.

March 17: John went for medicine for Chris. Finished two skirts for Lizzie and Dorothy.

March 20: Dr. Maclean came up. Chris declared much better.

March 23: Chris went outside [for the first time] after being ill. Bought dressing comb and buttons from a pedlar.

March 31: Very frosty. Repairing Jack's pants and jacket. Harry came up at dinner time. Jim went back with him. Chris still in bed [again] with rheumatics. Jack fetched a lotion from the Doctor's.

April 2: Sat 3 hens on geese eggs. A very nice day. Went to Chorley to get Jim's clogs. 3s 7d. We also went to the fair.

April 3: Went to St. Luke's in the afternoon, and in the evening had a walk round by Barnes's with Ellen and Dorothy.

April 4: Cold day. Washing and baking pies. Chris still in bed with rheumatism.

April 8: The white cow calved a roan bull calf.

April 11: Paid Dr. Maclean for attendance on Chris, £3 5s.

April 14: Chris took the table to Harry's and brought back the round table.

April 15: I carried Chris's bed back upstairs again.

April 19: Sent back the [dress] patterns to Noble's Ltd., Manchester. Father got eleven chickens out of one hatch.

April 20: Chris churned. Herbert Fowler bought a bull calf [from us].

April 21: Father took the calf down to Fowler's. Chris went down to Brinscall for the first time since being ill.

April 22: Made a sponge cake and a parkin. Then went to see chickens at **Fir Farm**. Went to Chorley with my old sewing machine and got a new one. Chris came to meet me [at the station].

April 27: Mr. Hargreaves brought my new sewing machine home for me. Father busy making hen coops across at **Fir Farm**. A cow jobber called from Egerton.

April 28: Chris started working again after being ill eight weeks.

May 3: Got a letter from Liverpool [Corporation] concerning the land at Blackhurst.

May 5: Father went to Chorley Cattle Fair. Bought a young heifer.

May 6: King Edward VII died at a quarter to 12pm.

May 12: Twenty-four years today since we first resided at **Marsden's Farm**.

May 13:   Father bought two heifers at Lamb's. He took the red cow to Bill Wilson's.
May 14:   Bought John [aged 11] cap, front, tie and boots at Chorley.
May 23:   White-washing the back kitchen. Baking pies and cakes in the evening.

June 8:   Father took the light-roaned heifer to Ridings.
June 11:   Bought Dora a hat, 3s 9d.
June 20:   White cow served [i.e. introduced to the bull].
June 25:   Sixteen little ducks arrived.
June 28:   Repaired Dora's corsets. Baking Day.
June 29:   Bill Hayes bought our Chris's hencote.

July 5:   Father mowing [hay-making] for B. Barnes.
July 23:   To Chorley with Dora. Got tried on for my print dress.

Aug. 16:   Tom Southworth un-roofed the house at **Fir Farm** and carted away the slates [or roof-flags].
Aug. 18:   Received a work-basket from Harlow [Essex] which I ordered the previous week.
Aug. 27:   Wrote to Mr. Critchley, auctioneer [about a sale at Marsden's].
Aug. 30:   Mr. Critchley called, also Robinson.

Sept. 1:   White-washing the front place.
Sept. 5:   Father hay-making at Bennet's, Heather Lea.
Sept. 6:   White-washing part of the house and putting back the pictures.
Sept. 7:   Father churned before going hay-making. I re-covered the sofa cushions.
Sept. 10:   Dora and I went to Brinscall Sports.
Sept. 11:   Went for a walk round Buckholes.
Sept. 12:   Father went to top the [hay] stack at Bennet's.
Sept. 13:   Mr. Critchley came up to take the Inventory of the Sale.

Oct. 1:   Went to Chorley with Lizzie. Bought two new chairs, 4s each, which we carried [all the way] from Heapey Station.
Oct. 3:   **Marsden's** Farm Sale. Fine but cold.
Oct. 5:   We went up to look at Mr. Nobblet's house [on Harbour Lane].
Oct. 6:   Ted Howcroft came up, agreeing for us to have the house. Went up to Harbour Lane, taking some pictures.
Oct. 7:   Nellie and Father went to clean the new house. Wrote to Aunt Charlotte, and Nat at East Liss [Hampshire].
Oct. 10;   Removed from **Marsden's** Farm after staying for a period of over 24 years.
Oct. 11:   Carting the remains away from **Marsden's** Farm.
Oct. 20:   Nellie and I went to **Marsden's** in the evening, carrying home some pots.

Oct. 24:   Father started working at the [Print] Works.

Oct. 26:   I went to pay Sarjent's for removing us from **Marsden's** Farm.

Oct. 27:   Father brought home some mustard seed from Ridings. I cleaned the mustard seed.

Nov. 2:   Went up [to **Marsden's**] for the crow for the fireplace. Also to fetch the rose tree and the willow tree. Made black puddings.

Nov. 5:   Father planted the willow tree.

Calender House, the Dixons' home from 1913 to 1928.

PART THREE

The Walks

The area of hill and moor that contains all 48 of the discoverable farms is so compact, relatively speaking, that I could have offered several different routes to prospective walkers, had I so wished. The five routes that I do offer are not intended to be absolutely obligatory or strictly adhered to, therefore, but they will provide the most efficient way of visiting all 48 via five separate expeditions (on five separate occasions, that is). The routes begin at a minimum number of suitable (and, increasingly familiar, perhaps) starting points.

   Nevertheless, please feel very free to make adjustments and, for example, to join part of Walk One (the Brinscall Woods Group) to part of Walk Two (the Central Group) if that appeals – bearing in mind that **Beardsworth's** and **Ripping** are actually quite close to each other, as are **White Hall** and **Whittle's**. Similarly, **Goose Green** (in Walk One) and **Fir Farm** (in Walk Three) are also quite close to each other. I confidently claim, however, that if you do walk the routes as I have shown them here, you will readily find, even during the walk as well as afterwards, that I had good reason for the grouping order and the sequence of visiting. If you follow my routes there will be interest and variety throughout. Please enjoy.

   As one who regularly walks the woods and moors, I firmly recommend the wearing of light, stout and waterproof shoes/boots or even light 'wellies', rather than heavier walking boots, since damp or soggy patches are more frequently found than craggy, rocky sections of a Lake District mountain kind. A compass will be very useful however, even in clear weather, to guide you from farm to farm, especially in Brinscall Woods. Throughout the walks, the OS Explorer Map 287 (West Pennine Moors) will provide helpful information.

The Brinscall Woods Group (12 Farms)

Start and Finish: Brinscall, the School Lane/ Railway Road Junction.

Distance: Up to 3 miles.

Time: Up to 4 hrs. 30 mins. if each farm is carefully examined, but down to 1 hr. 30 mins. if the route is more briskly walked.

Character: Not strenuous but requiring care and persistence. Some dampness underfoot is possible. A delightful woodland stroll in general, with occasional distant views.

IN DESCRIBING AND RECOMMENDING the walk round the 12 members of the Brinscall Woods group, I deliberately supply a good deal more precise detail of the ideal route than I did when presenting the 'Lost in the Woods' farms in Chapter Two of Part Two. Then I was addressing the reader as archivist, historian, sociologist. Now I am addressing the reader as walker, someone enthusiastically searching for hidden field walls and farm ruins in the midst, perhaps, of all the tangled foliage of high summer.

The starting point is at the foot of School Lane where, at a right angle bend, School Lane meets Railway Road. If you are arriving by car, there is convenient parking on Lodge Bank, just beyond the Brinscall Baths (or Leisure Pool) and overlooking the picturesque lodge with its resident ducks and geese and back-cloth of well-wooded hillside. This is a scene worth your attention before you begin your walk. I would recommend it for those who arrive by bus, too. The 124 bus (half-hourly sometimes, hourly most times) stops at the bottom of School Lane if arriving from Blackburn, round the corner and just at the start of Railway Road if arriving from Chorley.

From the School Lane/Railway Road junction, walk briefly eastwards, crossing the culverted Goit as if aiming for Butterworth Brow ahead of you. But, while noticing the old stone horse-trough on your left, ignore both Butterworth Brow and also Quarry Road on your left and aim resolutely for Well Lane on your right. Proceed up Well Lane, also ignoring the public footpath marked on your right just as you are beginning to climb.

There did indeed used to be wells on Well Lane, for instance one on your left, shortly after you have passed over the second of the modern "sleeping policemen"/ surface water deflectors. There was also another well on your left, 100-plus metres further up the lane, close to the fourth of the "sleeping policemen", more or less where the old track for **Greenlands** and **Cocker's Folly** (one of the hillside zigzags) leaves Well Lane by a grassy hairpin bend. There is no exact sign of either well, but a good deal of

dampness in the ground if, say, you were to turn briefly into the hairpin bend and walk up the zigzag for 30m to a stile. By doing this you would also be familiarising yourself with your future route to the Central Group of farms. For the time being, however, return to the firm tarmac surface of Well Lane and continue uphill. Bear in mind, by the way, that Well Lane, though of single vehicle width, is occasionally visited by drivers in vehicles hoping to go up to the very top of Edge Gate Lane, next to **Whittle's Farm**, and hoping not to meet head-on another vehicle coming down. There are few passing places. Where one of the vehicles is a large farm-tractor, towing a load of straw bales for the attention of hungry sheep, it does tend rather easily to get right of way.

Continuing up Well Lane on foot, as you are, notice, just after the fifth "sleeping policeman", a remaining single stone gatepost (with top hinge-pin) on your right, marking the point where a track left Well Lane to permit access to the sloping fields overlooking the former Bleach Works (whose lodge you have already seen). All such fields are now densely covered in small trees, mainly birch. The gatepost is easily missed by walkers such as yourselves perhaps when it is hidden by a luxuriant growth of nettles during the summer. To find it without being stung is your first challenge.

Well Lane, meanwhile, is still climbing, but less steeply than it was. As it bends to the left, you are about to see (or possibly hear before you see) the Hatch Brook waterfall on your right. When you find yourself at a junction – with the Heather Lea/Blackhurst 'carriage drive' departing via a metal gate on your right, and Well Lane continuing ahead and upwards (but now renamed Edge Gate Lane though there is no sign to say so) – there, on your left, is your first farm. This is **Ripping**, the least 'lost' of all the Brinscall Woods 12, in summer at any rate. [*Ripping was the home in the early 1890s of two persons, a widow, 75-year-old Margaret Shorrock, and her granddaughter, also Margaret, aged 29. Just the two where once it held seven. The senior Margaret, as a 35-year-old wife in 1851, had lived with her 37-year-old husband Thomas and their six children at **Solomon's Temple**, higher up on the moors. You can visit her former home on your Central Group Walk.*]

To look closely at the remains of **Ripping** with its low walls and obvious doorways on the far side, one into the house and one into the attached outhouse, step over the horizontal (but still living) trunk of a hawthorn bush, then over the stile, and walk carefully round the house, thinking of the two Margarets and then looking to your left to find the nearby ruins of a barn. Overhead are numerous sycamores, a few hawthorns and one upright and one rather twisted silver birch. Maybe in 1891 there was just one sycamore. Perhaps you could try to imagine the sylvan scene all around you with hardly any trees, with intact farm buildings and with upright field boundary walls. Or perhaps not, for it is a pleasant enough scene as it is. There are charming banks of wood sorrel flowers along Well Lane in the Spring, and Herb Robert for most of the year.

Now, back at the junction [*well-known, no doubt, to Alice Heyes of **Heaton's** and Mary and Rachel Shorrock of **Whittle's** before and after their day's work in the 1890s*], take the carriage drive on your right instead of walking up Edge Gate Lane. Almost immediately you will cross the Hatch Brook. Looking over the wall on your right you can admire the brook as it surges – or trickles, depending how recently rain has fallen – down over the high cliffs of the former quarry on its hectic – or placid – way to the Goit far below. I have never known the Hatch to run dry, I must say. In a rainy season you can hear its roar a mile away.

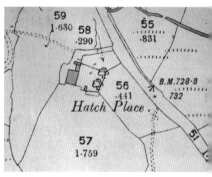

While observing the waterfall, you have been standing on a rough track, with occasional puddles after any of the aforementioned rain. But walk only another 25m and then look for a gap in the bank on your left. This is the start of the now grass-covered track that leads up to your second farm, **Heaton's**. Follow this track as it curves gently uphill but be prepared to make a detour round any wind-fallen tree trunks. You should be walking roughly south-eastwards. In only 100m or so you will see clear evidence of the ruins of a substantial farmhouse and barn. There are several gateposts, many with hinge-pins. In autumn, winter or spring you will easily find the well and the horsetrough just north of the main farm buildings, one on each side of the cobbled track. In the summer you will need to look especially carefully, peering through bracken or brambles or both. [*Young Alice, daughter of Thomas and Martha Heyes who lived here in the 1890s, could probably find the well perfectly readily when asked to bring in a pail of water. A small rowan tree stands helpfully close to the well these days.*]

Now walk due east, crossing a broken-down wall and then an open area of felled conifers until, in less than 100m, you find another wall and a pair of quite tall stone gateposts. Here is **Hatch Place**. [*This is where George, Sarah and David Shorrock lived in the 1890s. See the 1929 photograph of Sarah Shorrock aged 90 and living at **Ratten Clough**.*] The **Hatch** farm and barn longhouse is now the usual crumbled mass of stone but you can see its short walled track leading to the nearby Edge Gate Lane. No need to follow it. The exit to the lane is barred by barbed wire and there is now no bridge over the outside ditch. [*The seven daughters of Henry and Elizabeth Grime must have used it frequently in 1851, however, and known the small field and stone structures nearby.*].

You have now visited three of the 12 farms on the day's list. To reach the fourth requires a little deft manoeuvring in the woods. From the two gateposts next to the **Hatch Place** building follow an "unofficial" but clear path beneath the trees, going south-eastwards and slightly uphill and soon running along the edge of the smallish sycamores and conifers, with the area of cleared larger (as you can tell from their stumps) conifers visible on your right. After about 150m you will come to a substantial field boundary wall. Go through the broken section of this and almost immediately turn sharply left, to the north, and join a fairly indistinct (at first) but old-established path that is clearly marked both on present OS maps and on early nineteenth-century maps. It leads you gently down for about 40m through more trees to a plainly official United Utilities stile on to Edge Gate Lane. Notice, as you climb the stile, the two ancient stone gateposts on your left. This was once apparently a major entrance on to a large open field and a driveway up to **White Hall Cottages** (which you will soon visit anyway).

You will enjoy the short walk on Edge Gate Lane, I hope, with the increasingly open views up to the **Whittle's Farm** sycamore, across to the sycamores of **Ratten Clough** and, behind you if you turn quickly round to see it, the distant sea coast. At any rate I expect you have turned right on the lane and are now walking uphill, passing, on your left, two old gateposts (once a field entrance) and eventually reaching, on your right, a flat car park (or lorry park during tree-felling operations) where **White Hall Farm** used to be. Its surface is quite rough – stone and tarmac chippings mixed with tree-bark chippings. You will notice a field path a little higher on your left, departing over a stile for **Ratten Clough**. (This to be visited on another walk.) Beyond the car park there is a stile on your right, too, and a field path leading back towards Brinscall Woods and the boundary wall ladder stile. Unless you are determined to stand and walk on the flat space that used to be **White Hall**, climb the stile, take the field path and make your way to the ladder stile over the boundary wall, and climb it. You are now back in Brinscall Woods.

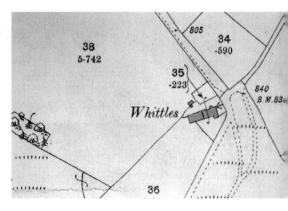

[However, as an alternative, just in case you might give way to a little curiosity about **White Hall**, *you could instead walk discreetly across the car park, standing briefly where the house was. The front of it was very close to Edge Gate Lane. Remember Ashworth and Ann Howarth of 1891 if you wish, or the earlier William and Mary Smith, or the earlier still Berry family of 1851, with Mary Berry aged 50 as Head of Household. Her household consisted of five children, one of whom, Lettice, aged eight in 1851, was by 1881 married to John Smith and living at* **New Ground** *with two children of her own.]*

Just beyond the western edge of the car park you might find three heavy stone slabs lying flat together in the grass, and evidently still concealing something rather significant. Lifting them, however, seems, as it should be, impossible, so you might as well walk on across the car park, and continue down a grassy path towards the ladder stile, keeping inside the boundary wall (a Liverpool Corporation structure) and about 5m from it until you reach the stile from the inside, as it were. There is no need to climb it.

You may have noticed that the ground hereabouts is damp. What you may not have noticed is that on your right, beneath numerous low trees, lies the mossy heap of stones that used to be **White Hall Cottages**. A low garden wall surrounded them. *[Think of James and Mary Bolton, if you wish, the tenants in 1891, or the earlier Thomas and Alice Loyd, or the earlier still (1851) Henry and Jane Fowler and their four-year-old son Richard. Henry had been a cattle dealer, whereas Thomas Loyd worked in a weaving shed and James Bolton was a quarryman.]*

It is now time to take a slightly longer walk and to come in due course to our sixth farm of the day, **Liptrot's**. It is an agreeable walk, shaded and sheltered by trees, parallel and close to the boundary wall with pleasant views over the open moors and sheep fields to your left. After a while, do stop to examine the ancient pair of gateposts you will meet. No hinge-pins there, for no gate ever hung on these posts. Hinge-pins require spare iron, and molten lead for the fixing of them. These posts just had incised slots to take wooden cross-bars that could be fitted in and then quickly released as required. A good 300 years old, perhaps? There are some other very similar examples in the lower part of Brinscall Woods near the bottom of the steep slope.

Continue your walk for perhaps five minutes on the easy and mainly level path, crossing four crumbled field walls on the way and noting on the left behind a silver birch one remaining and substantial gatepost (with hinge-pin) from a former exit point on to the moors. Then, after about a further 60 metres, you are suddenly upon the **Liptrot's** longhouse, with jutting porch (or dairy?) foundations to begin with and then the rest of the structure very close to your path. There is much bracken hereabouts in summer and a conspicuous damp area beyond the buildings, the relic of the farm's water supply. [*Can you imagine the four middle-aged siblings – three female and one male – living here in 1891, the sisters all farmers and their brother James Stalter, an iron broker and agent? Perhaps it is easier to imagine Richard and Ellen Taylor in 1851, farmer and handloom weaver, and their eight-year-old niece Ann Pilkington, working here as an errand girl.*]

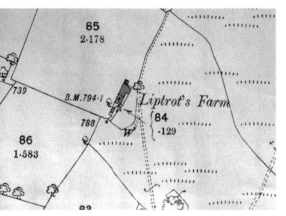

Now, after glancing upwards from the nearby stile to the rising moorland fields, turn to the west and plunge down again through the trees. Keep fairly close to the low wall on your left that accompanies you downhill. Beyond (to the south of) the wall is the damp and grassy former track that once ran up to **Liptrot's** via **Leigh Place** from the 'carriage drive' near Blackhurst. It is now too often muddy as well as shrub-and-tree-blocked to be worth trying to use. What you are doing therefore is crossing downhill what until as late as 1970 was still an open field. (I remember well the planting of new young conifers – mainly larch – here.)

Keeping your eye on the wall while also avoiding the twigs and branches of the young trees, you will soon see (after about 100m from **Liptrot's**) two low stone gateposts on your left. You will also find yourself striding over another low wall at right angles to the first one and into a short driveway beyond which is a small rectangular garden area that belonged to **Leigh Place**. At the northern end of the garden area is one small and ancient gatepost with the simple slots-for-poles system, rather than hinge-pins.

Just below and next to the garden area are the tumbled ruins of **Leigh Place** itself. These are worth a quick exploration. [*Quarryman Robert Grundy, his wife Jane and their four daughters were living here in 1891.*]

At the southern edge of the ruins you will see that the original track has made a dog-leg turn on its way down the hill. Hereabouts you will find the stone-built well arrangement if you search carefully. And now you have visited your seventh farm of the walk.

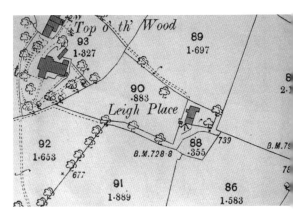

At this point, retrace your steps to the northern end of the **Leigh Place** ruins and find another wall, with ditch outside it, that you should follow for about 80m on its way down the hill until it meets another rather tumble-down wall coming in from the right. Step cautiously over this, for you are about to see and not fall into the subterranean stone archway below you which was part of the water-catchment scheme for the nineteenth-century grand mansion of Blackhurst. Blackhurst, clearly not at all a longhouse in plan, had a smart rock and grotto garden with paths, bridges and lawn, and a sweeping drive coming in from above and behind, so to say, the **Top o'th'Wood** entrance and buildings. It is **Top o'th'Wood** that I primarily recommend you to notice and examine, however.

Having walked over brambles and wood sorrel leaves down the former sloping field for about 80m from the underground archway, you will find yourself on the edge of a high wall overlooking the drive to the front (western) side of Blackhurst. Below you on the far side of the drive you will see two small, narrowly spaced pedestrian gateposts leading into the small garden area of **Top o'th'Wood**. Now go a little to your right and drop carefully down eventually to the remains of the **Top o'th'Wood** drive and then walk, stepping cautiously over old tree trunks, into the 'carriage drive' beyond. You last saw the 'carriage drive' when leaving it to take the **Heaton's** track just after the Hatch waterfall.

Turn left now to see the end of the **Top o'th'Wood** barn (rough, random stone walling) and then notice the quoins that mark the start of the farmhouse (domestic) building. [*Allow yourself to think, if you wish, that in 1881 this small Top o'th Wood group of buildings whose remains you are now looking at contained three distinct households numbering 24 persons altogether.*] Behind you, for your further interest, on the lower side of the 'carriage drive', are the underground stables belonging to Blackhurst. It is possible quickly to walk round and then down either side of these to look into the well-built, sophisticated accommodation provided for the horses.

At the top of Brinscall Woods, an old gatepost into which wooden bars could be inserted.

After a brief survey, return for a final look at the **Top o'th'Wood** barn and house, noticing, on the upper side, where there is a retaining wall holding up the added drive to Blackhurst, another low stone archway in this retaining wall – which you might have missed earlier. Was this a well supplying the needs of the **Top o'th'Wood** kitchen? Was it using the same water supply that had been piped down to Blackhurst from the underground archway higher up the hill? If so was it a Woods family compensation to the **Top o'th'Wood** dwellers for the building of the new Blackhurst drive high above their house?

Whatever the answer to these questions, you have now visited eight of the 12 Brinscall Woods farms. It is time to enjoy a relatively long and easy stroll along the 'carriage drive' right through to the south end of Brinscall Woods. You are beginning the search for **Marsden's**, farm number nine on our day's route.

In the 'Lost in the Woods' section, I did warn that the former direct route from **Top o'th'Wood** to **Marsden's** no longer existed – blotted out by afforestation. Even if you attempted it you might well have to deal, under the trees, with a swiftly flowing Sour Milk Brook cutting across your path. And even if Sour Milk Brook has run dry, scrambling across its stony course can be awkward. By the route I am now advising you can safely cross Sour Milk Brook by a bridge. (There is no parapet.)

So, from the **Top o'th'Wood** site (noticing on your right a tall single gatepost with large hinge-pin that must once have held a gate dividing **Top o'th'Wood** ground from Blackhurst ground) walk along the 'carriage drive' in a southerly direction. Walk past and below the Blackhurst garden area and come shortly to a junction with the old track coming down on your left from **Liptrot's** and **Leigh Place**. Here take the route to the right and proceed gently downhill. After 100m you will effortlessly cross the Sour Milk Brook flowing (or not flowing) through two wide pipes beneath you. Once you have crossed it you have left Wheelton and arrived in Heapey. Continue down the clear wide path through pleasant mixed woodland. Eventually you will pass several tall, spreading beech trees, magnificent specimens, indeed. Continue until you reach the end of the wood and see ahead of you the formal Goose Green double-arched stone bridge over the Goit. Ahead, also, is the superior wooden "kissing gate" giving access to the **Goose Green Farm** ruins and to the valley through to White Coppice.

The partner gatepost into which wooden bars could be firmly clamped.

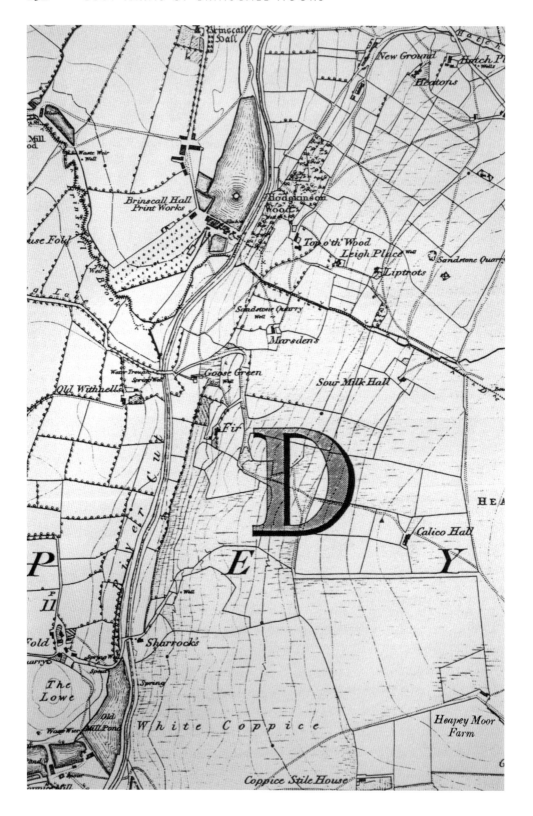

At this point there is no need to go through the "kissing gate" but do notice the farm gate (five-barred and wooden) to its left which once allowed vehicles to reach **Goose Green Farm**. For the moment you might well wish to have a quick look at the Goit while you are here. It will be your first sight of it as an open water channel on today's walk.

Now, from a point near to the **Goose Green Farm** gate take the clear if 'unofficial' path running uphill under trees and inside the post and barbed wire fence which separates woods from open sheep fields. Your direction is just north of east. Follow this path, keeping quite close to the fence (beyond which you can see the old 'sunken road' making its zigzag way up to **Fir Farm** and **Calico Hall**).

There is just one important instruction now. If, after some 160m or so, you find a small stream crossing your path, stop and retrace your steps briefly. If you were to continue at this point you would come to an outflow from a square stone tank which can produce a morass of a bog at times, a deep enough bog to lose a welly in. So, retrace your steps for just 15m until you see a branch of the path that takes you towards the fence on what becomes an 'avoidance' route. You will be briefly 'outside' the old stone wall which used to mark the edge of the wood, but you will still be inside the post and wire fence. Continue upwards and eastwards for 200m, rejoining the previous path in a while, and soon you will have sight of the south gable wall of **Marsden's**.

Rejoice in this. It is the most complete set of ruins in Brinscall Woods. The full shape and extent of the farm-and-barn longhouse and its details, its outer steps, its well, its subordinate structures, its (western) garden area are all there to be seen. A lovely place to be, no doubt, before its site became so densely tree-clad. [*If you had been Thomas Dixon in 1891 you might have been reluctant to leave it and your wife and four youngsters every evening in order to go down to be a night-watchman at the Print Works. A living had to be made, however, though the Dixons had to adjust their priorities by 1902, given the birth of eight more children.*]

With nine farms now discovered you can make your way back and down to the **Goose Green** area by the same paths by which you have just climbed up to **Marsden's** – remembering to take the avoidance route bringing you near to the post and wire fence at one particular point instead of unintentionally sampling the depth of a potential bog. Then, rejoining the main path beneath the trees down to the five-barred gate, approach the "kissing gate" just beyond it and go through into the lovely valley leading to White Coppice. What you now seek, in addition to tranquillity and charm, is of course the **Goose Green** ruin. It is not far away – about 60m in a south-easterly direction.

The southern gable of Marsden's. Internal brick chimneys are visible alongside the bedroom window. Smart, sloping window ledges in the foreground.

In the winter and spring months you will easily see the built-up, stone supported banks and the two sycamores about 20 and 30m away which mark the edge of the farm's garden or close field. ['*Garden', by the way, in the context of these farms, hardly ever means 'flower garden'. Vegetables, yes, flowers, no. I do not think many of our farm dwellers grew roses and dahlias or planted a lilac tree, or at least not until the Dixons left Marsden's in 1910 and until Jimmy Bennett planted roses and laburnums at Grouse Cottage in the 1950s.*] Beyond the **Goose Green** garden square you will see the familiar longhouse foundations and the little heaps of grey-white stone which show the position of the house section (nearest the hillside) and barn section (nearest the Goit).

In summer or early autumn, however, shoulder-high bracken can conceal much of this detail. To find what you seek you must push your way boldly through the bracken in the direction of the largest ash tree you can see – not a modest mountain ash or rowan but a great fully grown giant of an ash tree. It stands just beyond but very close to what was the eastern wall of the house. [*A smaller version of the very same tree is there on the early twentieth-century photograph of* **Goose Green***, enabling you to stand at the point from which the photograph was taken, and imagine the farm still there. It*

At Goose Green farm, looking over the foundations towards the Goit.

is not quite so easy to trace the remains of the lavatory block.] If on a summer day you are pushing your way through the bracken to stand on the farm's foundations, do please take great care not to turn an ankle over on any loose blocks of stone which lie hidden beneath the lush greenery.

With 10 farms now located you should justifiably be feeling a certain inner satisfaction, even a quiet smugness about your powers as a navigator in the midst of much arboraceous profusion. A quiet lingering in the vicinity of **Goose Green** should perhaps be allowed, an enjoying of the glorious view along the sheltered valley, a sitting, indeed, on the soft mounds of bilberry and heather on the lower slopes just above the old farm. A well-earned picnic, perhaps? But then the hidden world of **New Ground** still awaits you in the northerly reaches of the plantation, and you must therefore return to the "kissing gate" and re-enter the woods. [*As you do you might think of the school teacher Sarah Hogg in the 1890s onwards, setting out as she did in the early mornings on her bicycle from this very spot on her way to Higher Wheelton or Brinscall, and looking forward to meeting her pupils for the day.*]

The major track (which I have called the 'carriage drive') running right through Brinscall Woods from the Hatch Brook waterfall to **Goose Green** is a clear, wide, pleasant route with, on the whole, reasonable gradients. You have already walked along a little less than half its length – from **Top o'th' Wood** down to **Goose Green**. I am firmly suggesting that you now walk along its whole length, from south to north, as your main means of returning to your original starting point – and the end of your day's walk – at the School Lane-Railway Road junction. On the way, as I have just reminded you, you will be able to discover, or at least note the position of, the two most difficult sets of buildings to find in Brinscall Woods in high summer, the **New Ground Cottages** and the **New Ground** longhouses, your final targets for the day.

[So far your grand walk of discovery round the farms should have taken you, with all the searchings, findings and assessments involved, between three and four hours, if you have devoted yourself fairly thoroughly to all the available details. A quicker, competitive 'orienteering' version might reduce this to an hour or less, of course, but your understanding of the lives of those who lived there would necessarily be far less complete.]

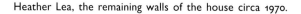

Heather Lea, the remaining walls of the house circa 1970.

The walk back now from **Goose Green** to Well Lane and then to School Lane-Railway Road should take just a little more than half an hour. Mind you, a really determined walking among the **New Ground** ruins (much easier to do in winter) could at least double that time.

Three other matters occur to me at this point. One: the first section of your return walk from **Goose Green** involves a continuous but gradual uphill progress past the Sour Milk bridge to the junction of tracks just before the Blackhurst garden. Do turn left and slightly downhill at the junction. Two: any former red building bricks that you see embedded in the surface of the 'carriage drive' are not evidence of nearby farm demolition but are simply the result of a strengthening of the drive's foundations when North West Water several years ago decided to import and lay down load upon load of cheaply available hardcore. Three: you will notice, en passant, at the highest point reached by the 'carriage drive', the position of the non-farm gentleman's residence 'Heather Lea'.

So do enjoy your returning stroll through the woods, and do remember to veer left when you reach Blackhurst rather than turning right at the junction and going back up to **Leigh Place** and **Liptrot's**. After passing **Top o'th' Wood** and the underground stables you will find yourself walking uphill for a short distance, passing a fine solitary gatepost (with hinge-pin) on your right. Once the drive has levelled out, look on your right for Heather Lea's garden wall coming in at right angles to your route. Next to it, notice one small laburnum and three small rhododendrons that tell you that this was once a 'suburban' garden. 30m further on, as your route bends slightly to your right and then to the left, notice a single rough gatepost on your left and a projecting infilled area that facilitated the reversing of horse-drawn carriages opposite what had been Heather Lea's formal gateway (with its two grand tall, square gateposts until their removal comparatively recently). You can see how the Heather Lea drive rose gently through the garden and circled round to reach a level tennis-court lawn, beyond which stood a fine mid-Victorian stone house with gables, bay windows and a small conservatory. Clearly there had been cellars. A large kitchen garden and orchard stretched uphill behind the house.

Photographs of the house suggest a date of 1860–70 for its construction, a little later than Blackhurst, but roughly contemporary with the present Brinscall Hall. Although it had by 1970 lost its slate roof and its decoratively carved barge boards to gables and porch, Heather Lea at that date still had substantial double-storey-high walls of refined stonework. These are well-remembered locally even though the house had last been inhabited in 1930. There are still considerable chunks of stonework – window-ledges, for example – to be found amid the debris in 2011. Never a farm, not on the list of our 48 to be visited, therefore, but nevertheless a house worth knowing of and a house still exercising a fascination among local people. A road nicely filled with elegant bungalows on Brinscall's hillside is named after it.

Walking on now from Heather Lea's former gateway, notice another single stone gatepost on your right (just beyond Heather Lea's northern garden wall) and enjoy the level walking along this, the highest section of the 'carriage drive' route. You might soon notice a small upright stone, also on your right, next to an enclosure wall, marking a very narrow former footpath entrance (wide enough for one slim human leg at a time, but too narrow for a sheep) that used to lead diagonally up to **Liptrot's** long before Heather Lea and its garden existed. Next, in 40m you will find the 'carriage drive' bending to the left and taking you gently downhill for 70m before levelling out again. At this stage, antennae need to be sensitized, for you are about to walk very close to the almost completely invisible **New Ground Cottages**. In front of you is a 70m section of straight and level 'carriage drive' before the drive takes another slight leftward bend downhill. Half way along this level section you would see below you on your left the roofs and chimneys of the five **New Ground Cottages** – if they still existed. You might now just be able to make out some 20ft (6m) below you a tree-cloaked (choked?) terrace where the houses stood. Do not go looking so hard that you fall down the 6m drop to the terrace. How then to reach the terrace and stride among the undergrowth and the foundations?

It is far easier in November-April than it is in May-October, so you could perhaps make a return visit at a later date but, if, undaunted and resolute, you at any time persist in seeking out the cottage foundations, here are some recommendations. With antennae still sensitized, walk to the end of the 70m straight and level section of the 'carriage drive' and then follow it to the left and gently downhill for another 36m. You will not then be at the end of the gentle slope but you should certainly see (if

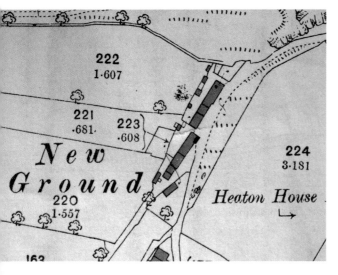

you are looking for it) the hip-height and ivy-covered single gatepost which shows you where the cottage track left the the 'carriage drive'. The gateway has been partially blocked by a row of small boulders but you can easily climb over these and follow the sloping track (with a low wall on its western side) for about 15m until it reaches the level terrace on which the five cottages stood in a row (parallel to the 'carriage drive' above them). Alas, masses of undergrowth and some fallen wind-overblown conifer trunks make

At New Ground, the high retaining wall below the farmyard.

progress difficult, but it is easy to see, and look over, the wall which edges the terrace and allows you to appreciate how high was the terrace structure above the former fields, now woods, below you.

Progress is difficult, as I say, along the cottage terrace but it is not impossible. So – watch your step at every stride. Avoiding large trees, small trees, trailing brambles and hidden stones, you will discover remnants of foundations (a row of five attached cottages – rather like the 'Brinscall Row' on School Lane) and also underground water-supply/drainage systems and the two pedestrian-exit gateposts at the southern end of the terrace. Feel the glow of satisfaction, of searchings rewarded, and then make your careful way back up to the 'carriage drive'.

[*You might spare a thought, as you leave, for the 17-year-old solitary weaver Esther Neville in 1851. From an upstairs window in her cottage (if that is where she did her handloom weaving) she would have been able to see right across the Brinscall valley to the stile (it would have been a stone version) near Harbour Lane from which you first looked over to*

the moors and woods on your preliminary walk from the Oak Tree. You will remember
that there were probably very few, if any, trees at all in 1851 around this New Ground
settlement. Fields sloping down before her, and fields sloping up on the far side of the old
Brinscall Hall, are what Esther would have seen when she glanced up from warp and
weft to the distant Windy Harbour Lane ridge.]

When you have scrambled back up the sloping track and over the stones blocking
the gateway – and said farewell to the ivy-covered gatepost – turn left on to the
'carriage drive' and continue down its slope, passing on your left the roofless barn.
After something like 75m you will find yourself at the lowest point on that section of
the 'carriage drive'. If only you could see through the mass of trees, saplings, nettles,
brambles, upturned roots and undergrowth generally on your left, you might see
that you are now level with one of the two **New Ground** longhouses. A new 'public
footpath' signpost stands at this point. In winter – a fine day in February, say – you
might be able to see something of this area, especially the artificially flattened yard
that culminates in a high terrace with spectacular retaining wall rising from the floor
of the Brinscall Woods. If all is, as it might be, obscure and impenetrable, worry not,
but walk on, slightly uphill, for another 35m until on your right you see a large sloping
slab of rock bearing the inscription 'PETE 96'. (This is next to a newly installed metal
seven-barred gate, part of the improved Anglezarke–Tockholes bridleway.)

Now turn immediately to your left. You must be looking at two, at least, of the
cross-wall foundation lines of the northernmost **New Ground** longhouse – the end
gable wall and the walls of the first two sections. Now go back five steps or so, and
then drop down from the 'carriage drive' straight into what might have been the farm
kitchen. It is a short step down. Then you can walk across the usual 20ft (6m) width
of the building and into a narrow yard (with the remains of at least three other stone
structures – lavatories?) and then over a low, mossy, crumbled wall into what was
once a field and is now just yet more of Brinscall Woods. (You will find the leaves
– and sometimes the flowers – of Claytonia [Montia Sibirica] on the 'forest floor'
here, rather than wood sorrel, celandines, anemones or stitchworts.) While you are in
this former field, walk south for 30m and you can look up to see the high retaining
wall supporting the terracing of the yard above you. Almost a castle outbuilding it
seems, but isn't!

Then, return over the low, mossy, crumbled wall and walk – push your way –
southwards along the narrow yard for 15m or so, and find two upright stone slabs
in front of you and a shoulder-height house wall on your left. You have now seen
enough to allow you to claim that you have visited, recorded and understood the
remarkable remains of **New Ground**. If, however, you had been strolling and chatting
merrily along the 'carriage drive' without reading instructions you might easily have

passed all these remains – the product of so much calculating, digging, upraising and labouring – not only unseen but even unsuspected.

With all 12 Brinscall Woods farms visited, all you have to do is step up to the 'carriage drive', turn left and walk uphill towards the Hatch waterfall. After 120m – shortly before you reach the waterfall – you will pass on your right the entrance to the **Heaton's** track up which you walked earlier – four or more hours earlier, perhaps. There are almost continuous if slow overflowings of clear water oozing from this grassy break in the bank throughout the year these days – but then there were wells, now waterless, at both **Heaton's** and **Hatch** farms, and the water has to go somewhere. (This particular oozing now makes its way down past the north end of **New Ground**, goes underground for a while, and emerges at two points in a little ditch by the track down to Bakehouse Lane bridge before entering the Goit.)

Now cross the waterfall bridge and go through the gate to meet the Edge Gate Lane/ Well Lane junction. Nod knowledgeably and appreciatively towards **Ripping** and stride easily down Well Lane back to your car or bus. You know that you will meet Well Lane again when you come back to climb the zigzags in search of **Greenlands**, **Cocker's Folly**, **Beardsworth's** and the rest of the Central Group.

The Central Group
(8 Farms)

Start and Finish: Brinscall, the School Lane/ Railway Road Junction.

Distance: Up to 3.5 miles.

Time: Up to 4 hrs., with special attention paid to some farms, but 2 hrs. or less if a brisker pace is adopted.

Character: An exhilarating walk over easy and open countryside. Many long views to the coast and mountains.

WELCOME AGAIN TO BRINSCALL MOORS. Your starting point for the second walk is exactly as it was for Walk One, the junction of School Lane and Railway Road, a start which allows you to proceed from the village to the moors via the convenient slopes of Well Lane, at least initially. Be assured that your task on this second walk is a lighter one, not only because there are fewer farms – eight instead of 12 – but because you will be walking in open country, without the challenges or delights of the tree-cover, the branches and the undergrowth, and without (of course) the extra excitements of discovering or failing at first to discover the hidden ruins, concealed by leaves and moss as they are in the woods. All eight of the Central Group farms are easy to find.

So, cross the culverted Goit as you did before, ignore Quarry Road, ignore Butterworth Brow (and its fine Brinscall Terrace) but tell yourself that you will be coming down it from the moors in two or three hours' time. Meanwhile walk up Well Lane, counting the "sleeping policemen" as you go, and after about 200m and at the fourth "sleeping policeman" turn sharp left off the tarmac surface, almost doubling back on yourself.

Cocker's Folly: the trees, the farm ruins and the gateposts.

You are now on a damp, grassy track that is part of the zigzag system. A slight incline brings you after 30m to a stile which you may briefly have visited on your previous walk. Over this you will now see on your right a crumbled field wall that keeps parallel, more or less, to the gently rising track. Very soon, having crossed the stile, you will see on your left a pair of tall stone gateposts (with hinge-pins) that lead you into the **Greenlands** farm yard and to the 20m long pile of stones that used to house all 15 of the farm's inhabitants. The ruins are now home to a mixed family of hawthorns, birches and sycamores. As you look at the former house you will see, between it and the track, the former barn, a separate square structure. Close to the house and barn are three more gateposts. And now you have visited your first farm of the day. (See map on page 124.)

Looking back at the hillside you will notice that the space between the rising field walls (which now run on each side of the track) is gradually widening. The track itself is also becoming partially blocked by flourishing clumps of rushes and then, higher up, by banks of gorse. To avoid these you might find it temporarily easier to walk in the edge of the sheep field on the lower or western side of the wall to the left of the track as you climb up to another pair of obvious gateposts (with hinge-pins). Beyond these another track can be seen ahead of you coming up from Butterworth Brow. When the two tracks meet, do not carry straight on as if towards the nearby quarry. Now is the time to make another zigzag, turning sharp right, passing an unevenly matched pair of gateposts and continuing uphill but avoiding more gorse bushes as you make for the three trees of **Cocker's Folly**.

Turning soon to the left, you will find yourself entering the short section of parallel field walls that you first saw on your early visit to the Oak Tree Inn when you were looking across to the Brinscall hillsides. At the end of this short section you will stand next to the three large trees – two sycamores and one ash – and a scattering of smaller types, mainly rowan, elder and hawthorn. You will also see two large single gateposts (with hinge-pins) and a pair of small gateposts for pedestrian use that led into the garden on the west side of the **Cocker's Folly** house. At your feet are some mighty chunks of fallen stone that seem to be the remains of an arched lintel over a barn door.

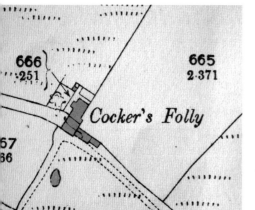

The ground plans, the shape and extent of the **Cocker's Folly** house and barn, are clearly obvious. [*There must have been plenty of room for the seven residents of 1891, the Counsells and the proud 84-year-old Ann Pilkington.*] To the west you have, as they had, extensive views over Brinscall village and the country beyond, to the distant centre of Preston, the mouth of the River Ribble, the Irish Sea coast and, in other directions, the far-off hills and mountains. Nearer at hand, to the east of the barn, is yet another pair of large gateposts (with yet more hinge-pins) in a long wall that continues, eventually, all the way to **Ratten Clough**. You might also notice that one of the two small gateposts at the entrance to the garden is a re-used ancient slot-and-pole one, as is another small post at the northern end of the former house. (Waste not

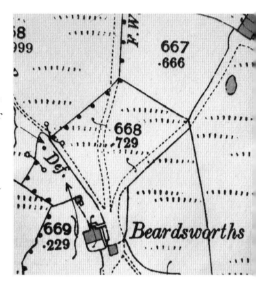

want not!) A short distance to the south of the farm is a small group of rather disturbed young rowans (formerly protected by fencing) next to the pond. [*On the trunk of the larger of the two sycamores are now affixed small memorial plaques recording the passing of Sid Edwards and Jacob Jackson, two gentlemen of Brinscall. The moors, the farms and their sentinel-like trees do have a special significance for many in the area.*]

Having completed your visit to the second farm of the day you should now walk in a generally south to south-westerly direction from **Cocker's Folly**, passing the pond and the rowans and finding a former cart track (obviously used more recently by farm tractors) with fairly frequent foundation stones indicating its originally intended use by horse-drawn carts and machinery. The track is marked on an 1848 map. It leads you in little more than 100m to the third farm, **Beardsworth's**.

The site of **Beardsworth's** is, as usual, indicated by the presence of a small group of trees – in this case mainly medium-sized hawthorns and elders. The track you have been following winds to the left just where you can begin to see, below you and at right angles to the track, the foundations of the main house, a modest rectangle of three main 'bays' from which elder trees currently sprout. A little way to the west are the remains of a barn, and to the east there has also been another separate structure of a barn or outhouse type. Near that building is one remaining hinge-pin-bearing gatepost. Beyond it, at the edge of a slightly higher field, is another pair of stone posts, while in the middle of a nearby lower field wall two old posts survive even though the original gateway between them has at some distant time been roughly infilled to make a continuous wall. At the north west corner of the house there was an interestingly curved retaining wall guarding a small flight of steps that led down from the track to the main house doorway. [*As a whole, **Beardsworth's** was clearly a relatively small set of buildings even for the eight Easthams of 1891, let alone the 10 Cottons of 1881.*]

Climbing back from the ruins up to the track you can now follow this as it winds back to the right on its leisurely way to Edge Gate Lane. Halfway there you will see

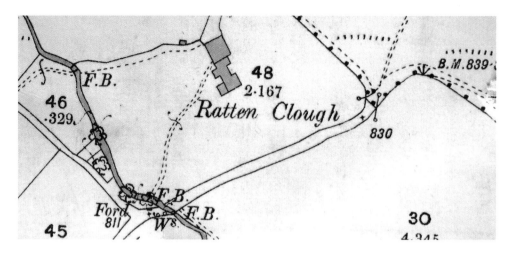

on your left a relatively new wooden post that bears four bright yellow arrow-markers, reminding you that this is a public footpath, and showing you that you could, if you wanted to, make a beeline for **Ratten Clough** from this point. But of course you do not want to do that. You would rather visit **Whittle's** on your way to **Ratten Clough**, I am sure, and that means continuing to stroll down the track till it meets Edge Gate Lane. It does that quite soon, at a seven-barred metal gate with a convenient wooden stile for you to climb over. You have now visited three farms and in rather less than an hour, I am supposing.

You have joined Edge Gate Lane at a point just a little higher than **Ripping** and a little below the small bridge (rebuilt in 2008) by which the Hatch Brook passes underneath the lane on its way to the waterfall. Turn to your left from the stile and begin to walk uphill in a south-easterly direction, right up, eventually, to the top of the lane. You will firstly cross over the Hatch Brook, then see on your right the two gateposts at the end of the short track from **Hatch Place** and then, also on your right, the two gateposts next to the stile that you climbed over on your first walk through the woods. From this stile you have already covered the next 100m of Edge Gate Lane when you were walking up to the **White Hall** site, with its car (or lorry) park. You have therefore just passed again the two old gateposts on the left-hand side of the lane before you reached **White Hall**. You now continue to walk uphill, not climbing over the stile which (by corner-cutting) leads directly to **Ratten Clough**, but noticing two more pairs of gateposts (impressively rugged) on your left before you finally reach the top of the road. Here there is a metal six-barred gate supported by a pair of cast-iron gateposts and by its side a "kissing gate" leading on to the high moor and ultimately (but not today) to Great Hill.

Pausing at the gate without so far going through it, you now have a full view of the lengthy rectangular foundation ruins of **Whittle's** with its prominent single sycamore and, near the tree, the ruins of a subordinate structure (a storage and lavatory block?). The photograph confirms what the ruins suggest, that **Whittle's** had a sizeable two-bay domestic section and beyond that an attached double-bay barn. [*It was a reasonably spacious dwelling even for the 11 members of the Briers family who lived there in 1851, and certainly for the five Shorrocks people of 1881 and the four who were still there in 1891.*] Now go through the adjacent "kissing gate" and inspect the ruins thoroughly while at the same time – as always – watching carefully where you place your feet (on account of occasional loose stones). The view to the west and north is spectacular and far-reaching. (See map on page 127.)

So fine and wide a view as that from **Whittle's** does deserve at least several minutes' attention and enjoyment before you walk on. No wonder the farm was sometimes referred to as 'Whittle's Heights'. Nevertheless with four farms so far visited there are still four more waiting to be seen on this second day – and some lengthy sections of walking between them. Therefore, go back through the "kissing gate" and look forward to making the acquaintance of **Ratten Clough** (spelt 'Ratencluff' by a census enumerator). From the top of Edge Gate Lane, cross the wooden stile (next to another seven-barred metal gate) and begin to follow **Ratten Clough's** own special track which runs downhill slightly (towards the upper Hatch Brook valley) and in a north-easterly direction. It is enclosed on each side by walls which, here and there, retain some of their original height. Soon after you have set foot on the track, however, your attention will almost certainly be captured by a strange grassy mound just beyond the wall on your right. You will probably need to know what this is before you can continue.

[*It is no prehistoric burial mound, you might be relieved to find. It is not at all ancient, and is most certainly rather modern. If you had been here 40 years ago you would have recognised it right away. You would have known it immediately as a surviving Second World War semi-underground air-raid shelter, with brick walls largely turf-covered and concrete steps leading down into its dark interior. Why should the War Department provide such a shelter in the middle of the moors for a few remaining farmers at* **Ratten Clough** *and possibly at* **Solomon's Temple** *– or for Brinscall village-dwellers caught out during a moonlit moorland stroll? The answer is at once simple and intriguing.*

Those needing a bomb-proof shelter up here in the 1940s were not locals but military personnel who had two clear duties. Firstly they were look-out men, observers watching over a wide area of West Lancashire whose responsibility it was to report a possible landing of enemy paratroops. Secondly they were decoys whose regular job it was to light the flares, the runway landing beacons, which might persuade the Luftwaffe to drop their night-raid bombs harmlessly on a make-believe airfield in the hills rather than on the real targets, the vast Royal Ordnance factory at Euxton and the hidden storage facilities at Heapey by the Chorley-Brinscall-Blackburn railway line.

A young Vera Mayor with a grazing sheep at Ratten Clough.

A more mature Vera Mayor heaving a sheep out of a snowdrift at Ratten Clough.

The smooth-mound outline of the former shelter with its infilled underground room and access steps is simply another eventual application of the sometimes quite wise Health and Safety approach to life. It may have taken over 30 years to get round to it, but there has not been any possibility of a falling-in of the roof once the shelter was largely demolished and its material remains were roughly landscaped in the 1970s. Nobody probably ever was, but nobody is ever going to be buried alive there now. For the potentially adventurous, I think it is still possible to work out where the mock-up landing lights were positioned in the neighbouring fields, however.]

But it is high time to move on swiftly down the track to **Ratten Clough**. If you do so you will soon be arriving at a bridge over the infant Hatch Brook and also at two stiles on your left, the second of which leads you on to the short, formerly cobbled path (and its collapsed field wall) to the waiting house remains and the barn. Still stirred, however, by the unexpected presence of the air-raid shelter it is possible that you will just momentarily have been distracted while crossing the Hatch Brook by the realisation that there had been a Second World War strengthening in concrete of the little bridge so that it could take heavier weights than a flock of sheep or a farm cart and horse. There had also been a constructing of a brick-and-drainpipe wall to control water flow and prevent flooding over the bridge on some desperately dark and stormy Second World War night. This momentary distraction is forgivable and is indeed a sign of alertness to surroundings and developing powers of observation and interpretation. Yet really, of course, the very buildings of **Ratten Clough** can provide an even better test of an inquiring mind and a capacity to make good sense of what one is looking at. There is a lot to be said about **Ratten Clough**, once you look closely at its walls, the upright and the fallen.

In the first place, although the whole of the 'front' (and 'end') walls of both the cottages have collapsed and a good deal of their stonework has been removed, this is still much the most complete of all the 48 farms for you to explore. To work out now the chronological sequence of its construction I advise you, once you have followed the access path and reached the obvious south 'front' of the building, to walk round to the north side where most of the 'rear' walls survive and tell a clear story via the quality of their stonework. Then, having drawn some conclusions, continue to walk along the north side and work out the history of the barn. Go to the west gable end of the barn and realise how it has been doubled in size. Finally, continue round to the south side of the barn and look in through the main doorway. By now you have seen almost all the evidence you need. (Incidentally but significantly, your circuit of the buildings has shown you that they – and you, therefore – are protected from damage these days by the presence of a firmly erected barbed wire fence running right round, keeping buildings and persons appropriately apart. Respect the fence, and take care meanwhile not to fall over any loose stones in front of the houses.)

Peter Mayor with sheep, older ones shorn, younger ones not shorn, at Ratten Clough in the 1930s.

So, what have you concluded about the sequence of construction? Plainly, the original eighteenth-century barn was the same length as the present one but was only half its width. The former outer (north) wall now runs down the middle of the present barn, and under the main cross beams of the fine late-Victorian machine planed steel tied roof timbers. The outer stonework of the present west gable wall also shows you where the new stones abutted the old (between the two blocked doors). Once you realise this, you can then work out (you can see it if you look carefully) the lower roofline of the original gable with its old window which was high up near the centre.

Next, you can see that the original **Ratten Clough** was very like **Coppice Stile** – a two-bay length barn with a small single-bay domestic end, that is a tiny one-up, one-down house about 6m square. You can see that the house was the same width as the first barn. Slots high in the east barn wall for the main roof beams of the house tell you this. The outer stonework on the north side of that original one-up, one-down house shows it was 6m square or thereabouts. The quality of the north side stonework is more refined and certainly quite different from its immediate neighbour's – the first extension or second-bay cottage. To prove the case beyond doubt there are good quoins on what was once its outer north-east corner – that is quoins (corner stones) now in the middle of what eventually became a much longer outer wall. And when you look from the front of the building at the quality of the partly broken-down dividing wall (as it is now) between the first cottage and the extension cottage, that wall clearly was originally an outer eastern-end wall – both in thickness (i.e. double thickness) and in quality of layering of carefully shaped stone.

Next, you can see that the extension cottage is obviously of the same dimensions as the original cottage. It has a roofline of the same height. It had two small windows downstairs and one upstairs in the south-facing wall (as shown in a convenient – and rare – photograph). As you can now see while standing next to the ruin, it had on the north side one quite long mullioned ground floor casement window (most of it having been filled in later). The original cottage by, say, the early nineteenth century perhaps, had gained a porch on the south side, but with an entrance doorway unusually facing at right angles to the normal arrangement – facing west in this case, that is, rather than south.

So much for the first extension cottage. What is at least as fascinating, however, is the examining and analysing of the second and final extension cottage, the third bay, as it became, of a domestic end which was now of greater length than the barn. It is at first difficult to determine even the approximate date of that final extension. Help is at hand, however, and of more than one type. Firstly, the final extension was similar

The double-width west gable wall of Ratten Clough's barn in 2010.

Ben (left) and Harold Mayor at Ratten Clough, circa 1930.

in length to its predecessors but it was a good deal wider (and seems to have been two-up, two-down), had a distinctly higher roof-ridge line and had no sign of mullion casement windows. Secondly, the neatly squared-off corner edges of the quoins on its porch (some of which still survive in situ) suggest that it is very much of the later Victorian period and therefore likely to be contemporary with the grand doubling in size of the barn. (Its porch also had the doorway in the normal place.) Thirdly, and crucially, on an Ordnance Survey map of 1848 there is no sign of that final extension nor of the doubling in size of the barn. Both these changes had happened, however, by the time that the new Ordnance Survey map appeared in 1894.

So, we can be fairly sure that what is still by far the largest and most complete set of ruins on Brinscall Moors, was not finally completed until the 1870s, say, having been enlarging gradually from 1700 onwards. **Ratten Clough** was abandoned in 1960. It therefore lasted in its final form for rather less than 100 years – very like the Brinscall railway, as it happens. What is encouraging and exciting for walkers and historians is to realise how much one can work out just by looking at a building. 'Reading a building' is almost as easy as reading a book if you train yourself to notice everything that could possibly be helpful. Having an occasional old photograph or an occasional old Ordnance Survey map is a welcome bonus, of course, just to support other evidence and, one hopes, confirm one's intelligent hypotheses.

With **Ratten Clough's** mysteries fairly resolved so far as may be, what else might merit a last thought and a last look round before tearing oneself away and heading for the sixth farm of the day, **Solomon's Temple,** with its own special problems of interpretation? It is true that I find pleasantly aesthetically satisfying the rounded corners of the north-east end of **Ratten Clough's** enlarged barn; but while walking once more right round the set of buildings, I would also recommend a quick inspection of the probable sheep-dip trough (what else can it be?) near the barn's western gable and then, of course, of the loo building. (All it needs is a new wooden seat and a new roof – and a lockable door and an underseat tub …) Then, in addition to the well-known sycamore that stands next to the barn, there is that special line (unusual on the moors) of mature trees (five large sycamores and one smaller one, plus a dozen pleasant hawthorns) that follow the course of the Hatch Brook and provide a soft and welcoming fullness in summer to the surrounding edges of the fields.

The route away from **Ratten Clough's** buildings and up to **Solomon's Temple** takes you at first back down the path to the concrete bridge and on to a continuation of the track coming down from **Whittle's.** (Barbed wire fencing for the containment of sheep as well as walkers restricts short cuts.) [*In any case, as you leave the buildings you might give a thought to those who have lived here over the centuries, including the Bennetts, the Catlows (with Mary Beattock) and the Shorrocks, plus the Mayors who were here while the concrete bridge, the flood-control brick wall and the air-raid shelter were constructed and utilised during the Second World War.*] Having reached the track and the bridge, do turn left up the now gently rising track instead of going ahead over the stile by the flood-control and into the field beyond. For a few remarkable metres as you walk in a north-easterly direction you will have the rare pleasure of walking on a track between field walls that still retain their full (and impressive) height. You might well notice how almost completely these 6ft high walls block the force of the wind coming to you, otherwise, from the east or from the north-west. They briefly provide quite a shelter if you are walking in a winter's half-gale. Efficient barriers indeed. In their glory days they stood at their full height for long miles across the hillsides and moors before at last beginning in recent times to collapse or at some points to be pulled down.

Enjoy this walking between the walls, then, but after about 100m from the Hatch bridge, with walls by that stage much diminished, turn smartly at 90 degrees to the right into the fields between **Ratten Clough** and **Solomon's Temple.** Walking now in a south-easterly direction and breasting a slight rise in the field you will soon see your next farm ruins (the sixth of the walk) clearly ahead of you about 150m away. An abandoned (it has been there for at least 25 years) and slowly rusting piece of agricultural equipment (originally a muck-spreader, looking rather like a junior dinosaur when seen at a distance) tells you that you are going the right way. To reach

Ratten Clough in 2010: the barn, the sycamore tree and the remains of the cottages. The loo block is on the left.

The impressive ruins of Solomon's Temple.

the ruins you need to walk the 150m as if making a beeline for the distant (one and a half miles distant) curved dome of Great Hill. It is usual to be able to see the summit, 1249ft (381m) high as it is, on most days in the year.

Solomon's Temple is well worth the 'reading'. Obviously, as the variety of stonework quality tells you, it was originally a medium size longhouse, but with, by the early nineteenth century, a projecting square extension (a dairy?) at the north-east corner of the domestic (northern) end. It had a comparatively small barn at the southern end of the main block. It also had a well at the south-east corner of the farmyard and an outside lavatory block to the west of the farmyard. Then, in the second half of the nineteenth century, a considerable enlargement of the barn happened, with additions to both length and width. Thereafter, alongside part of the domestic end, a two-windowed, large, probably lean-to-roofed room was added, opposite which a considerable free-standing block was built on the east side of the farmyard (whose surviving quoins deserve attention). Overall, it was eventually one of the largest of the 48 farms, and its present ruins are second only to **Ratten Clough's** in extent and in height of some of the surviving walls.

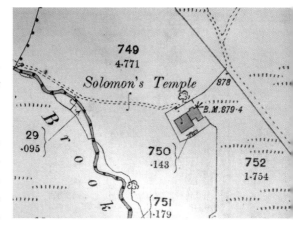

[*There is no evidence at all that* **Solomon's Temple** *has ever been even a part-time ecclesiastical or sacred structure, though occasional visitors to the area seem to want to hope so. It manifestly has always been, from the early eighteenth century until its twentieth-century abandonment, a busy working farm. The far more reasonable and likely explanation for the 'Solomon' designation is that one of its early tenants had the name of the tenth century BC Israelite king at a time when Old Testament names – Abram, Eli, Isaiah and the rest – were fairly popular and certainly more common than they are now. And of course any even half-worthy building endeavour was likely to be gently mocked by being compared to a famous and grand temple. (Members of eighteenth- and nineteenth-century farming communities did have a sense of humour too.)*

There is a similar but different background to another Solomon's Temple near Buxton in Derbyshire where a farmer and landowner, Solomon Mycock, provided work for unemployed labourers in the early nineteenth century by persuading them to build a folly – a prominent stone tower – on a Bronze Age site at 1,440ft in the Peak District. His tower was rebuilt when it began to collapse in 1896 and was restored again in 1988.]

What we particularly owe to the Shorrock tenants and to their predecessors at 'our' **Solomon's Temple** and to their successors too – the Rossalls and the Isles – is the efficient system of drainage ditches that make the level fields up here so firm and dry in almost any weather. This applies to the **Solomon's Temple** fields and also to the neighbouring fields of **New Temple**, our next farm 180m away to the south east.

On the way as we now walk from one 'Temple' to the other, the first feature to notice is the ditch next to the line of hawthorns (a former hedge) which goes off directly to the south and then turns again south-westwards to lead any surface waters safely down to the Hatch Brook. The next feature is the number of surviving gateposts which remain more or less upright in this area although the field walls connecting them have mainly collapsed. In addition to two single posts close to **Solomon's Temple** buildings, there are no fewer than four pairs that still stand where field gates used to be. At least one of those pairs, just north of the **New Temple** ruins, leans dangerously (or provocatively), each towards the other, as if endlessly seeking a stony embrace. (On your third walk you will find a similarly mutually attracted pair – although one is keener than the other – at the start of the short track to **Fir Farm**. One might be put in mind of the poet John Keats and figures on a Grecian urn.) More prosaically it has to be said that just over 100m along your short journey to the **New Temple** ruins you will find a pair of posts that are now permanently at rest; at least they have assumed a decidedly recumbent posture. You will find another pair in this condition just next to the former **New Temple** house when you reach it.

The third feature to notice in the area is that **New Temple** still has its trademark couple of tall sycamores to lure you on. To reach them you will have to climb a stile where a post and wire fence has replaced a former field wall. With the 180m (from Temple to Temple) now completed and the stile climbed, you can stand next to, and walk round, your seventh farm of the day. It does justify attention, analysis and assessment, but the intellectual challenge is minimal compared to the other farms you have just visited. **New Temple** is reduced to the 'fallen heaps of stone' condition but its foundation lines and four separate bay sections are easy to see. Unlike some, it never grew beyond its original longhouse dimensions except in so far as it gained two modest extensions, one at each end. These might have been a porch and a lean-to shed (or two porches or two sheds) and I confess that I cannot tell which might have been which. It was a dry and level site, however, and there is still one surviving (and upright) small gatepost where the wall, formerly coming up from the Hatch Brook, used to enclose the farmyard or vegetable patch next to the house.

The quality of the turf almost obliges you to stroll across these high but well-mannered fields east of **New Temple**. If you do stray a little further towards the south-east you will find that you eventually come to the end of the eighteenth-century enclosure

The tree and ruins of New Temple with one grazing sheep. Drainage ditches on the distant Old Man's Hill.

where fields meet rough moors, where there is a clear boundary between sheep-cropped turf and the high tussocky wasteland beyond. Where the boundary runs between them there has been a good deal of human digging and shaping of the earth. The sheep fields are protected by high banks and hedges and here, remarkably, there is almost a meeting of two streams which have in fact been firmly kept apart, which remain separate and flow eventually in quite different directions: north-westwards towards the Goit in the case of the Hatch and north-eastwards to the Rake reservoir in the case of the 'Rushy' Brook.

The 'Rushy' reminds us that it is time to visit our eighth and final farm for the day – **Botany Bay**, a farm watered by this same Rushy Brook while on its way, ultimately, to **Pope's**, **Dale Fold**, **Snape's** and **Twist Moor House**. So now we return to **New Temple**, cross the stile and make our way back to **Solomon's Temple** where there is a footpath sign suggesting that we turn right and go firmly to the north. This we do, more or less.

You have two main options as to precise route, however, given that there is no continuously marked path on the ground (or through the long grass). You can either follow the OS map and walk in a north-north-easterly direction for about 200m until

The ruins of Botany Bay in 2010, with the solitary tree.

you reach a straight boundary wall coming in from **Ratten Clough**, and then follow that wall for about 100m north-eastwards until you can see your target a little way along a track to your right. Your target, an unmistakable one, is the lone **Botany Bay** beech tree. On an alternative (and independent) route, you can walk immediately north-eastwards from **Solomon's Temple**, crossing the marginally higher land that was about 200m away (there are some hollows there too), and aiming just to the left of the distant Pendle Hill's summit, if you have a clear day. From the marginally higher land you can make your own way to the **Botany Bay** beech tree which will soon be in view. Leave the 'Rushy' Brook and some sections of very Victorian boundary wall well to your right.

There is nothing like the **Botany Bay** beech tree in these particular surroundings. It certainly tells you that you are near to where the farm buildings were. It also tells you very plainly what the prevailing wind direction is. On future walks in the Twist Moor area (looking from near **Scott Hall**, say) you will certainly recognise it, far away and over there, a solitary reminder of **Botany Bay's** distant presence.

Near to the tree you will find the former farm drive, now rather covered by grass and rushes except where these have recently been scraped away (by machine) and some of the cobbled surface has been exposed. Briefly follow the drive slightly downhill and between the two flat-sided gateposts and pause to look at the remains of the farm buildings next to you. There is an unusual ground-plan: two major 'rooms', two times two, side by side, the northern rooms having been built later and having single-storeyed lean-to roofs next to the double-storeyed and earlier southern rooms. There seems to have been a small extension at the western end.

There are some sizeable and splendidly decorative quoins at the eastern corners of the buildings, where the walls still stand up to 5ft (a metre and a half almost) high. There is one small blocked doorway at the eastern end. Near that there are two gateposts of very different style and age, the one from the other. There was at least one separate outbuilding.

Photographs suggest that there were occasionally some very jolly gatherings of quite large numbers of farming folk at **Botany Bay** (when it was acquiring its '**Summer House**' designation?) in the later years of the nineteenth century. It is also apparent that gatherings – at least of grouse-shooting parties – continued to be seen there even after the entire upper storey of the house had been removed. The clumsily re-roofed version was not an especially pretty sight. But **Botany Bay** was, and is, one of the most remotely sited of all the 48 farms. Often, as you will have seen on these walks, there was only 100m or so between one farm and another.

However, your day's searchings are now completed. You may say 'farewell' to the eight farms of the day, and there is just the matter of the return to the School Lane-Railway Road junction. It will be more than a mile's walk but the whole of it, apart from the first 50m or so, will be on the level or downhill. You can hardly get lost, but there is variety and there are features of interest all the way. First of all there is a brisk moorland walk of about three quarters of a mile down to the public road near Norcross Farm. At the start, what had once been a much-used roadway – certainly a firmly surfaced and very clear cart-track – has in recent years acquired a goodly number of clumps of grass and rushes in the immediate vicinity of the farm. Nevertheless, rising slightly past and to the left (or south) of the lone beech tree and aiming in a north-westerly direction, you will soon find that you are following

Members of the Robinson family at Botany Bay, circa 1930.

a regular track which, like some deeply rural country lane (except that you are high on the hills here) does just happen to have grass in the centre. You are on your way over this high moor to Twist Moor Lane and Butterworth Brow, eventually passing Ramsden's Farm cottages and Withnell Villa, and actually being quite close (on your left) to the boundary fence and warning notices of the otherwise fairly well-hidden Brinscall Quarry.

After the first half mile or less you will find your grass-in-the-middle cart track now has a more obvious surface with a mixture of old cobblestones (the small, rounded type), flat lumps of rock (some of this placed there, some of it just the exposed and naked sub-stratum) and some fairly recent deposits of broken-up old tarmac (good for grip). The fine view ahead has now opened up, with Withnell's Bury Lane and St. Paul's church spire in the near distance, and then the familiar vista with Hoghton Tower's wooded hill-top, the centre of Preston, the sea coast, the Bleasdale Fells …

Just before you reach the only stile you have had to climb since leaving **New Temple**, you will see a pleasing feature on your right, a significant copse (fenced-off like a former tree nursery) of mature beech trees looking rather less tormented than the single example up at **Botany Bay**. After climbing the stile you will next see, on your right, Ramsden's, now in its row-of-cottages form, and on your left Withnell Villa, sitting on top of the original and 1888-demolished **Richmond's**.

A further 60m down the moorland track you will find yourself at last meeting a public highway. This is that Butterworth Brow or Twist Moor Lane that was (before Railway Road existed) the main continuation of School Lane. The two roads, Butterworth Brow and Twist Moor Lane, were, before 1801, part of the only main route from Chorley to Bolton if you did not go by way of Horwich but used the Belmont pre-turnpike roads. If you now cross the road and look down the little path ahead of you through the trees you will see Norcross, the newly restored former farm and barn, sitting below you on its own brow. [*Do not, however, go down the little path, for that was the path that the Vachre family from Dorset must have used on their way to work at Withnell Mill.*] In other words, you have, probably without knowing it, almost arrived at the site of **Whave Gate**. It is part of Walk Number Four, the Twist Moor Group, so you will certainly be visiting this spot again in due course.

For now, however, please do turn left, away from the entrance to the little path, and begin to walk southwards towards Butterworth Brow – for that is the way to the day's finishing point. When you have walked for about 30m, you might in passing care to realise that it is just here, on your right, hidden now not only under trees but also under a thicket of saplings, bracken and brambles, that the modest heap of **Whave Gate's** longhouse ruins can be found. They are far more easily seen in winter or spring than in summer or autumn, just as the **New Ground** ruins are; but I would in any case recommend leaving them for the Number Four Walk, just noting now for future purposes their position in relation to Norcross Farm, and seriously promising to explore them as part of a Twist Moor survey.

So, walk on, past the two cottages of Church View (which used indeed to have a view of St. Paul's church – built 1841 – before the trees grew) and then start looking to your left for the first sight of the great depths and breadths of Brinscall Quarry. There is a special reason for this. You might actually be standing on air at the moment.

Once the main railway was built along the valley to your right, a remarkable piece of engineering ingenuity allowed loads of stone from the quarry to pass through a tunnel beneath the Butterworth Brow road (as I say, possibly just where you are now standing) and to be conveyed to Brinscall Station's marshalling yards by means of a special bridge ('The Gantry') over Railway Road. Parts of this system are still visible, though the bridge itself has long gone. No doubt several former residents of our moorland farms were employed in this quarry and in the sending of stone by this means across Railway Road for despatch by freight train.

The gantry over Railway Road connecting the Brinscall Quarry to the railway marshalling yard, circa 1930.

Continuing your walk, and passing the main entrance to the quarry (with no sign of the mid-air ghostly **Richmond's**), you have just two further structures to notice before you complete your stroll down to the School Lane-Railway Road junction. The first is another pair of smart cottages on your left, one of which became the eventual home of Fred Mayor, **Ratten Clough's** last tenant. The second, while you have just perhaps been glancing up the steep fields to the **Greenlands** trees where the day's visits to farms began, is the smoothly designed and rebuilt version of Crosby's which appears on your right and is known as Butterworth Barn.

And so to your bus or your car after a walk of three or four hours, probably – or only two hours if you were rushing. Your next walk, your visits to the nine farms of the Heapey/Great Hill group, will require a different starting point. Suitable parking is available at or near the White Coppice cricket ground. Please park courteously. There is, as you will probably know, no public bus service to White Coppice.

Sharrock's by the Goit, at the foot
of the White Coppice hillside.

The Heapey/Great Hill Group (9 Farms)

Start and Finish: White Coppice, the Cricket Ground.

Distance: Up to 5.5 miles.

Time: Up to 5 hrs. – or longer if you decide to linger on Great Hill. Could be completed in 3 hrs. if determined.

Character: A glorious moorland hike, with interesting farm buildings, splendid wide views but more intimate woodland and valley sections as well.

WELCOME TO WHITE COPPICE and the start of a fine moorland walk up to the highest of all 48 of our farms – **Great Hill Farm** – and then gradually down over the broad open space of Heapey Moor, returning finally to White Coppice via the quiet charm of the Goit and its valley.

For the most part your progress will be along clear, firm paths with only minor wetter sections. But three farms in the middle of Heapey Moor, with excellent foundations and sections of walling well worth seeing, do require the following of precise to-and-from routes if tiring clamberings over mighty tussocks and the involuntary finding of old watercourses are to be avoided. These three farms are **Heapey Moor Farm** itself, **Calico Hall** and **Sour Milk Hall**. Then, unless you enjoy gleeful galumphings downhill over more big tussocks, bilberry humps and substantial chunks of heather, I do recommend the route I offer you from **Sour Milk Hall** across and down to the beautiful but solitary **Fir Farm** site. My suggested route will not be shorter but will possibly be quicker and certainly easier.

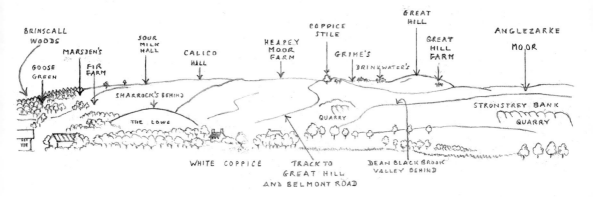

Looking east and north-east from Higher House Lane.

However, let us now make a start from the White Coppice cricket field. Having walked along the track round the southern edge of this, cross over the Goit bridge. Go through the kissing gates and then turn left, to the north, for a little way, noticing the broken former reservoir dam on your right (once holding back water for a long-demolished White Coppice textile factory) and avoiding some damp patches underfoot. Then start climbing the stony path (probably no need to sit on the stony seat) and take the direction to the east (to Belmont Road) at the Ramblers' Association sign. A fairly steep but really quite short section takes you past the former White Coppice quarry workings and then to an easier gradient (still climbing of course) up to the open moor. Occasional stops to admire the unfolding view behind you, or just to recover your breath, are quite in order.

Eventually you will arrive at a significant stone wall coming up from the Dean Black Brook valley on your right and crossing your path at a gateway before continuing firmly northwards to your left in the direction of Brinscall. Actually, if you look at the wall carefully you will see that this gateway facing you is not very old, and that a few metres to your right it is possible to make out the now-blocked previous gateway as referred to in the name 'Coppice Stile'.

Through the modern gateway, however, is your first farm of the day, **Coppice Stile House**. It is a typical heap of fallen stones at first sight, but after a quick walk round it (and over it) there you can find the clear outlines of a longhouse of three sections, one for the house at the west end and two for the barn and shippon: the whole structure about 17m long and 6m (at the most) wide. One main hawthorn tree and four wind-blown smaller ones perhaps offered some protection from westerly winds.

[*With copies of the* **Coppice Stile** *photographs in your hand for making comparisons, it is possible to stand by the 'new' gateway just 'inside' the wall and, looking carefully, to* *indulge in 'then and now' sensations, remembering that this is no artificial game and no fantasy but a being for a while in the exact spot where that entirely real father stood with his wheelbarrow full of peat, that mother raised her arm as she scattered food for her poultry, and that line of three well-behaved and carefully attired little girls stayed still for the camera. Just one of them watched the photographer. Ah well….. the mysteries of time and space. Their view of Great Hill itself, had the three young girls turned to look at it, could not have been very different 120 years ago from the view you have of it now as you raise your eyes from the ruins and begin to look up to where you will be in little more than an hour's time.*]

Four more farms to visit now, however, before you will reach that highest point of your day, and then four more on your way back to White Coppice. Your immediate way forward is at first the obvious one – to walk along the level track ahead of you with Great Hill as the eventual target. However, in order to enjoy a dry-shod and easy visit to your second farm, the splendidly but slightly awkwardly positioned and damply sited **Heapey Moor**, you need to be leaving your present track and turning to the left very soon. Here are precise instructions.

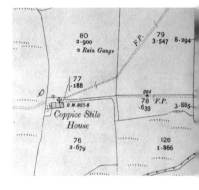

From **Coppice Stile** walk east along the track but notice, shortly, a first wall coming at right angles to meet you on your left. Continue your progress but look out for a second wall, quite soon, also coming on your left to meet you at right angles. Here, stop, leave the track to turn left in a northerly direction and walk next to and along the wall on its far (or east) side. You are walking along the edge of a former field and gradually gaining height. Next, your wall will meet (at right angles) what looks more like a banked-up (earth and stone) boundary line that is actually one side of a pair of mini-ramparts that enclosed (one on each side) the former main approach road coming up to **Heapey Moor Farm** from the White Coppice valley below. The road itself is no longer passable, but you can make good use of the raised bank (or mini-rampart). You should now step up on to it, turn right and walk single-file along it as it runs eastwards and straight towards the farm ruins that you will be able to see only a little distance away.

Once your mini-rampart comes to an end, you have the substantial ruins immediately in front of you, the great length of the house and barn, with a projecting terrace plus one detached structure. There is one small hawthorn and one remaining gatepost at the southern end. To the north-east there is a pond, with open water among the rushes. To the south-east there is an impressively large, rectangular well. The whole is a much more considerable establishment than was **Coppice Stile**. [*The Scamblers from the Lune Valley must have been quite delighted by it in the 1880s.*] There are five

Looking towards Great Hill from the ruins of Coppice Stile.

separate bays or sections. Some lengths of outer and interior walling retain a height well above the foundation level – at the south-east gable end, for example. It is well worth the detour from the **Coppice Stile-Great Hill** track.

For a farm site that did not initially have the benefit of an adjacent and naturally occurring stream it is remarkably well-watered, so to say. Original builders and early residents must have dug very effectively in the gentle slopes from Brown Hill in the east, capturing water-flows and leading them to the farm across what is now a generally very damp expanse of tussocky moorland to the west of the major Great Hill-Brinscall track. Do not attempt to cross that section of moorland unless the Brinscall area has been enjoying an extended spell of dry weather.

There is an additional feature in terms of water-capture in that, from the farm and running due north past the pond, there is a single artificial bank or mini-rampart which would be very useful if your immediate intention and destination was a dry-shod arrival in Brinscall rather than – as it is – a return to the **Coppice Stile– Great Hill** track and a discovering of the **Grime's**, **Drinkwater's** and **Great Hill** farms. If ever in future you do walk along that artificial bank running due north from the **Heapey Moor** farm you will find that there is a drainage channel running all the way along the eastern side of it, and also that it does, by design, after about 200m, make a junction with the main Great Hill-Brinscall track. We will return to this point along the track later when we are on our way to find **Calico Hall**.

For the moment we must now find our way from **Heapey Moor** down the grassy slopes towards **Grime's**, the third farm of the day, with its equally prominent ruins. It is the case that the mass of rushes and long grass immediately to the south of the **Heapey Moor** buildings suggests that there is a good deal of wetness in the land there too, as well as on the eastern side. Fortunately there is also a drainage ditch which, though it could benefit from a cleaning-out, does take surplus water reasonably efficiently southwards down eventually to the Dean Black Brook valley. To follow it as it curves slightly and then runs straight downhill, all you have to do is walk again for a little way in single file along the top of or very close to another raised bank which has been built up on the western side of the ditch. As you walk you will notice that

The remains of the south gable end of Heapey Moor farm.

Looking towards Great Hill from the ruins of Grime's.

this ditch quickly becomes a veritable little canyon (grassy rather than rocky) some 5m deep, with water audibly and occasionally even visibly tumbling eagerly down.

After, I hope, an easy downhill stroll through the grass you will soon meet the main track that you left a little way back when you took the diversion up to **Heapey Moor**. Now turn left on this track towards the east, cross over the carefully constructed drain which carries the outflow from your little canyon, and then accompany the wall on your right which is leading the track slightly downhill on to the **Grime's** buildings. As you look at the lie of the land hereabouts it is obvious that the builders of **Grime's**

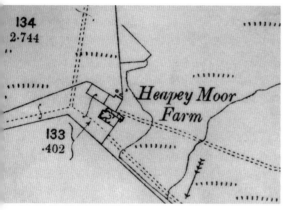

set the farm, high as it is, in what might be called if not a hollow at least something of a slight declivity. Try noticing this again when you have gone on, say, another 200m beyond the farm ruins, and look back at the lie of the land. **Grime's** has got whatever element of shelter from winds it might be possible to enjoy on this generally very exposed moor.

Meanwhile take a good look at the farm's interesting features. On the line of the field wall you have been accompanying there is one single happily surviving gatepost in front of the farm, guarding the entrance to its yard at a point where a field wall from the north would have come down to meet it. Near the top of the post on its western side two quite deep holes had been hollowed out, the lower deeper than the upper. Can we work out their purpose? There are no hinge-pins on the post. Then, considering the ruins of the main building, we have another longhouse of the **Heapey Moor** kind. There are, again, five separate bays or sections, each of the usual five-plus metres width. Parts of the lower walls survive, with the usual carefully laid courses. Close to but quite separate from the south-east corner was a detached building of a slightly larger size than **Heapey Moor's**. One can imagine that on a warm, sunny day in summer it would have been quite pleasant to sit next to the long south side of the main building, overlooking the valley and the far hillside up to Round Loaf's prehistoric mound and beyond – if anybody ever had time or excuse to sit, that is. It would have been a decent place for shearing sheep, anyway.

When we leave **Grime's**, our third farm of the walk, to move further east, we will very soon be walking uphill, not especially steeply but enough not to mind pausing and turning round to assess the lie of the land around **Grime's** farm as I suggested earlier. This will also be, for much but not all of the year, an occasionally muddy uphill progress, but one can invent one's own diversionary routes. The immediate

Before shearing
– Harold Mayor
and sheep at
Drinkwater's.

After shearing
– Harold Mayor
and sheep at
Drinkwater's.

target is the point where a field wall comes up from the right to join your path at the well-known junction where another Ramblers' Association sign announces that Brinscall lies to the left and the Belmont Road to the right. We will take the road to the right. This junction is also the point where if you are veering to the right you leave Heapey and enter Wheelton. (That is significant information for those for whom it is significant.)

Your way forward now is, for a while, a level one or even briefly, and slightly, downhill – where a little surface water sometimes gathers. Basically, however, you have before you a path with (for the most part) a good, firm cobbled (small cobbles) surface that takes you past the beech and fir plantation on your right, and up to and well

The ruins of Drinkwater's in 2010.

beyond **Drinkwater's**. **Drinkwater's** (the fourth farm on your walk) announces itself by presenting a row of four trees up on your left and a row of five trees on your right along the edge of the terrace. It also welcomes you by inviting/obliging you to walk on to the yard and terrace by passing between two sturdy gateposts where the left-hand post still bears an attached metal catch waiting for the closing (with a 'click') of the gate. Alas, no gate survives. You will see the spring water in the well on your right, however, if you look over the terrace edge at the appropriate point (near to the 'Joe's Cup' sign).

Drinkwater's as a building has clear signs of modification and enlargement. There was originally a house of two bays (each bay about 6m wide by 3m long) and a barn about 6m wide by 9m long. The house seems to have had a south-facing porch. Then the barn was much enlarged by the building of wide new (lean-to?) additions on the north and east sides. Finally a cottage was added on to the west end of the house, supplying two additional rooms, each of 3m by 3m, on both the upper and ground floors. It is interesting to see that no attempt was made to key the outer front wall of the cottage into the front wall of the house by integrating the stonework. Instead the two sections simply abutted, and such gap between them as might develop was concealed by a line of cement or common mortar. As a solution it seems to have worked. In any case one can clearly see the division between the house lived in in 1881 by the Bibby family and the cottage lived in (after they had left the house) by the Jacksons. Did they do all the building work for themselves?

Without a final answer to this question, you should now leave **Drinkwater's** through the eastern gateway with a single upright gatepost (with attached metal catch) on your left and a decidedly recumbent gatepost lying nearby on your right. It is now probably an hour and a half since you left White Coppice. You have a walk of probably no more

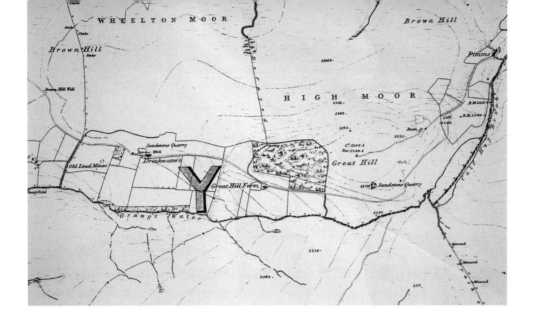

than 10 minutes on the track up the gradual slopes of Great Hill before you can see and get to know the marvellously sited ruins of **Great Hill Farm**, your fifth farm of the day. So, rise with the track and with a wall alongside you on your right. Notice another wall coming up from the valley on your right and then, shortly afterwards, further walls joining from both right and left. Very soon after that, a fine path of sheep-cropped grass leaves the cobbled track and descends to the right towards the farm which is now appearing in the valley a little way below. The path's smoothness is irresistibly attractive. So allow the main track to continue its own upward journey over a stile towards the still-300m distant summit of Great Hill (to be visited later if you wish!). Enjoy the smooth grass path and the downhill stroll towards the group of trees and the low walls of barn and house that await your attention.

If you did not have a refreshing drink and bite in the shelter of **Drinkwater's** then surely this is the place for a picnic. Here is a grand outward view to the south and west but also a deep inner sense of being in a very human habitation, in a wholly reassuring spot where for centuries people made a home and found comfort and security in what had once been a wilderness. Look carefully around the barn and, at right angles to it, the house, with projecting porch and at least one outhouse.

[*Ann Pilkington, aged 84 and living at* **Cocker's Folly** *in 1891, had been a 43-year-old farmer's wife here, at* **Great Hill**, *when the 1851 census returns were completed. She had still been here as a mother, a widow and a "retired farmer" in 1881. Her memories of this place must have been long and full.*]

The barn we can now see is a separate oblong structure of about 10m by 5. The domestic block seems to have had four bays with an overall length of about 16m and with a width of 6m. At least two of these four bays must have been storage spaces for animals or hay. There are two groups of trees: one of a single sycamore and two hawthorns on the east side, and one of two sycamores and three hawthorns on the south side. The presence of rushes below the terrace suggests no shortage of water supply. It is in every sense uplifting to be here. This is not only your fifth farm of the day but easily the highest of all farms on Brinscall Moors.

After a short or a long lingering at the farm [*where seven people lived in 1851, seven in 1881 and six in 1891*], it is time to retrace your steps up the path to the point where you left the track from **Drinkwater's**, and there to make a decision. Of course you could turn to the west and make your way back downhill passing **Drinkwater's** and the plantation, glancing quickly at the curious row of lead-mine craters crossing the field on your left down to Dean Black Brook, and turning right (and back into Heapey) at the Ramblers' Association sign towards Brinscall. Or... you could take advantage of being almost on top of the world in these parts and turn to the east where you could quickly climb the stile and conquer Great Hill's 381m summit.

There are three bonuses to enjoy if you do this. Firstly, you really will be aware of having a completely all-round view – north, south, east and west – from this genuinely separate summit, giving you views not only to Winter Hill and beyond but also deep into Rossendale and East Lancashire, as well as towards all that you have previously been seeing to the west and the north. In particular you also have a view of just about the whole of our grand triangle of Brinscall Moors, the ancient and high wastelands in the foreground and the moorland slopes and edges where the 48 farms were once worked and occupied. Secondly, if you find that the summit is an extremely windy place, as it might well be, there is an excellent cross-shaped (in plan) stone shelter-wall, giving you at least one if not two calm quadrants in which

The ruins of the main house and barn section of Great Hill farm in 2010.

to find a temporary refuge (you can even sit down on stone seats behind this most effective wind-break structure). Thirdly, if you would like to see at close quarters not an extra ruined farm but at least the remains of an unexpected high-level barn, all you have to do is to continue eastwards past the summit for a further 100m plus, and there, suddenly, it is on your left, with the clear foundations of a barn of about 17 by 5m. Never a permanent habitation, of course, but I should not be surprised if in spring or

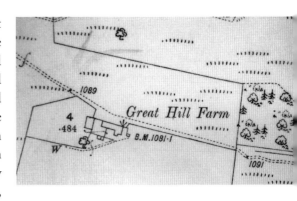

summer the occasional shepherd spent the occasional night up here. Quite a resource in a winter emergency too. From here, looking to the north-east, you will also have a view, far below, of **Pimm's Farm** – to be visited on walk number five.

But now you should turn back to the west, to walk past the summit, over the stile and down the track past **Drinkwater's**, turning eventually to your right at the Ramblers' Association sign. All that downhill section of the walk will not have taken long – 10 minutes, perhaps. At the junction, ignore the track back to White Coppice by which you climbed up past **Coppice Stile** and **Grime's**. Once you have turned right at the junction and on to the broad track to Brinscall you will have before you the extensive, almost level but much tussocked Heapey Moor. If you look carefully to your left you might be able to make out the position 200m away of the ruins of **Heapey Moor Farm** that you visited nearly two hours ago. What you must do now is to follow the Brinscall track, winding a little as it does at first, but then going in a generally north-westerly direction until it very definitely turns to the north. At that point stop! Here, the bank and ditch, mentioned earlier, that leads due north across from the pond at **Heapey Moor Farm** now meets the Brinscall track. At this point, also, a significant wall departs (at 90 degrees) to the left, going due west, in fact. Leave the Brinscall track here and follow this wall on its far (or north) side. In 100m or so it meets another wall going north. Turn right here and follow this new wall which leads you in a short time directly to **Calico Hall**, the sixth farm of the day. And by the time you arrive at this sixth farm, assuming you had a picnic lunch, say, at **Great Hill Farm** and/or climbed to the summit of Great Hill itself, the likelihood is that it is some three hours, at least, since you left White Coppice.

The large **Calico Hall** was an excellent example of the complete longhouse with no major, separate, additional structure. There was just a small lavatory block at the edge of the farmyard to the west of the main building, and a small square structure (incorporating a well?) at the northern end of the farmyard. The main house and barn was at least 6m wide and at least 25m in length. The walls are not especially high now,

Calico Hall, with foundation lines of the barn's eastern side showing clearly on the right.

but the foundations are beautifully clearly displayed rather than being reduced to an indeterminate heap of rubble. The domestic sections do seem to be at the north end with the barn sections at the south end of the main longhouse. The two northernmost bays of the house are about half a metre wider than other bays, and project a little towards the east. They also have extra internal support walls or dividers at foundation level. On the other side of the house the two central bays project for about a metre towards the west as if they included porches, or carried an overhanging roof covering a wide barn door. [*Given the name **Calico Hall** and its probable textile-manufacturing heyday (the late eighteenth century and the first half of the nineteenth) it must have been an important producer of hand-woven cotton cloth. In 1851 a family of 11 (two parents and nine children) lived here, many of them involved in handloom weaving.*

*I suppose it ought to be pointed out that no undue or special significance should be attached to the use of the word 'hall' in this case or in that of the nearby **Sour Milk Hall**. There should be no eager confusions as to the possible meanings, no illusions about grand houses up here for the landed gentry, with Georgian panelling, curtsying servants, harpsichord recitals in the music room…. A 'hall' in medieval or early modern times might refer simply to the main living room, or even the only living room, in a small vernacular house. While it is the case that **Calico Hall** had 11 inhabitants in 1851, it had only two in 1881 and none at all in 1891. I remember that it did have one surviving tree in the 1970s, a small one, a gnarled hawthorn, whose blossom arrived late and clung but briefly on this open moor. It has now blown down.*]

As you prepare to leave **Calico Hall** via the little triangular field to its north, you have two possible routes to **Sour Milk Hall**, your seventh farm. The first takes you via particular lines of field walls, and also on a stretch of the main Great Hill-Brinscall track. The second suggests that you dare boldly to take the direct route which, though more or less on the level, does involve your striding determinedly over tussocks. They are not by any means the largest or wettest tussocks on the moors, however.

If taking the first route and aiming for the main track, go from **Calico Hall**'s ruins to the north-eastern end of the little triangular field. Then follow closely the wall which continues just east of north from there for 100m or so. You will now meet another wall coming from both left and right across your path. At that point turn right, towards the east, and take the short walk alongside this wall as far as the main track. Then turn left, to the north and walk easily ahead on a decent surface. You are walking alongside the old moorland enclosure wall on your left, and passing numerous shooting butts, also on your left. You will pass five of these. (You missed the first four of the total of nine while you were visiting **Calico Hall**.)

Soon after the last of the shooting butts, the track will bend to the left. Before it quite quickly turns to the right (the north) again, you must turn left and leave it. You must join what the OS map shows to be a path – in fact what on the ground is a damp grassy space between another and occasionally still quite high wall (going west) and the incipient trickles and pools of the very young Sour Milk Brook. Going west-north-west as you now are, you will find the path and the wall soon beginning to go gently downhill. As soon as you see, ahead and slightly to the right of you, a couple of old gateposts (the only obvious ones near here), you should stop downward progress, turn left, cross the trickle, or flow, of the very narrow Sour Milk Brook, and walk southwards (on a sheep track if you like) into the rough field there. (Your stepping across the brook has taken you back from Wheelton into Heapey again, as you may, or may not, wish to know.) Staying at roughly the same height, you should not need to walk more than 100m before the ruins of **Sour Milk Hall** become apparent. Again, the walls are not very high but the foundations are very clear indeed.

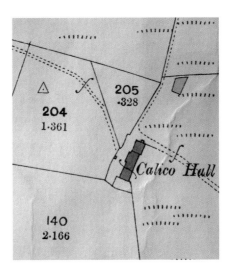

If, instead of this slightly roundabout route, you decide on a direct approach from **Calico Hall**, you will do, frankly, what I have always done rather than troubling to return to the Great Hill-Brinscall track. I confess I have enjoyed the journey over the tussocks, happily and straightforwardly aiming due north from **Calico Hall**, firstly crossing the low wall at the northern edge of the little triangular field, and then striding out over tufts of grass and heather. The tussocks are of ankle height, and never of waist height as they can be in the **Heapey Moor Farm** area. If by any chance you do trip, your landings on grass and heather will be soft and safe, and even controlled. Companions are likely to be entirely good-humoured and helpful about this.

Having crossed the low wall when you left the triangular field there is just one more low wall to stride across, running east-west about 120m into your short journey. The fields here are more or less entirely level, so when you have crossed this east-west wall, you may walk unimpeded (but still due north) for another 170m, thereabouts, when suddenly you will be able to see to your left the low walls round the small intake fields (for gathering sheep) next to and to the east of **Sour Milk Hall** itself.

A smaller establishment than many is this seventh farm of the day, and in plan a junior version of **Calico Hall**, you might say. It is a characteristic longhouse of three bays only, like **Coppice Stile** in that respect. The domestic section does appear to be at the north end, which juts out a little to the east and at 25ft (7.5m) is wider than the 20ft (6m plus) of the barn section. The length of the complete longhouse is less than 14m. There seems to be an internal doorway between the living room and the barn. As at **Calico Hall** there is a farmyard on the western side, with a lavatory block in a similar position just by the field wall. Everything in terms of foundation walls is there clearly to be seen, unlike the mossy tree- and undergrowth-covered ruins in Brinscall Woods. There are three adjacent fields of small size, and three larger ones. **Sour Milk Hall** appears to have been not only empty but derelict by 1891, alas.

I probably state the obvious when I mention that the very name – Sour Milk – is, as it is in the Lake District, a reference to the nearby occasionally rushing waterfall that appears after an outburst of heavy rain when the mixture of earth, air and water produces a colour of foaming spray that is more creamy yellow than white, more sour milk than fresh. You may see this rushing torrent from time to time in Brinscall Woods when the Sour Milk Brook in spate thunders beneath the bridge on the 'carriage drive' while you make your way down to **Goose Green**. It is almost as impressive as the Sour Milk Gills to be found in the Buttermere valley, in Borrowdale or in Easedale. People even come specially to Brinscall Woods to take its photograph.

Meanwhile, you need now to walk, I suggest, in a fairly restrained and sensible fashion from **Sour Milk Hall** down to **Fir Farm**, the eighth farm of the day, on its hillside shelf above the Goit valley. There is theoretically a direct route from one farm to the other, but it involves galumphing downhill over a long steep and deeply be-tussocked slope and is not to be recommended except for the most experienced and determined of galumphers. The combination of steepness and the great width (and depth) of tussocks means that it is hardly possible to make progress without feet being frequently entangled and ensnared by big clumps of grass, heathers, bilberries and finally bracken. Here are precise instructions, therefore, for a longer, smoother, easier journey that takes you into the southern edges of Brinscall Woods and down to **Goose Green**, and then up by a short, comparatively easy slope to **Fir Farm** itself.

From **Sour Milk Hall** you need to walk across the field in a northerly direction for about 100m and then cross the Sour Milk Brook near to the only two stone gateposts hereabouts and the partly broken-down wall ahead of you. If you had arrived at **Sour Milk Hall** directly over the fields from **Calico Hall**, this means crossing new territory. If you arrived from **Calico Hall** by means of the Great Hill-Brinscall track, this means simply retracing your steps towards the two gateposts. Once you cross the brook (back into Wheelton), turn left and walk downhill on the path past the little delph and its roofless storage-workshop (you will be walking in a north-westerly direction) and climb over the stile very close to **Liptrot's Farm**. You are now once again in Brinscall Woods.

Here, turn left and enjoy walking easily under the high fir trees, following the 'unofficial' path and keeping fairly close all the time to the outer post and wire fencing. This boundary fence between wood and moor takes five right angle bends – right, left, right, left, right. At the second of these bends you will find yourself crossing Sour Milk Brook by walking along the top of a wall and holding on to the smooth wire fence if necessary. At the fourth bend you will find yourself approaching and then passing **Marsden's Farm**, and therefore on a familiar path, remembering to take the 'avoidance' route close to the fence as you continue the downhill walk. Very soon you will arrive at the "kissing gate" and the view of the **Goose Green** ruins. Go through the "kissing gate".

As you look along the valley towards White Coppice, do look particularly at the number of quite large individual trees at varying heights along the hillside on your left. These are mainly sycamores but there are oaks and hazels as well as the big ash tree next to the old **Goose Green** farm. Some of those that from this angle seem to be highest up the slopes are actually very close to the ruins of **Fir Farm**. There are few trees higher than **Fir Farm**, though the mainly tree-less hillside above this goes on rising for a further 400ft without being visible from the "kissing gate".

To find **Fir Farm**, the easiest way is first of all to stand on the **Goose Green** ruins and then, leaving the big ash tree on your right, to begin climbing up the hillside in a south-westerly direction. A low wall accompanies you briefly. A century ago there did used to be a pedestrian footpath between the two farms (**Goose Green** and **Fir Farm**) by this direct hillside route – in addition to the zigzag route for horses and

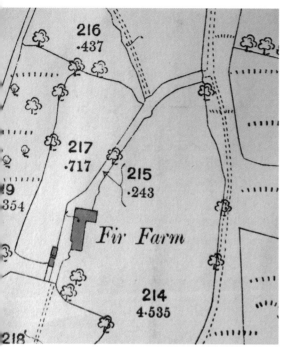

carts via the 'sunken road'. But now you can easily find your own way upwards through the bracken, heather and clumps of rushes, if you aim towards some of the higher trees. Make sure that you eventually see the walls on each side of the zigzag above you, and then look for two distinctive if quite small trees just higher up than the walls. One tree is a rather bent-trunked oak; the other is an oddly bulbously trunked rowan. Just opposite and below these two trees you will find **Fir Farm**'s gateposts leading from the zigzag 'sunken road' into the farm's drive. One of these posts is leaning at an angle of 45 degrees towards the other, more or less upright, one. Not quite a love match then!

The **Fir Farm** drive, now with lots of little tussocks between its two stone walls, leads gently downhill at first until it crosses a shallow grassy canyon-like drain coming down from the hillside above and continuing down towards the valley floor on your right. At this point there is on your left an intriguing little structure, a low curved wall, more like a garden feature than a well. From this point onwards in summer, much healthily vigorous bracken has rather taken over the now level drive and the wide shelf you will soon come to, where the farm's fallen cross-walls and foundation rubble can be found. The drive section is overhung on your left by (in this order) a hazel tree, three hawthorns, another hazel tree, two more hawthorns and a sycamore. Thereafter we can walk up and down over the rubble divisions that separate the six bays of the longhouse, with domestic sections (probably) at the northern end, and barn at the southern end. Half way along the ruins, cut into the hillside to your left, is an obvious, square-shaped, stone-lined well. Beyond the ruins is one more sycamore and, finally, an uncompromisingly dead tree (which very probably was also a sycamore).

The steepness of the slope to the west, when you look down from the edge of the shelf and its buildings, is quite dramatic. The farm had been poised on the brink, more or less. But the views, far and near, are delightful. It must have been quite an exciting place to live and work in, though hardly any of the fields making up its 39 acres could have been other than – how shall we say? – sharply inclined. [*I wish I could ask the opinion of the two 27-year-olds, James and Elizabeth Warburton, husband and wife at* **Fir Farm** *in 1881, parents of two-year-old Margaret and one-year-old Robert.*

I wonder what Jessie Benson, their nine-year-old visitor from Manchester on the day of the census, thought about life in a farm on a hillside above this lovely valley.]

Sharrock's, however, the ninth and the one remaining farm of the day's walk, was, like **Goose Green**, comfortably sited in the low fields at the foot of the slope. You will want to make your way there now, and so back to White Coppice, but you will need to take especial care as to precise route. There used to be (and the OS map still shows) a pedestrian path in a straight line directly down from **Fir Farm** to **Sharrock's**. It is important that you do not attempt to find it. All that is to be found where you might think it should be is a narrow sheep track meandering precariously among tussocks, taking the walker along the edge of considerable slopes – not quite vertical but certainly impressively steep slopes, where one can look down to a much better path a 100ft or so below.

Therefore, make your way back down to **Goose Green** by the route by which you had climbed up from it to **Fir Farm**. Then, from the **Goose Green** ruin go a little way to the west, to the bottom of the former garden area, and join the path that starts at the "kissing gate". This is the obvious path that runs southwards extremely pleasantly along the foot of the steep slope, nicely above the lowest fields next to the Goit, and runs along a wall for quite a lot of the way, eventually leading you exactly

Fir Farm: the well next to the hillside.

Fir Farm, looking across the foundation lines of the barn and house.

to the **Sharrock's** site. As you see **Sharrock's** ruins, you will join a zigzag track coming down from the moor-tops (from **Calico Hall** and **Heapey Moor Farm**, actually) and aiming for the **Sharrock's** bridge over the Goit. That is your route back to the White Coppice cricket field, i.e. over the bridge and then along the newly constructed path that comes all the way from 'Waterman's' Cottage. But first you must have a good look at **Sharrock's**.

Long before the Goit existed, **Sharrock's** had been built beside a major track which ran right from 'Warth' (the original settlement by the White Coppice ford), behind the small round-topped hill, The Lowe, past Tootal's Farm and then, via **Sharrock's** itself, up the steep Ice Age edge by a special zigzag route eventually as far as **Calico Hall**. Since 1857 **Sharrock's** has had its own Goit bridge, but there are no surviving attendant trees apart from small-scale sapling types near the Goit, and no distinctive additional structures except perhaps on the north side where the track ran past. It had been an entirely conventional and relatively small longhouse, comfortably sitting on a slight east-west slope. It had been a farm of 19 acres. The building had four separate bays. There are signs of an internal doorway between the first and second bays at the upper end. The overall width of the longhouse was just over 5m and the length was about 15m. Clearly the main water supply was a stream on the southern side running now into the Goit. [*The house, larger than* **Goose Green** *but smaller than many, did contain 10 Pilkingtons of varying ages in 1881, and three Hindleys, a Brocklehurst and one Pilkington in 1891.*]

As you prepare to leave the **Sharrock's** ruin and its quiet and sheltered valley site, it might please you to know that just a little of your day's walk still remains, just a little more of your relaxing stroll through the valley. It is a charming Goit-side progress that you will find on a new path leading you by gently flowing waters straight to the cricket field where your day's expedition began. So, go through the new "kissing gate", cross the **Sharrock's** bridge and, as the cricket field and its pavilion come closer, remind yourself with a smile that today you have visited both the highest and the lowest of the Brinscall Moors farms (and seven other farms between them): **Great Hill** at 1070ft and **Sharrock's** at 480ft – 329m and 155m, thereabouts. Which might you have preferred, for the raising of your sheep and the upbringing of your children?

Finally, while you are driving carefully away from White Coppice along the narrow but charming Hollins Lane and Higher House Lane, or past Causeway House Farm and along Tithebarn Lane, you might find yourself beginning to plan for the start of Walk Number Four – the Twist Moor Group.

Looking north from Fir Farm down the slope to the Goit and across to the Harbour Lane ridge.

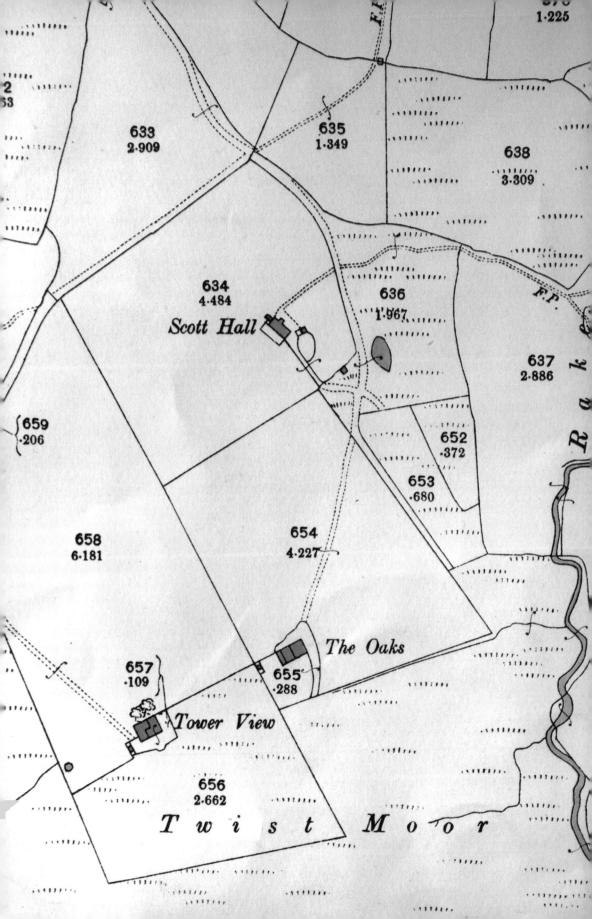

The Twist Moor Group
(12 Farms)

Start and Finish: EITHER Roddlesworth Lane car park OR Abbey Village, the Hare and Hounds area.

Distance: Up to 5 miles, depending on starting point.

Time: Between 3 hrs. 30 mins. and 4 hrs. 30 mins.

Character: A stimulating and varied walk over high moors, by small, leafy valleys and tumbling brooks, and briefly along roads including pre-turnpike lanes.

A N IDEAL PLACE for car travellers to begin this fourth walk is the small car park on Roddlesworth Lane, adjacent to Lower Roddlesworth Farm. Here you are on the continuation of Twist Moor Lane, the pre-1801 route that ran from Brinscall's School Lane via Butterworth Brow and then via the Roddlesworth Valley and Hollinshead Hall to Belmont, Sharples and Bolton. It is a location rich in historical significance. Among other things it tells you much about the typical width and meandering qualities of pre-turnpike roads. If, however, this car park is already full, it is usually possible, if you park responsibly, to find space near Abbey Village in the vicinity of Dole Lane and the Hare and Hounds Inn. In any case you could return there for refreshment.

Supposing that you are able to park on Roddlesworth Lane car park, however, I recommend that you then walk south-eastwards for a mere 20m or so to climb a stile on your right leading you south-westwards and downhill into a pleasant pasture which you may happily share with a small stream and, from time to time, with assorted groups of sheep, ducks and geese. Cross the stream and walk uphill to a stile next to the A675. Traffic moves quickly here, so take great care when crossing the road to a gateway on the far side with another stile, beyond which is a path which was originally, and is still, an obvious continuation of your path from Roddlesworth Lane up to farms on Twist Moor.

If you have arrived by the 124 Chorley-Blackburn bus at the Hare and Hounds or have parked your car in that area, I recommend that you walk south-eastwards from there along the roadside footpath that accompanies the A675. You will eventually pass close to the Rake reservoir on your left. The roadside footpath then becomes narrower just as the A675 bends quite sharply to the left, so take particular care at that point. Single-file walking is absolutely essential. You might meanwhile notice that it is just here on the opposite side of the A675 that the pre-turnpike Twist Moor Lane comes down from the fields to cross the Rake Brook and join the 'new' 1801 road briefly at the bend. You yourself will arrive there in two or more hours' time at the conclusion of today's walk, having by then visited 12 more ruined farms on the moors, and made your way back via Twist Moor Lane.

For the time being, continue round the bend along the narrow roadside footpath while the A675 straightens itself out and begins gradually to climb. Notice, opposite, an old and carefully levelled track leading off to the former Birch Clough quarry. Very soon on your left you will see that a slightly re-aligned Roddlesworth Lane (the continuation of Twist Moor Lane) departs from the A675. It makes sense for you not to follow it but instead to continue along the now slightly wider roadside footpath for another 140–150m at which stage you will see the stile on your left which you might have climbed if you had used the Roddlesworth Lane car park.

Look across the A675 now to see the gateway opposite (with surviving stone gate post that, near its top, has a large through-hole as well as a hinge-pin) and close to it a wooden stile for you to climb. Before you cross the road to climb the stile, look at least twice in each direction – to Preston to your right and to Bolton to your left – and be quite sure that no traffic at all is approaching. Then cross quickly, remembering that vans and lorries, in addition to cars, can appear very rapidly even though the road is now subject to a 50 mph speed limit. Once you have climbed the stile you might reflect on the fact that the rough track that you are now standing on is a far older route than the A675 you have just crossed. It was once, in the old pre-1801 days, on its quiet way over the hillside from Roddlesworth towards **Keck**, **Mosscrop's** and **Aushaw's**, among other places.

Leaving the A675 behind, walk uphill in a south-westerly direction to climb yet another stile and then continue with a post and wire fence on your left and a collection of roughly quarried stones on your right. As you reach the top of the slope notice on your left an old wall beyond the fence which is leaving you and following the line of the former track to **Keck** and **Mosscrop's**. You will continue to follow the fence which will lead you downhill to a wooden bridge over the Rake Brook. It is a charming and entirely rural scene among mature trees, the only sound being the chatter of the stream as it tumbles down among the rocks below you. Cross the bridge and climb the path up the opposite bank. Keep the fence on your left. In two minutes you will arrive at the considerable ruins of **Aushaw's**, your first farm of Walk Four.

There are several tumbled field walls hereabouts including lines of parallel walls leading into the farmyards. What you will also easily find are the bases and low walls of two adjacent but quite separate sets of buildings involving both domestic and barn structures. One is on a line SW–NE; the other is on a line NW–SE. Below them are the clear remains of a well.

*As you stand there among the ruins it is not difficult to imagine times when the farmyards here were busily filled by the many adults and children of the Southworth, Waring and Fazackerly families in the later years of the nineteenth century – once these people had returned at the end of a working day from their labours in quarry, print works, spinning mill or weaving shed. Not much farming work would have been carried on. There are probably a good deal more sheep in the fields round **Aushaw's** now than there were in the 1890s.*

Before leaving, do glance down at the Rake reservoir ahead of you and, further to the left, at the great square block of Abbey Mill, and then, to your right, at the Birch Clough Quarry and above it, on the sky-line, the narrow pencil (or stone sky-rocket) of Darwen Tower. On your far left, the trees of **Grouse Cottage**, your next farm of the day, are welcomingly close.

Walking from **Aushaw's** next to the post and wire fence in a westerly direction you will very soon (in less than three minutes) meet the cart track that comes up to **Grouse Cottage** from Twist Moor Lane. Here you need to turn left at the gateway and climb over the stile, the gate itself normally being closed and locked, as indeed also is the gate lower down the track where it meets Twist Moor Lane. The pattern of closed gates, stiles, post and barbed wire fences and the lush green colour of the grass tells you that these are important sheep fields where ewes meet tups (rams) and where lambs are subsequently born and suckled every year. Not far beyond the stile that you have just climbed are the sheltering trees and the significant ruins of **Grouse Cottage**.

A short driveway on your left allows you to visit and explore the remaining house walls that sheltered the Snapes in the 1890s and provided such an up-to-date and improved house for Jimmy Bennett and his family in the 1940s and 1950s. Not much remains of the Bennett garden but what does remain, apart from signs of an oven and a sink, is the still just-about-roofed outside loo.

Thereby hangs a tale of life here in the 1950s – an entirely true one, I am told. The journey from within the house to the outside loo involved leaving the kitchen via the main front door and its porch (half way along the cottage's north side) and then walking past the store room door at the end of the north side and round the corner to the out-of-sight loo door. The trouble was that the Bennett poultry hovered possessively around the store room door, and the cock was fiercely protective of his hen-harem. The only way that a loo-bound householder was going to get past him was to carry and determinedly brandish in his direction a stout broom handle. The broom handle, normally kept in the kitchen for the purpose, had to be taken into the loo, and the return journey then involved more firm brandishings before the safety of the kitchen could be regained. Presumably the Bennetts did not make more frequent visits to the loo than they absolutely had to. How their visitors might have fared I know not.

*Nevertheless, **Grouse Cottage** seems overall to have been a most happy place to live, though it could sometimes seem rather lonely once surrounding farms were abandoned, and did so seem to Mrs Bennett when her husband was away from home for long periods on active service during the Second World War. There were times, too, when Mrs Bennett used to wait in the dark near Wood's Fold to meet her daughter as she walked home from school alone on winter early evenings along Twist Moor Lane.*

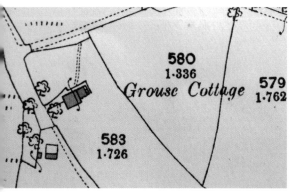

However, it is now time to have a look at some of **Grouse Cottage's** former neighbours. The cart track you have briefly used from the stile continues in a south-easterly direction, passing initially the ruins of the separate barn. Follow it and look shortly for a wooden post with yellow direction arrows. When you first see the post you will see beyond it the single sycamore tree that stands immediately next to the ruins of **Scott Hall**. (There is another but in this case irrelevant sycamore further over to your left where there never has been a farm.) Both **Scott Hall**'s ruins and its sycamore tree are more or less in line with the distant dome of Great Hill (properly pronounced by local inhabitants as 'Gretel' – Hansel's sister, that is, and perfectly rhyming with 'kettle').

Aushaw's, with the ruins of two houses and two barns. Abbey Village and its mill are seen in the distance.

By the time you reach the wooden post you might be inspired not only by the sight of Great Hill but also by your first sight since Walk Two of that unmistakable though distant solitary beech tree next to **Botany Bay**. Great Hill is to the south of where you stand by the post. The **Botany Bay** beech tree is to the south west. Almost you might feel you ought to go and greet it, so distant and alone the tree seems across the moor. However, there are other obligations closer at hand.

One of the yellow arrows on the post indicates a path to the left which eventually crosses Rake Brook by another wooden bridge on its way to Watson's and the Belmont Road – but this is not a route you require on Walk Four. You will use it on Walk Five, however. The other yellow arrow indicates a path to the right which leads to **Pope's** Farm and the stepping stones across the 'Rushy' Brook. You do want to go in that general direction. There is no sign of paths on the ground here. But then these are sheep fields. Rather than trying to follow an artificially straight line, pushing your way through large groups of grazing or resting or suckling ewes and lambs in the Spring, say, the country-style way to make progress is quietly to divert, and negotiate a way round the sheep, causing minimal disturbance while making eventually for a stile and marker post by **Pope's**. Dogs must most certainly be entirely under control.

James Bennett at age 16, before he went to live at Grouse Cottage.

As you walk you will be quite close to **Scott Hall** with its obvious longhouse-shape heap of stones and its rectangular well and ruined outhouse. [*Here was the small world in the 1880s of the young Moss family and in the 1890s of the Gregorys. Four acres, only, belonged briefly to them among all these fields. A one-year-old Mary Ann Moss might have sat comfortably on her mother's lap under that very **Scott Hall** sycamore tree in the summer of 1881. A one month-old Robert Gregory in 1891 must almost certainly have breathed his first breaths just here, very close to where you are now. Humbling thoughts, these, as one strides out, a temporary visitor, over land they knew.*]

While you make your way towards **Pope's**, you will meanwhile notice on your left (looking in the general direction of Great Hill) four distinctive circular metal-railed animal-feed units; but you will also see the quite close, shoulder-high (in parts) ruins of **The Oaks**, 200m or so beyond **Scott Hall**. [*It is not difficult to imagine the six young children of the 1891 Stephen Miller family running playfully about **The Oaks** fields on cool winter days.*] On the other hand you will not from this point find it easy to identify the nearby ruins of **Tower View**, hardly distinguishable as they now are from the several sections of fallen field boundary wall hereabouts. But we do have an easier position from which you can soon see **Tower View**, once you have first visited **Pope's** and then taken a short additional stroll in the 'open access' land beyond the barbed wire fence, having crossed the fence by climbing the **Pope's** stile. Details follow shortly.

Its tall yellow-arrowed marker post allows you to recognise the **Pope's** stile a good 100m away. Not until you climb and stand on the stile, however, will you see the heaps of collapsed stone that once made up the **Pope's** longhouse, the house at the far end, the barn below you. [*A small hidden gem, you might once have thought it, with its own stream running sweetly by the front door, thereafter plunging safely and steeply down to Twist Moor Lane and beyond; a place for a proud and solitary farmer – William Dewhurst living there alone for more than 20 years, from the 1850s to the 1880s.*]

Having climbed over the stile and taken a good and thoughtful look at the **Pope's** remains, I suggest you take advantage of the fact that you are now on the south side of the post and barbed wire fence and on 'open access' land. Walk in a south-easterly direction next to (or quite close to) the fence for about 200m. You will find yourself walking on firm, mainly well-drained land (lots of minor drainage-ditches doing a good job) and on short good quality grass. A little distance up the hillside on your right is much damper and rougher land, but there is no need to explore this. Soon, having passed two metal gates, you will see exactly what you seek, just a few metres to your left on the other side of the fence – the ruins of **Tower View**. [*Here are the buildings and fields belonging to Thomas (or Doctor) Nowell and Alice his wife and their five children in 1891. And here, just at your feet as you stand by the fence, is the mass of rushes that mark exactly the area of the circular pond that provided the Nowells' water supply. The pond is clearly shown on the 1894 Ordnance Survey map.*]

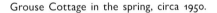

Grouse Cottage in the spring, circa 1950.

You have now seen six of the 12 farms on Walk Four, and I would guess that between 50 and 60 minutes will have passed since you began this walk. If from your position close to **Tower View** you now take a general look over the area of land you have just been getting to know – from **Aushaw's** right up to **Tower View** – it might occur to you to wonder why any group of families should choose to live up here in such a high and potentially windswept location. But before you dismiss life here as intolerably hard and demanding by twenty-first-century standards, take a look at the moors to the right of Darwen Tower, over a mile and a half to the east of where you now stand. There you will see, more or less due east indeed, the very firm and secure buildings of New Barn, still inhabited and still a working farm. These stand at exactly 310m above sea level (1,007 ft), no less. **Tower View**, the second highest of the ruined farms you will see in today's walk, stood at a mere 245m (796 ft).

The sight of New Barn should meanwhile inspire you to walk a little further along (but outside) the post and barbed wire fence while you are on its southern side, and therefore on 'open access' land. If you do this you can soon enjoy a really good view of **The Oaks** as well as **Tower View**. Even more significantly you can also see the foundation wall remains of that otherwise most elusive of ruins, **Mosscrop's**. **Mosscrop's** was built on a gentle slope just east of the Rake Brook, but it is not now on 'open access' land. Nor is it close to a public footpath. All this means that

Ths ruins of Grouse Cottage in 2010.

it cannot be seen from **Keck**, its near neighbour, which you will visit on Walk Five. The lie of the land and the modest height of the farm's foundations means that it is invisible from all other directions apart from the area you are now in. Even from the path coming over the hill from Watson's, which passes very close to its ruins, **Mosscrop's** remains out of sight. It does not have the benefit of an attendant tree.

But from the point that you are now at, quite close to **The Oaks**, and exactly where the nineteenth-century enclosure wall passes through (as it were) the post and barbed wire fence and then turns through it again, **Mosscrop's** is clearly visible. It is precisely in line with New Barn, away above it in the distance. The ground where you are now standing, where wall and fence meet twice, is often rather wet, the drainage system not working very well here. I assure you that if you were boldly to press on into the area of tussocks, rushes and wet wilderness in an attempt to reach Rake Brook and come closer to **Mosscrop's**, you would regret the increasingly waterlogged walk. So do stay at the point you have now reached, and consult the OS Explorer 287 map where you will find the small rectangle representing **Mosscrop's** standing on the 250m (812ft) contour – and apparently close to a sheep fold whose walls now seem unfortunately to have been scattered. The National Grid Reference 649210 should confirm your sighting of the farm.

The substantial ruins of The Oaks, 2010.

The Mosscrop's foundations tell you that it was another typical longhouse of approximately 16m by 6m. It was set on an east-west alignment, and it had three main sections. There was a small (lavatory?) block at the lower (west) end, and a separate barn-like building a little further west. A driveway left the nearby track as it came up from **Keck** and led into the farmyard on the north and west sides of the main building. [*In 1881 and 1891 Thomas and Mary Miller lived here with their five children. By 1891 four of the five were employed in a cotton factory – as spinner, weaver or cardroom hand. The fifth child was a 10-year-old girl. Mosscrop's was a farm of 28 acres. It seems that Thomas Miller, aged 47 in 1891, worked the farm single-handedly, unless he had any assistance from the 37-year-old Stephen Miller of The Oaks, which was a farm of only three acres.*]

With this in mind, it is time to turn round and retrace your steps to the **Pope's** stile. Climb over this and begin to make your way back to the direction post and ultimately to **Grouse Cottage** and the second half of the walk. On your way to the post, notice another feature of these fields, a very straight section of double parallel walls roughly half way between **Pope's** and **Scott Hall**, and apparently leading towards **Grouse Cottage** though not continuing all the way there. Very much a means of leading sheep from one section of the moors to another, I presume, yet in this case actually built exactly on the line of a dotted boundary marker (pre-dating the walls themselves) which is shown on a map of 1831. The map concerns land sales in that year, the dotted boundary marker line showing the western edge of an area of land not yet enclosed but numbered '355'. This is an area of land which subsequently contained the newly built **Tower View** and **The Oaks**. It is across the Rake Brook from the four fields marked as belonging to **Mosscrop's** in 1831.

Having now made your way down the track to **Grouse Cottage** with its easily recognised trees and surviving loo block, climb the nearby stile and turn left on to the path by which you had an hour or so earlier arrived from **Aushaw's**. Keep close to the post and wire fence on your left, and within two minutes, having walked 100m or less, see, beyond the fence, the artificially flattened field that is the site of **Dale Fold**. Surrounding the field on its east, south and west sides is an earth and stone embankment plus ditch in part, looking almost like the outer defence line of an old Roman fort. Apart from this and a couple of low ridges plus a broken-topped former gatepost at one corner, there is nothing like the usual heap of collapsed stonework to show that from the eighteenth century up to the 1890s there used to be a considerable longhouse (barn, house and cottage) here. [*Any descendants of the Dorset Joy family who come here now to seek out their Dale Cottage home of the 1870s and 80s would find that flat green field a sad disappointment. So might any members of the John Miller family who were hoping to find the Dale Fold Farm.*]

However, with four more vanished (or almost vanished) farms to be visited on today's walk you need to leave the **Dale Fold** site behind you and continue along the post and wire fence (now joined by the **Dale Fold** wall) down an increasingly steep slope towards the 'Rushy' Brook and its wooden bridge. As with the Rake Brook bridge you crossed earlier on your walk, this is another charming rural scene, with trees and the tumbling stream below you on its spectacularly rocky bed. Having crossed the bridge, the first thing to do is to climb a stile and then proceed uphill with the post and wire fence now on your right. As you climb the hill you will soon realise that beyond the fence lies the great excavation, the huge hole in the ground, of the former Central Quarry, now mainly used for storing piles of newly felled logs. You may also notice that all the former fields that once belonged to **Snape's Farm** have quite recently been transformed into a plantation of young, rapidly growing conifers. The timber business is a significant one, locally.

As the slope you are climbing gradually levels out you will probably notice another post and wire fence appearing a little distance away on your left, but this is one that you do not need to approach. The fence to your right is the one to keep in view. Beneath your feet you will also become aware of increasing numbers of sizeable quarried rocks that are unevenly scattered about. For the sake of your ankles these are to be avoided. You will soon, however, cross a field boundary wall, and then you must veer to your right (towards the north-west) as your post and wire fence goes gradually downhill. Looking ahead you will notice a mile away the spire of Withnell's St. Paul's church on Bury Lane. Then you will see, closer to you on your right, a small rectangular reservoir. You are now very near to the site of **Hillock Farm**. (**Hillock** seems to have been known as Brook's in the eighteenth century.)

Depending on the precise route you have chosen in order to avoid the scattered rocks and the breaking of ankles, you might now have found yourself with three stiles to climb, or just one or possibly none at all, in order to visit the **Hillock** ruins.

Looking north-west from Roddlesworth Moor.

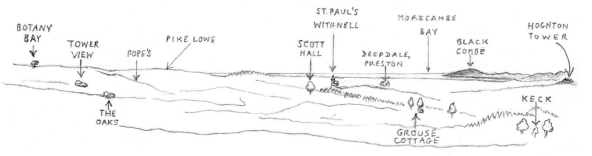

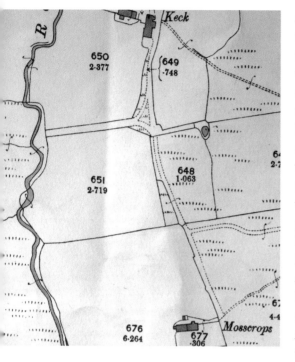

At any rate, take care among the rocks, take care not to trespass upon the area of the small reservoir, but do look at the **Hillock** remains, while acknowledging that they are not, alas, so extensive or meaningful or grand as many we have seen previously on our four walks. In particular there seem to be the ruins of a small barn in the western part of the site, while a small, but particularly level area of grass nearer to the reservoir, and with a boundary wall round two of its four sides, might very probably mark the position of the main house. It seems most likely. Indeed, the higher of two large and unusual cast-iron gateposts probably stood next to the south-west gable end of the **Hillock** farmhouse. [*Certainly **Hillock**, your ninth farm of the Walk Four day, did contain 12 members of the Cookson family in 1891.*] From the ruins there is a fine view of the five storey high spinning section of Abbey Mill and of the attached single storey weaving shed on its south side. [*If Abbey Mill was the daily destination of a majority of the younger members of the 1891 Cookson family, they quite clearly did not have far to walk.*]

Interestingly, the small reservoir next to the farm was a recent construction (circa 1850) built to provide compensation water for Withnell Mill (at the bottom of Bury Lane) once streams that used to serve the mill had been diverted into the Goit by Liverpool Corporation. [*Any Cooksons working at Withnell Mill would probably realise that their little local pond helped indirectly to guarantee a textile job day by day.*]

When you leave **Hillock** do not turn right or walk to the north and Dole Lane and Baron's Fold. Instead, walk north-westwards on a path, muddy in places, between a relatively new post and wire fence on your left and an old wall on your right. Keep near to the fence until you can see, 200m to your left, the group of cottages that Ramsden's has been turned into, and near it the considerable copse of beech trees that you noticed on your walk down from **Botany Bay** (Walk Two). Then follow the wall on your right which leads down to a five-barred wooden gate with a stile and 'public footpath' sign next to it. Climb the stile. You are now on Twist Moor Lane at a point where it has just been joined by Norcross Brow as it comes up from Bury Lane. At this point Twist Moor Lane is briefly a bus route (the 124, Chorley-Blackburn). On the far side of the road is a bus stop, and immediately opposite the stile is a seat which is useful either when waiting for a bus or simply when wishing for a short rest or to enjoy the view over Abbey Village to the distant Bleasdale Fells. Do not yet cross the road, however, but do turn left and follow Twist Moor Lane as it continues straight on while Norcross Brow descends to the right with the bus route.

As you walk along Twist Moor Lane you will have a clear view to your left of Ramsden's Cottages, an original farm longhouse now extended and nicely renovated. You will soon also recognise the end of the track on your left down which you walked from the high moors when you were returning from **Botany Bay** and the Central Group. On your right and opposite the moorland track is the little path which provides a pedestrian shortcut down to the refurbished Norcross Farm. What you are looking for now, however, are the undergrowth-covered remains of your tenth farm of the day, **Whave Gate**.

Cross to the western side of Twist Moor Lane and then, from the point where both moorland track and little Norcross path join the old main road, walk along the road for 30m and look carefully to your right for all the remains that you can see. There is nothing dramatic or even obvious. What you will see, very close to the road, is that, for another 20m beyond the 30m point you have just reached, the ground level under the trees and undergrowth is distinctly higher than it is elsewhere, almost up to the height of the Twist Moor Lane surface.

What this amounts to is a long (20m long), quite narrow (6m wide) heap of rubble made up of stones from the fallen walls of **Whave Gate**. If you then walk about experimentally (and cautiously) on this rubble, you will realise what it consists of and roughly speaking what its shape and extent was. It was yet another longhouse and it ran parallel to, and very close to, Twist Moor Lane. I cannot tell which was house and which was barn, but it does seem to have been one continuous (and long and narrow) building. I must remind you again that it is easier to identify in winter rather than in summer any possible evidence of a former structure. Saplings, bracken and brambles as well as trees provide a thorough summer camouflage. If, however, having stood on **Whave Gate**'s ruins you then move to stand next to the ruins but on the surface of Twist Moor Lane and looking to the south at the field opposite, you will see that **Whave Gate** was exactly in line with Withnell Villa and therefore with the pre-1888 **Richmond's** before it. The relative positions of **Whave Gate**, **Richmond's**, Norcross and Ramsden's farms as shown on nineteenth-century maps are exactly those that you can see as you stand by the **Whave Gate** rubble heap. [*Those four farms made a close little community, a small quadrilateral,*

*in the mid-nineteenth century and earlier. This was the welcoming neighbourhood that provided a home at **Whave Gate** for the 10 members of the Vachre family from Dorset in the 1870s and 1880s. Maria Vachre was born here in 1874.]*

Having now seen and understood all that can be deduced from the sight and touch of **Whave Gate**'s rubble, you should retrace your steps, returning to the junction with Norcross Brow and the bus route. Then, watching carefully for traffic, cross Twist Moor Lane to its bus stop, or northern side. Take advantage of the roadside pavement and its quite generous footpath. Take advantage, also, of the seat if you would like to spend a little while contemplating the scene to the north, over the Ribble Valley and the far hills. Moving on in due course, you have an interesting final stage of the walk to complete, given that Twist Moor Lane will now provide almost the whole of the route back to your original starting point, much of this being along the line of the venerable pre-1801 route that you are already following. On your way you will also be able to see the sites of your eleventh and twelfth farms of the day, **Snape's** and **Twist Moor House**.

I am assuming that your journey so far, up to and including **Whave Gate**, will have taken a total of between an hour and a half and two hours. The remaining section of the walk will take an additional 30 to 40 minutes at the most. Any variations in timing will depend on whether you have parked your car in Roddlesworth Lane or in the Hare and Hounds area, or are intending to catch a bus from Abbey Village to Chorley or Blackburn. In any case, continue your walk now along the easy roadside path, with Twist Moor Lane falling gently downhill for 100–110m before swinging to the right and rising again. It then appears to turn sharply to the left, to Baron's Fold farm and Abbey Village, but it is not Twist Moor Lane but Dole Lane which makes this turn. It is Dole Lane which from this point carries the main motor road and bus route down to a junction with the A675 opposite the Hare and Hounds Inn.

What Twist Moor Lane does instead of turning left here is what it has always done, that is go straight ahead, just south of east in direction, aiming for Wood's Fold and, ultimately, for the upper Roddlesworth valley. The fact is that, in 1800, say, there was no other road here apart from Twist Moor Lane. There was no such road as Dole Lane, not even a minor cart track beyond the Baron's Fold buildings. There was no Gladstone Terrace, of course. (Gladstone was not even born until 1809.) I am simply urging you to continue eastwards along the traditional route, doing no more than glance at Baron's Fold in passing. However, what I am also urging, and most emphatically, is that you do not cross from the roadside pavement and path over to what appears to be the approach to Wood's Fold without double-checking that there is no main road traffic arriving from any one of three directions. Traffic here can include not only cars and occasional buses but also lorries to and from the timber yard, lorries to and from the Brinscall quarry and farm tractors to and from Baron's Fold. It is the presence of the bends in the road that requires the extra care to be taken, rather than the simple frequency of the traffic.

Having safely crossed the road, do walk happily along what, as I say, does at first look like, and is, the welcoming approach to an interesting timber yard, but is also an ancient pre-turnpike route of importance to farming communities and itinerant traders over many centuries. Beyond Wood's Fold it certainly does assume the characteristics typical of a non-Roman road of the middle ages or the seventeenth century at latest.

The first thing to notice is the entrance, on your right, to Central Quarry, an impressively large and once-busy place of employment for several of the inhabitants of our farms. The next thing to notice on your left, is the barn and restored farmhouse of Wood's Fold itself, one of those worthy survivors that do prompt 'What might have been' and 'What if?' remarks. [*The Marsden family were farming at Wood's Fold in 1881 and the John Duxbury family in 1891.*] A third item of interest, although there is almost nothing to be seen apart from a fragment of walling, is that on your right, just opposite to Wood's Fold farm, were two small Wood's Fold cottages. They were demolished long ago and their site has been totally overtaken by the densely packed trees of a flourishing plantation. [*Their occupants in 1881, the Beardsworths and the Oliver Duxbury family, were cotton weavers and labourers, while in 1891 Robert Duckworth was a quarryman.*]

Now, having moved a little further along the road, you will have found Twist Moor Lane rapidly becoming a narrower and more modest track. A delightful country lane indeed it quite suddenly seems, with sheltering trees and views of gently sloping fields. While the lane itself begins to go downhill in order to cross the 'Rushy' Brook, you might be sufficiently distracted by the view ahead to miss the turning on the right which led into the **Snape's** farmyard. If you find yourself walking distinctly downhill, turn round and go back to the one now obvious point where a gateway from the lane gave access to the rubble humps of **Snape's**.

These rubble humps suggest that the main length of house and barn was at right angles to the lane, and that between the lane and the humps there was a small 'garden' area. It is apparent that there was a small projection to the east at the front (or lane) end of the building, and another more prominent eastwards projection at the rear end. There is almost no exposed rubble or foundation stonework, as there is, for instance, at **Aushaw's** or **Pope's**; all is matted in a clinging undergrowth of grass, supplemented here and there by brambles and hawthorn. But there is no doubt at all that this is precisely the site of **Snape's**, farm number 11 of the day's walk. [*You are certainly standing exactly where the Southworth couple and their lodger*

Bernard Foy, in 1881, and the cotton-weaving Bolton family – all six of them, plus Mrs Bolton's elderly sawyer father, in 1891 – lived, moved and had their being. It is a most conspicuously quiet and private place these days, lying still and silent among the young conifers.]

Returning to the lane, do continue downhill, and watch for the appearance of the 'Rushy' Brook on your right and its eventual departure beneath you down to the A675 and the Rake reservoir. However, before you cross the brook, do also notice in the middle distance on the fields ahead of you the recently visited trees and surviving loo block of **Grouse Cottage**. And notice these not just on account of the pleasure of seeing old friends again but because, directly in line between where you now stand on the Twist Moor Lane slope and **Grouse Cottage** is the ruin of **Twist Moor House**, your twelfth and final 'lost farm' of the day.

Apart from a straight edge low down on its southern side, this is not a substantial ruin with surviving wall sections or foundation plan. It is simply a rectangular heap of rubble, crowned by three thriving hawthorn trees, and prone to extra decoration by active nettles in the summer. It is, nevertheless, as is **Snape's**, as is **Whave Gate**, a precise relic in the exact position of the original building. There can be no doubt. There is no need of guesswork even of the intelligent kind. On nineteenth-century OS maps **Twist Moor House** was undoubtedly a pair of semi-detached cottages with a combined size larger than the combined size of both house and barn at **The Oaks**, say. A storehouse/lavatory block stood on the opposite side of the track. There was a small garden area on the north side of the cottages.

On the other hand, **Twist Moor House** seems not yet to have existed in the eighteenth century and seems not to have had any regular tenants in 1881 or 1891. Some degree of unexplained mystery still exists therefore. Moreover, to visit and stand by or on the ruins requires the following of a special track up from Twist Moor Lane – a clear and original track which used also to lead to **Grouse Cottage**, **Scott Hall**, **Pope's** et al. But the gate to this track is closed and locked. This is a sheep field, not 'open access' land, apart from the one footpath running across the top of the field which you have already used in connecting **Aushaw's** ultimately with **Dale Fold**'s site and with **Hillock**. Therefore, look your fill now at the ragged rubble of the hawthorn-betopped ruin, and continue your walk along the delightful Twist Moor Lane down, eventually, to the A675. Enjoy the privilege of walking along a stretch of a major pre-turnpike route which still looks and feels very much as it must have done in 1801 or 1701 or 1601. And you now have the benefit of knowing another 12 of the 'lost farms' of Brinscall Moors.

Assuming that you do continue your walk along the lane, as its cobbled surface bends gently to the left, downhill and between ancient walls, you will eventually cross the Rake Brook just before arriving at the A675. Now you have one immediate priority and that is to cross the A675 safely. The only pavement and footpath leading to one or other of your starting and finishing points is on the far, or eastern, side of the road. Crossing the road, either as a single walker or as a member of a group, will require special care.

Once you and any or all fellow walkers are standing safely on the footpath, and looking briefly and happily, for instance, at the Rake reservoir, then, clearly, you will turn towards Preston if you are taking the short walk back to Dole Lane and the Hare and Hounds Inn for your car or to catch a bus. You will turn towards Bolton if you are going to return to a car parked on the Roddlesworth Lane car park.

It might interest you to know, however, that there is a possible alternative route back from the **Snape's Farm/Twist Moor House** area to the Dole Lane/Hare and Hounds area for anyone preferring not to have to cross the A675 near to the Rake reservoir bend, though this would involve missing out some of the pleasantest final sections of Twist Moor Lane. If this is what you would prefer here are details.

Having looked over the field to the **Twist Moor House** ruin with its three hawthorns, all you need to do is retrace your steps back to Wood's Fold and from there follow the yellow arrow sign next to the barn on your right. This leads you across the yard and then via a left-right dog-leg into a field path which takes you down (between parallel stone walls at first) northwards to emerge by the A675 about 100m east of the Dole Lane junction. If you do follow this route, you might find it easier to cross the A675 near the Hare and Hounds, if indeed you have to cross it at all. Certainly you will have a longer view of approaching traffic on its way from either Bolton or Preston. Of course you ought to keep a look-out for traffic emerging from Dole Lane as well.

With Walk Four now complete, your thoughts will be turning to the start of Walk Five – the Roddlesworth/Calf Hey Group. The starting point for this final group is, conveniently, exactly the same as for the Twist Moor group, that is, either the Roddlesworth Lane car park or the Dole Lane/Hare and Hounds area. In any case, the walk really begins with a long-ish stroll south-eastwards along Roddlesworth Lane, and then up to the Calf Hey Bridge for the visiting of the three ruined farms in that area.

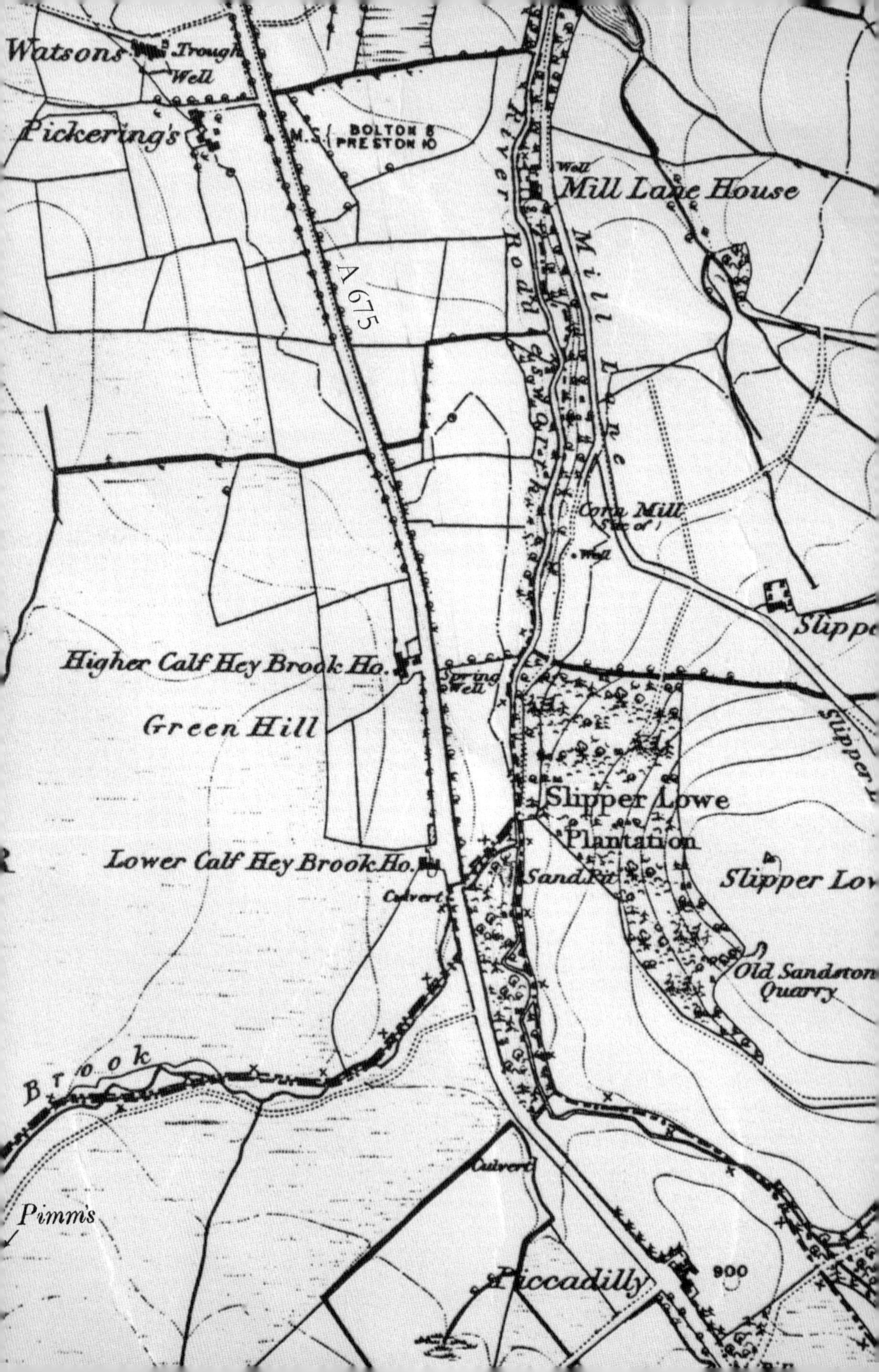

Watsons   Trough
Well

Pickering's

BOLTON &
PRESTON 10

M.S.

A 675

Well

Mill Lane House

River Roddlesworth

Mill Lane

Corn Mill
(Site of)

Well

Slippe

Higher Calf Hey Brook Ho.

Spring
Well

Green Hill

Slipper Lowe
Plantation

Slipper Lo

Lower Calf Hey Brook Ho.

Sand Pit

Culvert

Slipper Lo

Old Sandston
Quarry

Brook

Culvert

Pimm's

Piccadilly

900

The Roddlesworth/Calf Hey Group (7 Farms)

Start and Finish: EITHER Roddlesworth Lane car park OR Abbey Village, the Hare and Hounds area.

Distance: Up to 7 miles, depending on starting point.

Time: Between 4 and 5 hrs., depending on pace and starting point.

Character: A lovely woodland and river walk plus sections of fine moorland walking with minimal damp and muddy patches and with splendid views over north-west England.

THIS WALK BEGINS along Roddlesworth Lane, the delightful pre-turnpike route that takes us between pastures, through woods and by river cascades on our way to Calf Hey Bridge and **Pimm's Farm**. I am assuming that you will have arrived by bus at the Hare and Hounds or will have parked your car either in the small Roddlesworth Lane car park or in the Dole Lane/Hare and Hounds area of Abbey Village. Roddlesworth Lane is part of that pre-1801 route that came from Chorley via Brinscall's School Lane and Butterworth Brow, and then via Twist Moor Lane down to what is now the A675, the post-1801 Sharples-Hoghton Turnpike route. The Roddlesworth Lane section then leaves the A675 just south-east of the Rake reservoir bend.

Your walk properly now starts just before you pass, on your left, the entrance to Lower Roddlesworth farm, with its cottage and its two fine stone barns of 1674 and 1755. (The bigger farmhouse was demolished by Liverpool Corporation in 1914.) This is still a busily working farm with sheep and with plenty of poultry including geese. Opposite to the farm entrance you will see on your right another of those unusual cast-iron gateposts that you saw at **Hillock**. (And we shall see some more later on

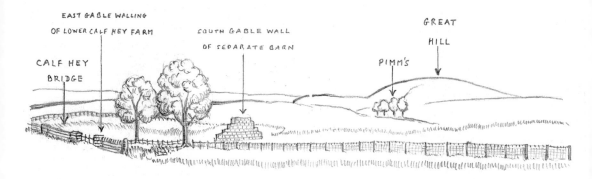

Looking south-west from the Lower Calf Hey ruins by the A675.

this walk.) Meanwhile, in another 200m you will pass, again on your left, Higher Roddlesworth farm, a grand square house with central doorway that was once also a 'Public House' (as shown on the map of 1831). On your right you will see not only a second cast-iron gatepost but also traces of a gradually rising track, now grass-covered, that ran from the 'Public House' across the fields to join the once newly constructed Toll Road (the A675). This track was intended to persuade horse-drawn travellers in the nineteenth century to pause and sample the local ale here, as they had more easily been able to do when Roddlesworth Lane had been their only available route.

Looking again across the fields to your right you will see a pair of telecommuni-cation masts atop a small hill. Even more importantly you will see on the hillside a gathering of slightly straggly birch trees with, just at the near side of the A675, a large, well-rounded and dominant sycamore. Immediately to the south of this sycamore are to be found the ruins of **Besom Hall**, a site we shall visit at a later stage of today's walk. The footpath to it leaves Roddlesworth Lane just as we meet (on our left) the impressive and newly reconstructed houses of Cliff Fold. For the time being we carry straight on, having ignored also two invitations to take paths on the left that allow walkers to visit the very attractive Roddlesworth reservoirs – a pleasure to be deferred to some future occasion, no doubt.

Soon after Cliff Fold we enter the woods as the lane gradually drops down to cross the Roddlesworth river at Halliwell Fold Bridge. Cross the bridge and take the road to the right which is now not only Roddlesworth Lane but also the Witton Weavers' Way. Take a good look at the bed of the river, too, as you cross it and walk south alongside it. Quite frequently the river is flowing directly over smooth, bare and solid slabs of rock rather than over a more usual bed of loose stones, soil and gravel. This is quite different from the Rake or 'Rushy' or Hatch brooks, for instance. On the other hand the woodland surrounding you is at least as delightful as the Brinscall Woods on the far western side of the moor. As you continue your walk you will soon notice that the lane with its traditional cobbled surface, is steadily rising, leaving the river eventually far below you on your right.

Just as you think you are going to lose touch with the river, do be sure to notice, about 350m beyond the bridge, a wooden post on your right with an arrow directing you to leave the lane (and the Witton Weavers' Way) and to take a track leading gradually downhill and back towards the river and its sounds of tumbling waters. Eventually you will arrive at a damp patch on the path, with the remains of a small (pre-woodland) quarry on your left, and then a little mound to climb and a flight of six wooden steps to descend. Damp, even muddy, patches persist on the path here and there, but the river is worth your attention with several minor cascades and one particularly impressive waterfall (marked on the modern OS map), as the Roddlesworth leaps from one rock slab down to a lower one. Traffic on the A675 now makes itself heard, and suddenly you arrive at a watersmeet where Calf Hey Brook joins Roddlesworth River (two streams of, by now, roughly similar size). Just to the south of the confluence is a convenient pedestrian bridge (a level slab of solid concrete) allowing you to walk by the Calf Hey up to the stile next to the main A675 road bridge.

A firm construction of 1905 this bridge is, an early engineering achievement of the famous Leonard Fairclough building company of Adlington, easily carrying lorries of far greater weight than could have been envisaged in 1905. When you have left the wood behind you and climbed the stile you will find that the eastern parapet bears an inscription confirming that the bridge and the Calf Hey Brook mark the old boundary between Withnell (in the Hundred of Leyland) and Turton (in the Hundred of Salford). When you have, with appropriate care, crossed the busy A675 you will find that the western parapet's inscription assures you that this is indeed the Calf Hey Bridge and that it was re-built in 1905. Modern roadside signs tell you that this is still a significant local authority boundary.

The Pimm's trees, looking north.

Having established yourself safely on the western side of the A675 you will have time to notice that you are in sight of three more of our ruined farms. **Lower Calf Hey** and **Higher Calf Hey** are very close at hand. Indeed the 9ft high remains of **Lower Calf Hey**'s southern barn gable are very obvious in the nearby field. We will return to look in detail at these two farms, but for the time being our first priority is to visit the more distant **Pimm's** farm whose four trees are clearly visible away to the south west in line with the summit of Great Hill which rises behind them. Your walk from Lower Roddlesworth will so far have taken between 30 and 40 minutes. In another 20 to 25 minutes you will stand next to the considerable house and barn ruins of **Pimm's**.

Staying on the western side of the A675, walk towards Bolton (i.e. southwards) along the roadside grassy verge for about 100m until you reach a stile and public footpath sign. Take this path, which would lead you over Great Hill and all the way to White Coppice if you continued beyond **Pimm's**. On this occasion, of course you should aim to return to this stile and to the Calf Hey Bridge within the hour, even allowing for a leisurely examining of the **Pimm's** ruins.

Your path is accompanied on your left by a recently installed post and wire fence and on your right by the Calf Hey Brook and its adjacent boundary wall, which is still its original 6ft height in parts though crumbling and fallen in other parts. There are stepping stones for your use in a damp area where a small tributary stream makes its way down to the main brook. Just at the point where another impressive boundary wall comes in on your right to join the first wall, your path begins to veer distinctly to the left – following a bend in the Calf Hey Brook. You soon will be walking in a more southerly direction, with the **Pimm's** trees plainly in view some 300m ahead. Ignore a wooden kissing gate through the post and wire fence on your left, but tell yourself that you will go through it on your way back, giving yourself a slightly different route to the A675 on your return from **Pimm's**.

The high (in parts) boundary wall has been keeping some 20m away on your right for a while, but soon you should find yourself approaching it while first using stepping stones to cross the Calf Hey Brook (quite narrow by now) before walking towards a gap in the wall near a pair of surviving gateposts. There are the remains of hinge-pins on the left hand post. Having passed through the wall you will find your path rising determinedly towards the **Pimm's** trees. A boardwalk has been provided to allow you to cross easily over a particularly damp patch. Meanwhile the wall, though badly broken in places, can be seen making its way onwards and upwards to pass over Great Hill to the left, or south, of the summit.

In two minutes you will arrive at **Pimm's**. The site and the stone remains of the buildings are all that you might have hoped for. This is much the most complete of all the farms you will visit today. The walls retain sufficient height to enable you to identify domestic sections and barn sections and to appreciate how orderly and agreeable life must have been at 1002ft (305m) above sea-level. [*This was home for well over a dozen years in the 1880s and 90s for the Brownlow family, including Miles and his wife Alice, as well as their 12-year-old son Miles junior and his brother John in 1891, and 70-year-old grandmother Lucy in 1881. They knew this place very well a century and more before you ever thought of setting foot here.*]

Looking out at the Calf Hey valley now, and seeing on the opposite bank of the brook another path which particularly leads over to a restored farm (by the A675) known as Piccadilly, you should say farewell to ruins and trees here, and make your way back to the boardwalk and the gateway in the wall. Retrace your earlier steps until you reach the kissing gate and then pass confidently through this. A fine path meets you and allows a swift and mostly level walk to the south of your earlier approach – except for one steep little grassy ravine which has to be negotiated. This contains the rushing tributary stream you met earlier when using stepping stones to cross a damp patch. Beyond the ravine you walk on as if making for Piccadilly until meeting a ditch surrounding an enclosure wall which must once have contained pasture belonging to Piccadilly.

Here you must veer left, without trying to cross ditch or enclosure wall. You are now walking to the north-east rather than the east, as you have been doing since the kissing gate. As you draw close to the A675 you will notice that there is no easy access to a roadside verge at this point, so your path turns clearly to the north and brings you precisely to the stile over which you climbed 40 or so minutes ago. Make your way back to Calf Hey Bridge, and prepare to visit the two nearby farms.

Both of these, the **Lower** and the **Higher Calf Hey** farms, stand on 'open access' land. Nevertheless, if you are to visit their sites, there are gateways and post and wire fences to be sensibly negotiated, and this will involve a little, but only a little, careful walking on the grass verge alongside the busy A675. For the moment, stand at the north end of the western parapet of the Leonard Fairclough bridge. You can see, close to you, one of the two large sycamore trees and beyond it the southern gable wall of the **Lower Calf Hey** barn. Immediately in front of you is a little broken-down field wall continuing from the bridge parapet. Then, you might suddenly realise that a further section of really well-laid stone walling just to your right and in easy touching distance is not what you at first assumed it was – more field boundary wall. It is actually the remaining four to five feet high gable end wall of the main **Lower Calf Hey** house. It is at a slight angle to the A675, but no more than two metres from the road surface.

Looking over Cold Within Hill, with the Pimm's ruins next to the trees.

This wall is quite an exciting discovery, in its own way, so close to passing traffic, even the occasional horse-drawn traffic of the nineteenth century. Just at the other side of that very wall was the kitchen in which a farmer and his family lived out their lives. The OS map of 1929 shows that the farm was still inhabited at that comparatively late date, even though **Higher Calf Hey** was not. [*In 1881, Thomas Phipp from Rochdale and his wife Alice had lived here with their five children aged from 12 years to just eight months. In 1891, John Nelson from Kendal was living here with his wife Agnes from Mardale and their three children, Tom aged seven, Lilian aged five and Marion aged one.*]

With thoughts of these young people in mind, move carefully on now in a northerly direction along the narrow grass verge and see, even before you reach the second sycamore, a blocked gateway into what had been the farmyard, the gateway's position being given away by yet another cast-iron gatepost. Continue along the grass verge (which is widening a little now) for 50m or so before reaching an open gateway (with wooden posts). Go through this gateway. As you walked along the verge you had been following, on your left, an old post and barbed wire fence. There is another newer post and barbed wire fence some 10m inside and parallel to the old one. There is also a metal gate next to which is a section of wooden fencing which is easily climbed. Do climb this. You are now in an 'open access' field, suitably distanced from the A675's traffic. The ground is an interesting mixture of clumps of rushes, plus small tussocks, large molehills, short grass (sheep-nibbled) and occasional damp patches. Walk easily back to the **Lower Calf Hey** site. The plan of the buildings is readily visible, with the barn (whose south gable survives, though with a distinct lean) being at right angles to the main buildings of farmhouse and original barn. There seems to have been a pond to the west of the buildings. Water oozes from this and makes its way gradually down to join the Calf Hey Brook close to the bridge.

Now turn round and walk back through the 'open access' field (keeping close to the newer post and wire fence) as far as the two distant sycamore trees of **Higher Calf Hey** farm, about 150m to the north. As you walk back you could establish firmly in your own mind the fact that the site of **Higher Calf Hey** farm is indeed higher, though only marginally higher, than the site of **Lower Calf Hey** farm. I mention this for two reasons: firstly because the farm close to and within, as it were, the valley of the brook is naturally lower than the farm in a field above the valley of the brook; secondly because an OS map of 1848 quite firmly uses exactly the names for each farm that I have used, even though I have to acknowledge that a 1929 OS map does actually call the surviving **Lower Calf Hey** farm buildings '**Higher Calf Hey**'. But then the otherwise excellent West Pennine Moors OS Explorer Map 287 of 2004 prints the name 'Watson's Farm' quite wrongly next to Pickering's instead of next to Watson's.

On your stridings-out from **Lower** to **Higher** you will make good progress even through the clumps of rushes except perhaps at one point where there is a regular outflow from the **Higher Calf Hey** pond. When you arrive at the site of the farm, the position of foundation walls and rubble heaps makes it quite easy to establish the basic plan of the buildings, even though there are no surviving gable ends of the **Lower Calf Hey** kind. A good-sized straightforward long house it has been, with small westward extensions at the northern end. There is one stone gatepost near that end. Two major trees stand guard over the ruins, one near the farm, one near the old post and wire fence close to the A675. And while we are looking in the A675 direction, what else might one see where the driveway from the road used to come into the farmyard? Not one but two cast-iron gateposts.

[*Just two members of the Park family, uncle and nephew, lived and worked here in 1891. In 1881, however, it had been a very full house. It housed Richard and Margaret Cookson and their nine children – before they transferred to* **Hillock** *in pursuit of jobs in textile factories and quarries where only a short walk to work was required.*]

Somebody did a good job on the field wall here, however, which retains its full waist-height quality for much of its length as it stretches out west to meet the big enclosure wall separating fields from wild moorland. You will see this as you leave **Higher Calf Hey** and retrace your steps to climb the wooden fencing and return via the gateway to reach the grass verge by the A675.

Your immediate purpose now is to re-visit the Calf Hey Bridge and then carefully to cross the A675 with the object of walking down the wooded valley of the River Roddlesworth as far as Halliwell Fold Bridge. From there walk back along Roddlesworth Lane up to Cliff Fold and at that point take the public footpath on your left which, as you saw earlier, leads across a field to a large rounded sycamore.

You are about to visit your fourth farm of the day, **Besom Hall**.

Like **Lower Calf Hey** farm, **Besom Hall** had one gable end which almost touched the road surface of the A675. Unlike **Lower Calf Hey**, the rest of the **Besom Hall** longhouse was built on a sloping field whose slope fell away quite steeply from the road. This allowed the insertion of an extra storey below the immediate roadside level of the kitchen/living room – which is why I declared earlier that **Besom Hall** appeared to lean up next to the road, to be "hutched up" against it, as the Lancashire expression has it. All this is apparent as you walk across the field from Cliff Fold. When you reach the slope, do not immediately make for the stile in the roadside fence ahead of you. Instead, walk a little to the right as if aiming for the rounded sycamore tree. There, just before you reach the tree, you will see the **Besom Hall** ruin. I cannot promise you clear foundations, but there is an undeniably longhouse-shaped heap of rubble, quite a prominent feature once you realise what you are looking at.

[*It must have seemed a pleasing, modestly elevated site in the eighteenth century when there was no A675, and the nearest road was Roddlesworth Lane 300m away to the east. It would not have been unpleasant even after 1801, as for example in 1881 when Ralph Brownlow and his wife Jane lived here with their three young daughters Lucy, Mary and Sarah. Ralph, however, was a quarryman as well as a farmer of 10 acres. But then Miles Brownlow up at* **Pimm's** *was also a quarryman in addition to farming 30 acres. In 1891* **Besom Hall** *had only two residents, Robert Bateson, a quarryman and not a farmer at all, and his wife Margaret who, like Agnes Nelson of* **Lower Calf Hey***, had come to Withnell from the rather special valley of Mardale in Westmorland.*]

By now it could be up to three hours since you originally left the Lower Roddlesworth area to make your way up to Calf Hey Bridge and the grandly remote **Pimm's** farm. There are still three more farms for you to find, but the distances remaining to be walked are much shorter than those you have already covered. Having looked your fill at **Besom Hall**'s rubble-ruin, do walk along now to the nearby stile overlooking the A675. Do not cross it as yet, for you can first take a look at **Stake Hill**, your fifth farm of the day, from inside the **Besom Hall** field. **Stake Hill** is not on 'open access' land. There are no surviving buildings, nor is there a path to it. But there is a quite obvious heap of grass-covered stones if you look now from the stile in a south-westerly direction across to the land on the far side of the A675. There, outlined against the sky at the top of a smoothly sloping field, is a little tuft of rough grasses and weeds, about 10m in length. I have, with the farmer's permission, stood on those ruins. I can vouch for there being all the stony evidence of yet another typical longhouse, domestic quarters and barn combined in one single structure, where the extent of the stonework – the outer edges of external walls – can easily be found.

[*From your present position by the stile it is also easy to imagine the farm as it was in 1891, a solitary but not remote building with its three occupants, the elderly widow Mary Smith, her middle-aged daughter Margaret and her 80-year-old brother William Dewhurst, formerly of Pope's.*]

As you now climb the stile and walk carefully along the roadside verge in the direction of Bolton (i.e. to the south), do glance now and then sympathetically at the grassy ruin and think kindly of the mature trio who once lived there. Your objective now, however, is to join the public footpath that rises up to and then beyond Watson's farm. Watson's is the exceptionally long Victorian longhouse not very far away on the opposite side of the A675. It is a working farm, home to both sheep and cattle.

Your walk along the roadside verge is not a long one. Soon you will see the public footpath sign by the Watson's gateway. You will also observe that you are being invited to cross the A675 at a particularly safe and relatively high point on what is rather a switchback road

Robert Moss, circa 1907. He was born at Stake Hill in 1882, and was grandfather to Barbara Butler.

formation. You have a clear view of approaching traffic coming from either direction. You will also see, before you cross the road, that there is another public footpath sign on this eastern side of the road indicating a path that is theoretically to and from the Halliwell Fold Bridge, deep in the woods. The path is marked on OS maps. I have deliberately not advised you to use it, for there is no continuously visible path, and the extent of wetness over most of the assumed route makes for an awkward journey unless you actively enjoy splashing through quite deep surface water for its own sake.

Of more, if minor interest on the east side of the road is a cast-iron gatepost where once there was a gateway leading into pasture that is now totally tree-clad. And – no great surprise, this – across the road, at the bottom of the Watson's track, is a further cast-iron post, painted white a while ago. It is time to walk past this and up the track to the farm (where there is another white-painted cast-iron post – which you might well think should be the final one for the day).

Veer to the right past the farm, past the lengthy barn and then through the (sometimes muddy) farmyard and between the cattle shed and another barn. You will pass a (sometimes closed) gate and make your way out into an open field. The two telecommunication masts are visible on your right, close to the **Stake Hill** ruin. As your path goes across the middle of the field you will see an enclosure wall over on your left which makes a right angle bend and then comes across to meet you. There are some small conifers here and there beyond the wall. Just across that wall is 'open access' land from which you might think you ought to be able to see **Mosscrop's**. That farm, or rather its foundation stonework, remains quite invisible, given the lie of the land, however, and **Mosscrop's** does not have a tree to identify it. Oddly enough you will soon be able to see not only the **Scott Hall** tree but even the far away **Botany Bay** beech tree. (See plan on page 193 and map on page 194.)

You are now, in effect, moving away from **Mosscrop's**, a complex combination of post and wire fencing and surviving field walls encouraging you to make straight for **Keck**, your sixth farm of the day. Your path largely follows the line of overhead cables that are on their way past **Keck** and **Aushaw's** to the world beyond. At the corner of a second field you will find not only a stile and a stone gatepost but also a set of yellow direction arrows attached to one of the overhead cable posts. These arrows direct you across another field to another stile and then down a slight slope to the fine double heaps of stone that are the remains of **Keck**'s two longhouses.

Before you come close to these you will notice the lines of parallel stone walls which for a while run along each side of the track coming up from Lower Roddlesworth to **Keck** and going on towards **Mosscrop's**. At right angles to these there is another shorter set which lead down to the ford across the Rake Brook.

Now, however, it is **Keck** that deserves your attention. There are, as at **Aushaw's**, two quite separate large structures placed at right angles to each other. The more easterly one is alongside and parallel to the track from Lower Roddlesworth. Both of them sit on a field that is sloping very slightly down to Rake Brook. Your path today takes you directly past both buildings on your way to the ladder stile and wooden footbridge that will allow you to cross the brook. Each building is roughly 6m wide by 19m long. There is plenty of fallen rubble about, but the foundation walls are clear enough. Each building is divided into several sections (seven in one case, six in the other) of which two are slightly wider than the rest. I assume that these contained the domestic or family accommodation. There are several adjacent trees. [*The chief residents in both 1881 and 1891 were the farmer (of 18 acres) William Moulden and his wife Mary. 'Moulden Water' is an older and alternative name for the River Roddlesworth, by the way.*]

Having crossed the Rake Brook by the footbridge, your first need is to look to your right to find a second ladder stile and thus escape the steep banks of the brook and walk on easily in a mainly level sheep pasture. Another arrow on a fence to your right points you towards **Grouse Cottage** by way of the familiar (from Walk Four) wooden post with yellow arrows that you met when on your way to **Pope's**. You will see **Scott Hall** (its tree and its heap of stones) on your left before arriving at the wooden post. Then continue on the obvious track down to the **Grouse Cottage** stile. From the stile follow the path on your right via **Aushaw's** and the Rake Brook bridge (used on Walk Four) to the A675.

You now have one more farm to find today before your walk is complete. It has so far been a four hour walk? But a pleasantly varied and picturesque one? At the A675 it is another case of very carefully crossing the road to the footpath on the eastern side. There, do not cross the stile as if making for Roddlesworth Lane but instead turn left as if for Abbey Village. Walk on down the roadside footpath and soon pass the entrance to Roddlesworth Lane, continuing on the now narrowing footpath round the sharp Rake bend. Glancing right at the bend you might just make out the remains of the field boundary wall of **Rake** farm itself. (There used to be no trees just here.) In another few metres you will arrive at the point where fishing (and walking) persons are able to stride over the Liverpool Corporation wall that separates the A675 from the Rake reservoir. Do stride over this wall.

All you now have to do is walk forward for about a dozen metres and then climb the low bank on your right to look over the boundary wall. There, especially easily in winter, you will see, quite close to you, the crumbled outer walls and the rubble heaps of the house, cottage and barns of **Rake** farm. You will also – can you believe? – see a cast-iron gatepost with hinge-pin.

[*Here, before your very eyes, is that large collection of buildings, mainly hidden from passing view now, that housed the 12 members of the Richard Waring family (plus their one lodger) in 1881, and then the 13 members of the Richard Marsden family plus four members of the Joseph Waring family in 1891. In its abandoned condition, you must agree that this is a rather quieter, less hectic place now than it was 120 years ago, in spite of the A675's twenty-first-century traffic. The Rake reservoir was already here (from 1857) but there must have been many fewer trees in the 1890s, and more open fields leading up towards Lower Roddlesworth farm.*]

Your walk for today is now concluded. All that remains is to return to Abbey Village (and Dole Lane or the Hare and Hounds) or to the Roddlesworth Lane car park. A walk of four and a half hours it has been, depending on your pace, I expect? Five hours, surely, if you have stopped for a picnic lunch? And if you happen to turn left for Roddlesworth Lane car park when leaving **Rake**, do not be surprised if you see near the old boundary wall two ivy-clad cast-iron posts, positively the last of the day. Why, you might ask, have we seen so many of these on this particular walk, and so few on earlier walks?

One possible answer I have heard from a local farmer is that these gateposts – or metal cylinders – had become surplus to requirements at the gas works formerly run by the Parke family at Withnell Fold, and that the Parkes probably distributed them among (grateful?) farming tenants in the north and north-eastern parts of Brinscall Moors at some stage before 1898. So, several but by no means all of the Withnell farms received some cast-iron gateposts, but, so far as I can see, no farms in Wheelton or Heapey did.

There are, however two metal posts supporting the six-barred metal gate at the top of Edge Gate Lane, which is certainly in Wheelton. But this is a modern gate on to the moor, and is not at all in the position of the former gateway which used to lead from Edge Gate Lane into the **Whittle's** farmyard. The two metal posts were surely not a gift from the Parkes to the Shorrocks of **Whittle's** in the 1890s – or so a well-balanced critical historian might reasonably conclude. But as to why in particular there are two metal gateposts at the top of Edge Gate Lane I have no clear explanation to offer – unless there is a link with the Second World War air-raid shelter.

I end my description of the five recommended walks on this light-hearted, perhaps mildly eccentric topic of cast-iron gateposts, as indeed I had earlier and quite frequently drawn attention to older stone gateposts and their hinge-pins. This has been no mere quirky gesture, of course. It has partly been a matter of ensuring that walkers knew they were on the right track when recognising particular features. It has partly been a reminder of the need for walkers and aspiring historians to enjoy being alert even to small details, to any and every piece of evidence which might otherwise be overlooked but which might reveal something special about the skills and the customs of farmers and their families.

Gateposts, after all, do survive on the moors more easily than field enclosure walls or the very buildings of farm houses and barns. They become the most obvious memorials, the signs and symbols of endeavour and hope and order and achievement. My hope is that through this book many of the people and buildings of Brinscall's farming community will live on in our minds and will never be entirely forgotten.

May I also express the hope that you, readers and fellow walkers, have not only found my descriptions of the walks helpful when you have actually been following the routes – walking the walks, so to say – but that you have also enjoyed that special additional pleasure that we call 'armchair walking'. I hope, while sitting at ease in an evening, you have re-read the text, re-visiting the scene imaginatively after the event, and recollecting in tranquillity all that you happily saw and felt on the moors, on the hillsides and in the woods.

Index

General Index

Index of significant farming families

About the author

B ORN IN HORWICH, and a graduate of Merton College, Oxford, G. D. (David) Clayton, as Senior History Master of Burnley Grammar School, published a significant academic work on 19th century international relations – *Britain and the Eastern Question: Missolonghi to Gallipoli* (Hodder and Stoughton) in 1971.

Following a career including 8 years as Deputy Head and 17 years as Headmaster in Burnley he has more recently turned his attention to local history, publishing a celebratory assessment of a new post-1944 Act grammar school's early years – *The Hayward Grammar School, Bolton: the first decade 1955–1965* (Phillimore) in 2008.

President of the Bolton Branch of the Historical Association since 1987, and a resident in the Lancashire village of Brinscall since 1965 he began in 2009 to explore the reasons why there are so many ruined farmhouses on the nearby moors. Why and when were the farms built, and why and when did they fall empty? Why were they demolished? Who had previously lived there and why?

As usual, events do have causes, in local as in national and international affairs. A fascinating story emerges in Brinscall – not only of irresistible economic change but also of positive achievement, triumph over adversity, and sadness mingled with success.